Fenjia

Fenjia

Household Division and Inheritance in Qing and Republican China

DAVID WAKEFIELD

UNIVERSITY OF HAWAI'I PRESS
Honolulu

Library of Congress Cataloging-in-Publication Data
Wakefield, David, 1950–
  Fenjia : household division and inheritance in Qing and Republican
China / David Wakefield.
     p.   cm.
  Includes bibliographical references and index.
  ISBN 0–8248–2092–4 (alk. paper)
  1. Inheritance and succession—China—History.   I. Title.
KNQ770.W35   1998
346.5105'2—dc21   98–26392
                                                           CIP

Book designed by Kenneth Miyamoto

Contents

v

List of Figures and Tables

Figures

Tables

Acknowledgments

I N *How Europe Underdeveloped Africa*, Walter Rodney, the great scholar of Africa, stunned me with this statement in his preface: "I will not add that 'all mistakes and shortcomings are entirely my responsibility.' That is sheer bourgeois subjectivism. Responsibility in matters of these sorts is always collective."

In the revolutionary spirit of the early 1970s, such a statement not only fit the context of the times, it was also true, and Rodney was brave enough to say so. Rodney's view is still every bit as true now as it was then, but times have changed, and I am simply not brave enough to follow in his footsteps. To those listed below, and to those I may have forgotten, my heartfelt thanks for your time, advice, and support. The book has been immensely improved by your efforts. All the errors that remain are mine alone.

To my professors at UCLA—Philip Huang, Kathryn Bernhardt, Ben Elman, Richard von Glahn, Herman Ooms, Francesca Bray, and Bob Brenner—you each played a unique role in shaping the book. Special thanks to Professor Shirleen Wong for her hours spent one-on-one helping me read classical texts and documents and to Professor Chang Wei-jen for his early encouragement and direction on the project.

To other graduate students and friends who helped, especially in deciphering Taiwanese household division documents: Ping-chun Hsiung, Li Rongchang, Liu Chang, Ni Daxin, Pan Ming-te, and Hiroshi Yoneyama. To Jiang Yonglin for providing Ming law documents. A large thank you to Richard Gundee for reading and commenting on the entire manuscript. To Clay Dube, Jeff Hornibrook, Brad Reed, and Matt Sommer for their ideas and support.

To friends, colleagues, and professors in China for their thoughts and varied roles in facilitating my two research trips to and around China: Professors Chen Yande, Chen Zhiping, Kenneth Dean, Jing Junjian, Li Bozhong, Shen Bingyao, and Yang Guozhen. Special thanks to Professor Zheng Zhenman for his time, encouragement, and friendship.

To my editor, Sharon Yamamoto, of the University of Hawai'i Press, for her belief in me, her timely calls, notes, gifts, and encouragement.

No project of this type can be completed without the nurture of grant funding. My thanks to the U.S. Department of Education for a Fulbright-Hays Dissertation Fellowship; to the Committee on Scholarly Communication with China for further dissertation support; to the University of Missouri's Research Council and Research Board, which provided substantial support toward turning the dissertation into a book. And a final thanks to the Pacific Cultural Foundation for funding to complete the manuscript.

On a more personal level, thanks to my parents for opening up their house and subsidizing us while I simultaneously completed my dissertation and fought my first round against bone cancer. They did this even as my mother fought her own battle against breast cancer. To Bud, who never showed his weariness at providing hospital taxi service to two cancer patients.

And finally and most importantly to my wife Su, who through the last six years has not only supported my completion of the manuscript, but has battled with me through the ups and downs of my personal war with cancer, educated her way to a B.A., an M.A., and a good job, and in the midst of all these difficulties has done a superb job raising our wonderful son Daniel. She has suffered much, and it is to her that this book is lovingly dedicated.

Chapter 1

Introduction

THIS is a book about Chinese inheritance, usually called *fenjia* in Chinese, and *fenjia* is best translated as household division. The basic issues I explore in the book are, first, the nature of household division and, second, household division's importance to Chinese history and social structure. I do this by attempting to answer several major questions regarding household division that have long bothered historians of China. The first perhaps deceptively simple question is, what was the Chinese inheritance regime? Since Thomas Malthus wrote in 1826, scholars have long assumed that at inheritance time Chinese family property was divided equally among all brothers (Malthus [1914] 1982:129–130). This assumption was never directly challenged, but it did come packaged with a sense of unease. Privately, many scholars felt that such an inheritance regime was economically "irrational" in that it created, indeed guaranteed, property fragmentation, downward mobility, and morcellated landownership. Why would Chinese families do such economically "irrational" things? Secondly, the increasing sensitivity to the vast historical and geographical variations in areas of Chinese culture such as language dialects, marriage patterns, and dowry practices led many to worry that perhaps inheritance might also contain regional variations. The knowledge that in some locations eldest sons or grandsons received some extra property often fueled this concern. Thus a major portion of the argument here is designed to answer the question, did Chinese families really divide the family property among all sons?

1

The evidence demonstrates that the Chinese equal-male-division inheritance regime was consistent over the centuries of Chinese history. It was also consistent in all regions dominated by Han Chinese in the Qing dynasty. To illustrate, I offer case studies of household division as it operated in two distinct cultural, economic, and temporal environments: Qing dynasty Taiwan and Republican era North China. Despite the differences in time and place, equal division was the rule. But I will argue that it was equal division with two twists. First, since household division most often took place while one or both parents were still alive, these living parents were guaranteed continued support in some form. Second, if any sibling remained unmarried at the time of division, he or she was entitled to marriage expenses (for a son) or a dowry (for a daughter). Thus equal division among the sons was the rule, but living parents and single siblings had rights as well.

The second question addressed is, was it possible, within the pattern of equal division, to strategize about the use of property? Here again the answer is yes. At household division time, it was legal in both law and custom to take property out of the division process, establish it as a set-aside or trust, and dedicate it to a certain purpose. Trust and set-aside strategies varied by region and class, and I have labeled them orientations.

The third related question addressed is, what, if anything, was the relationship between inheritance, the various orientations, and the larger society? The evidence strongly suggests that the variations in inheritance orientations had dramatic effects on landownership patterns, lineage property patterns, lineage strength, class formations, and even the level of state efficacy and penetration into village society. Thus I will argue that household division and its related strategies had powerful effects on Qing China's social and economic structures. In my conclusion I will speculate on the possible effects household division may have had on the pattern of development of Chinese history as a whole.

Influences

This study of household division in Qing (1644–1912) and Republican (1912–1949) China rests at the confluence of four academic traditions: a European tradition of political economy that links family and economic history in global syntheses; a Euro-American anthropological tradition analyzing Chinese family and lineage structures; and two distinct Chinese scholarly traditions, one emphasizing family documents and village-level studies, and another emphasizing the importance of the law, the state, and legal procedures.

Political Economy: Engels and Habakkuk

The first significant contribution to the European tradition of political economy is the work of Frederick Engels, who forges a grand synthesis of family history. Engels defines material life as containing two elements: structures of production and structures of reproduction, the latter synonymous with family. He argues that historical progress and the development of the family are closely related and that as societies move through the progressive stages of history, the structure and importance of family life change. In the early stages of history before the formation of social classes, family and sexual ties are the dominant institutions in society. In the later stages of history when class societies appear, state and "local groups" emerge as the dominant institutions, and the family is relegated to a subordinate position (Engels 1902).

While much of Engels' argument has been criticized, several strands of influence can still be detected in contemporary family history and anthropology. First, family structures are seen to be humanly constructed and changeable over time. There is a history to family life, and this history can be described, analyzed, and synthesized into a system. Second, the history of family is determined by and secondary to the deeper forces of historical change rooted in class structures and the stages of economic development. The changing pattern of class structures over time determines the change in family structures, and thus class structures must be understood if family history is to be analyzed properly. In simpler terms, economic history determines family history.

The work of H. J. Habakkuk is the second major contribution to this tradition of family history as political economy. Habakkuk is particularly important to this study because he inverts key elements of Engels' theses by assigning a critical importance to family and inheritance practices, and arguing that inheritance practices directly affect demography, geographical mobility, and economic development.

He divides inheritance into two ideal types: single-heir systems and partible inheritance systems. Single-heir systems, in which all family property goes to one heir, promote a single-heir marriage pattern in which one heir marries and receives all the family property. This single heir will tend to have many children, since there is no inheritance-based pressure to limit their numbers. Though families will be large, many children will not inherit, and they may remain celibate. These noninheriting, single children will form a highly mobile labor force and leave the area. This pattern produces an overall slower rate of population growth and a less dense population. This trend in turn leads to the likelihood of agricultural surpluses available for sale on a market. In sum, single-heir systems produce slower population growth, mobile labor, and agricultural surpluses, a constellation of social, economic, and cultural elements conducive to the development of capitalism.

Partible inheritance systems, in which property is divided among several heirs, do just the opposite. In these systems all heirs marry. This factor in turn produces faster population growth, fragmentation of property, and a less mobile labor force as each person has a property tie to the community. A denser population results, and any potential agricultural surplus is consumed. As land becomes scarce, families turn to handicraft production to buttress their subsistence, and these family-produced goods tend to resist the intrusion of industrial goods produced elsewhere. Thus, multiple-heir systems of inheritance result in dense, immobile populations that consume their surpluses and produce their own handicrafts. This social, economic, and cultural environment is inimical to the development of capitalism (Habakkuk 1955).

Just as in the case of Engels, though there is much to criticize, Habakkuk's influence is significant. Like Engels he argues that family history can be systemized, but as opposed to Engels, family structures and family history are key determinants, if not the foremost determinants, of economic development and economic history as a whole. Family and inheritance patterns determine which populations will develop and which will not; in sum, family history determines economic history.

In the ninety years since Engels wrote, scholars have produced a plethora of anthropological and historical studies on the subjects of family structure and history. Many of these empirical studies have revealed a vastly more complex world of family and inheritance than previously thought. A fine example of this mountain of empirical data and the intricate patterns it reveals is the volume *Family and Inheritance: Rural Society in Western Europe, 1200–1800,* jointly edited by Jack Goody, Joan Thirsk, and E. P. Thompson. That collection is particularly relevant to this study as it takes inheritance as its theme and treats it in historical and trans-European perspective.

The ten essays suggest strongly that neither Engels' nor Habakkuk's scheme can encompass the tremendous variety of specific inheritance and family forms in Europe alone. Lutz Berkner, for example, finds that inheritance patterns differed markedly by region in seventeenth- and eighteenth-century Germany, with Calenberg practicing impartible inheritance and neighboring Gottingen practicing partible inheritance. Emmanuel Le Roy Ladurie finds three basic geographic variations of inheritance in sixteenth-century France. The contributions from J. P. Cooper and David Sabean suggest that a family's class position affected inheritance as well. The overall impression is that the partible-impartible distinction is increasingly difficult to make in the European context and that there is no real pattern to inheritance at all (Goody, Thirsk, and Thompson 1976).

This increased research into the details of actual family and inheritance practices has not been kind to the grand theories put forth by Engels and Habakkuk. Regarding Engels, while family does indeed tend to decline in relative importance with the advent of class societies and states, still, in most traditional agricultural societies the peasant family was a critical institution in determining the economic, social, and political dynamics of the society. As to change within class societies, Engels is again right to suggest that as class formations change, so too does the family, though only on the most general of levels. Thus in peasant societies the family functions for the purposes of production, consumption, and reproduction, while in modern capitalist societies, most families function for purposes of consumption and reproduction only. Beyond these mundane generalities, however, close connections between the stage of economic development and family are more difficult to find.

Habakkuk's theory based on distinguishing partible and impartible systems and then making connections to economic development has proven less resilient than Engels' in the face of new evidence. Much new research suggests that even making the partible-impartible distinction may be difficult and that connecting inheritance practices to economic development may well be impossible. (Goody, Thirsk, and Thompson 1976).[1]

Anthropological Influence: From Maurice Freedman to Jack Goody

In Western studies of Chinese society and history, the topic of inheritance and family has been guided by the pioneering work of Maurice Freedman, who approached China from an anthropological perspective different from the economic development paradigm of the European tradition. Freedman drew inspiration from studies of African lineage systems, and thus his theoretical inclination was to stress the importance of lineage structures. He synthesized empirical accounts of lineages in Fujian and Guangdong by beginning with a quick, though instructive, discussion of family and then building to his extensive treatment of lineage.

He argues that Chinese lineages were based on the principle of patrilineal descent, and he systematizes the different types of lineages by analyzing such variables as their internal structures, ritual practices, and patterns of control over lineage property. He found a bewildering array of lineage types, which he attempted to model on a scale from A to Z. The A-type lineages were small structures with no corporate property except ancestral plots and that published no genealogy. The Z-type lineages were large lineages with many segments and much corporate property. Freedman simultaneously linked lineage relationships to structures of local control, local economic power, and state power (Freedman 1958, 1966).

In his latest work, Jack Goody attempts a powerful synthesis of much of the above historical and anthropological work. He simultaneously places the history of the Chinese family within a worldwide historical context and unites the Chinese family of the anthropological tradition of Freedman with that of the European tradition so influenced by Engels and Habakkuk. And Goody is not deterred from attempting to construct a new system by the growing volume and complexity of the evidence.

Goody argues that a theory of family is still possible and that a focus on family and inheritance, rather than the lineage so dear to Freedman, is the key to that theory. He states that Bronze Age agriculture allowed for the development of hierarchical societies with roughly similar family forms. The similarities lie in inheritance, particularly in women's inheritance and property rights, which Goody labels the "women's property complex." Analyzing Chinese women's property rights in their natal homes, their conjugal units, their wider kin groups, and their continuing ties to their natal homes, Goody argues that these elements of women's property rights do two things.

First, this devolution of conjugal property to women[2] unites the seemingly wide variation of family forms and inheritance practices of Europe and Asia that new research has unveiled. And while the women's property complex creates a Eurasian family form, it also distinguishes an African family form. While in Europe and Asia conjugal property devolves to women, in Africa only male property devolves to men and female property to women. Thus family forms are of two types: the Eurasian and the African (Goody 1990).

The significance of Goody's contribution are several. Like Engels and Habakkuk before him, he has constructed a system designed to encompass the entire history of the family. He also pointedly argues that class distinctions do affect family form and marriage practices. But Goody rejects Engels' notion of historical progress through stages; he also specifically rejects Habakkuk's notion that any particular family form is a precursor to capitalism and argues that a comparison of Japan and England based on unigeniture is misguided. In so doing, Goody is severing the tie among family, inheritance, and economic development so dear to Engels and Habakkuk. Thus Goody's argument incorporates the strengths of the models of the past, overcomes their weaknesses as revealed by new research, and synthesizes the new empirical data. It is the latest grand system of family history, and it unites the European tradition of family-centered family history with the Chinese tradition of lineage-centered family history.

Two Traditions of Chinese Scholarship

The third major influence on this study is a tradition of Chinese scholarship pioneered by Professor Fu Yiling of Xiamen University in Fujian province. In the course of his career, Fu Yiling stressed linking family documents (such as wills, contracts, and genealogies), village-level investigations, and major theoretical concerns in the writing of Chinese history. This combination of historical and anthropological methods has revealed a world of great variation in family, social, and economic life in Fujian alone. Fu Yiling has speculated on matters as small as the division of a water buffalo at inheritance time and as large as the theoretical implications of the fact that slave, feudal, and capitalist class relations existed in China simultaneously. The students of the "Fu Yiling School" have delved deeply into the question of inheritance, family, and lineage, and have done much to expand our understanding of how family and inheritance practices changed over space and time in Qing Fujian and Taiwan (Fu Yiling 1989; Fu Yiling and Yang Guozhen 1987; Zheng Zhenman 1984, 1989, 1992).

Another important influence from Chinese scholarship is a tradition practiced by Professors Jing Junjian and Chang Wei-jen that stresses the importance of law. These two scholars insist that in the Qing period the Qing Code was a central guiding document in the practice of inheritance and that any treatment of household division would be incomplete if it looked only at family and village-level practices, and slighted the law, the courts, and legal procedures (Chang 1983; Jing 1994).

In the United States at present, the field of Chinese legal scholarship is undergoing a renaissance. The contrast between earlier works such as Ch'u T'ung-tsu's *Law and Society in Traditional China* and the most recent work of the eight authors featured in Kathryn Bernhardt and Philip Huang's *Civil Law in Qing and Republican China* is so stark that it is easy to argue that the field is being reconceptualized entirely. The earlier scholars, while not ignoring civil law and changes in China's legal tradition completely, placed much more emphasis on penal law, the continuities embodied in abstract principles such as *li*,[3] and the pervasive use of law to buttress social stratification.

The opening of local Qing archives in the 1980s has allowed scholars to look anew at Qing law and legal procedures, and the results are a new emphasis on civil law as a major part of Qing legal procedures and a clearer picture of how the magistrates used the code to resolve civil disputes, of which household division was a part.

Though written in earlier decades, a major influence in shaping the debates contained within this renaissance of Qing legal scholarship is the pioneering work of the two great Japanese scholars of Chinese law Niida Noboru and Shiga Shūzō. These two doyens of Chinese legal scholarship have debated seemingly every important question relevant to their field. For this book, their debate on the nature of family property is particularly salient. Niida argues that family property was jointly or communally owned by all family members, male or female; Shiga, by contrast, argues that only the father, or perhaps more precisely the father-son unit, could be considered the owner of the family property (Schurmann 1956; Bernhardt 1995:269–270). A second debate concerns the nature of change in inheritance law in the Southern Song dynasty. In this context, Niida argues that daughters came to have rights to inherit family property equal to one-half of a son's share of the family property, while Shiga argues that this increase in a daughter's property rights simply never occurred (Birge 1992). A final area of debate, this one not between Shiga and Niida but between Shiga and the new view of Qing legal history, is Shiga's belief in the commonly held view that in civil cases Qing magistrates acted more as mediators than as administrators of the Qing Code. The new view argues that Qing magistrates did indeed use and enforce the code when adjudicating civil disputes (P. Huang 1994:142). This tradition of debate in Chinese legal history has been a fourth influence on this book.

The Synthetic Vision of This Book

This study draws from the strengths of these four approaches to the study of inheritance and family. From the Engels-Habakkuk tradition of political economy, while the issue of feudal to capitalist economic development may have faded, the importance of inheritance to economic issues, such as family survival strategies, upward and downward social mobility, and the preservation of wealth, remains of salient importance. So too does the importance of social class. From the Freedman tradition comes the importance of wading through the wide variety of Chinese family and lineage property practices; from Jack Goody comes the more recent focus on inheritance, women, and the nuclear family. And from the two Chinese traditions comes a concern with family documents, village investigations, and law. This study weaves these different yet complementary traditions into a new vision of how inheritance, family, lineage, and state interacted in China over the course of the Qing and Republican periods.

Chapter 2

Inheritance Law and Practice before the Qing

A BEGINNING, or entry point, to any topic in Chinese history is always a dilemma. I have opted for the simple answer. I will begin at the beginning, with the earliest recorded references to inheritance. Thus Chapter 2 is a quick overview of China's inheritance law and practice over a period of thirty centuries.

Legal Continuities: From Origins to Han

For inheritance in China's Western Zhou dynasty (ca. 1027–771 B.C.), some scholars have argued that primogeniture was the rule.[1] The system has been labeled the *zongfa*, with kingship passing through the *dazong*, or main line, and secondary and tertiary noble titles descending through *xiaozong*, or minor lines. This social hierarchical ordering of the elite is further reflected in hierarchical burial patterns of the nobility. Commoners were buried in hierarchical patterns as well, but whether commoners were part of the *zongfa* system is unclear. It is also unclear how property devolved to the next generation, because it is doubtful that private property in land existed. Thus, while kingship, royal titles, and fiefs passed down through the rules of primogeniture, the pattern of property devolution among commoners, if any, remains unknown (Eberhard 1987:50; Hsu and Linduff 1988:163–171).

It was not until the end of the Eastern Zhou dynasty (771–256 B.C.) that private property among the common people emerged and with it the possibility of inheritance (Cho-yun Hsu 1965:112). Thus China's recorded inheritance law regarding commoners emerges from the Warring States period (403–221 B.C.), in the state of Qin, during the reign of Duke Xiao (361–338 B.C.). The duke, heeding advice of his influential minister Lord Shang, implemented a series of social, economic, and political reforms designed to expand the Qin state's population, agricultural base, and military power. The essence of these reforms is recorded in *The Book of Lord Shang* (Duyvendak 1928), and their effectiveness as strategies of state building is affirmed by the Qin state's ultimate conquest of the other warring states and the first unification of the entire Chinese empire in 221 B.C.

On inheritance, the law reads: "Those families who have more than two men and do not divide will have their taxes doubled." In 350 B.C., Duke Xiao went one step further and banned the coresidence of a father and his grown sons (Qi Sihe 1981:140; Duyvendak 1928:15–18). These policies were designed to accomplish several related things: to encourage families to divide, force cultivation of new land, promote agricultural expansion, increase state revenues, and thus strengthen the state.

A second critical development in early Chinese inheritance law occurred in the Qin's successor, the Han dynasty (206 B.C.–A.D. 220). At the outset of the dynasty, the Han founder Liu Bang enfeoffed relatives and favorites as princes. Seven of these princes eventually became so powerful that in the year 154 B.C. they rose in revolt against central imperial authority. After suppressing the revolt, the Han state implemented policies to weaken future economic and geographic bases of noble power. Emperor Han Wudi promulgated measures that required all princes to divide their fiefs among their sons. He further mandated that princes could not circumvent the intent of the order by giving small shares to several sons and the major portion to one (Ban Gu 1975:395; Goodrich 1959:37).

These two acts of early Chinese statecraft placed the weight of law and state on the side of partible inheritance for both peasant and noble families. The record of the laws' effectiveness among the nobility is clear: following Han Wudi's orders, the nobles did indeed divide their fiefs (Ban Gu 1975:396; Goodrich 1959:37). And though the effectiveness of these laws among peasant families can only be guessed, a reference in *The History of the [Former] Han Dynasty* suggests that they worked: "After two years of implementation [of the new tax laws], the old Qin customs fell into disuse, and therefore, sons in rich Qin families grew up and had to divide; sons in poor families grew up and found families to marry into" (quoted in Qi Sihe 1981:140).[2]

The Chinese state's early and continued preference for partible inheritance is critical. Systems of unigeniture in Japan and England emerged to serve elite interests: in Japan to create samurai class military accountability between lord and retainer; in Europe to allow for either more effective feudal control, better manorial order, or greater family longevity. In these cases, elites and the state sanctioned unigeniture, and the practice then spread downward to the middle and peasant classes.[3] In China, by contrast, the state's consistent support of partible inheritance forestalled any such top-down emergence of unigeniture.

Legal Continuities: From Tang to Qing

For China's second great imperial period, the Tang dynasty (618–906), the extant law on inheritance is detailed and explicit. An edict of the Kaiyuan period (713–741) outlined the fundamental principles of Tang property division (see Appendix 1 for a full translation). The edict stated that, first, family property was to be divided equally among brothers. Second, if a brother died, his son or sons inherited the share. Third, unmarried sons were entitled to extra property to pay marriage expenses. Fourth, a sister-in-law's dowry property was not divided when her husband and his brothers divided their father's property. And fifth, a widow without a son received her husband's share of property. This pattern of property division would remain largely intact down to the twentieth century and the Republican revolution, so let us examine this extended pattern of continuity.

During the following Song dynasty (960–1279), the Song Code repeated the Tang Code almost word for word, with one significant addition, making explicit the punishment for unequally dividing family property (see Appendix 1 for a full translation). Thus Song inheritance was a fundamental continuation of the Tang tradition: all sons inherited equally.[4] During the Yuan dynasty (1260–1368), China was ruled by Mongol conquerors who practiced a very different type of inheritance, a variant form of ultimogeniture (Fletcher 1986:17). In Mongol custom, as each son matured and married, he was given a fixed amount of property, and he and his wife set up a separate household. The majority of the property remained with the mother and father, and it would devolve to their youngest son upon his parents' deaths. If the husband died first, the widow thus commanded considerable property until her youngest son came of age (Holmgren 1986:127–192). The Mongols also allowed polygamy, and it is possible that sons of different wives shared unequally. An "old substatute," probably of Mongol or Nüzhen origin, suggests an inheritance system based on shares: four shares for a son or sons of the wife; three shares for a son or sons of concubines; and one share for sons born of illicit sex with a worthy person or a favored slave girl (Zhang Xueshu 1986:53; Burns 1973:136; see Appendix 1 for a full translation). Only some written Mongol law has survived to the present, and what little is known suggests that in most areas of family custom, the Mongols allowed the Chinese to rule themselves in their traditional manner and did not attempt to impose either ultimogeniture or the varied share system on China (Paul Ch'en 1979:124). In fact the extant law contains several references to "equal division," and thus it is most likely that Mongol customs of ultimogeniture and unequal division had no significant effect on the fundamental equal-male pattern of Chinese inheritance (Zhang Xueshu 1986:53).

By the mid-fourteenth century, the Mongol state had weakened to the point where it could no longer suppress Chinese-led rebellions, and the Yuan dynasty was overthrown. Chinese political control was reestablished in the Ming dynasty, and the first emperor, Taizu, turned his attention to restoring order and law to China. Over the course of his rule, Taizu, often using the Tang Code as a model, would compile and issue a body of legal work that would "qualify him as one the great legislators of Chinese history" (Farmer 1995:10, 38). Taizu's laws on inheritance, as contained in the *Great Ming Commandment* and the *Great Ming Code,* were quite detailed and would set the legal pattern of inheritance for the entire Ming-Qing period.

On the subject of inheritance the Ming Code itself was terse, but it did follow the Song Code and specifically state that unequal division of family property was a crime punishable by twenty to one hundred strokes of the light or heavy bamboo, depending on the amount of money deemed misappropriated (*Da Ming lü* 1959, juan 4:10; see Appendix 1 for a full translation). But Taizu's *Great Ming Commandment,* which also carried the force of law, was much more specific: it stated that all sons, be they born of wives, concubines, or slaves, inherited equally. The *Great Ming Commandment* further elaborated on the position of the appointed heir, mandating that if a natural son was born after the appointment of the heir, the heir and the son divided the property equally. Thus appointed heirs were legally guaranteed an equal share of property, even if a blood heir was born later (Farmer 1995:159–160; see Appendix 1 for a full translation).

A likely Ming addition to the law was the notion of illegitimate sons. These were sons born of legally proscribed sexual relationships, probably outside of a father's household or households. Despite the illegal nature of the sexual union between their father and mother, these sons had inheritance rights to one-half of a legitimate son's share of the father's family property. This addition was a clear legal exception to the equal-share law from the Tang to the Qing; but if a family had an illegitimate son and an adopted heir, the two inherited equally. If there was no legitimate son, the illegitimate son inherited fully (Farmer 1995:159).

The code of the succeeding Qing dynasty (1644–1912) adopted most if not all of the Ming wording, though cash amounts were updated to account for inflation, and several explanatory lines were added for clarity (*Da Qing lüli,* juan 8:29; see Appendix 1 for a full translation). Relevant sections from the *Great Ming Commandment* were incorporated into the Qing Code, consolidating all inheritance law into one volume. The results show very little change in inheritance law from the Ming to the Qing.

Thus, for the vast majority of inheritance cases from the Tang to the Qing, the law was the same: all sons inherited equally. And while this general rule and its related corollaries went unchanged over the centuries, Tang law did not remain inviolate. In some areas affecting a significant minority of cases, there were changes in inheritance law.

Legal Changes: From Qin to Yuan

A first significant change in Chinese inheritance law related to the state's attitude toward the timing of household division. In the Qin, the state mandated early division by ordering division to take place before the death of the father. By the Tang this mandate had changed, and the law attempted to delay the timing of household division. For the Tang and Song periods, household division comprised two acts: the division of household registration and the division of household property. The former entailed the division of the household's registration with the state and the related tax liabilities; the latter, division of property owned by the family. At first glance, the law stipulated that children could not divide either registration or the household property while their parents and grandparents were living: "Whenever during the lifetime of the paternal grandparents or parents the children or grandchildren divide the household registration and partition the property, the punishment is three years of penal servitude" (*Tang lü shuyi* 236). The law further stated that, following the parents' deaths, the children could not divide registration or property until after the proper mourning period, usually three years. Thus Tang law delayed the division of household registration and property division until well after the parents' deaths.

The law that children could not divide registration or family property was copied into the Song, Ming, and Qing codes, with only minor changes related to the required punishment. But the state's stance began to moderate by the twelfth and early thirteenth centuries (Bernhardt 1995:290), probably allowing division if the parent or parents agreed. This change was codified in Ming Taizu's *Great Ming Commandment*, which states that a living parent or grandparent could legally permit division of household property among sons and grandsons (Farmer 1995:161). And by the Qing, the complete withering of the Tang-Song household registration system and changes in the tax systems allowed the prohibition on early division of household registration to fall into disuse. Recognizing this fact, the Qing Code incorporated Ming Taizu's law specifically legalizing early divisions of property ordered or allowed by parents (*Da Qing lüli*, juan 8:28).[5] Thus by the Qing, by contrast with the Tang, household division concerned solely the division of property and could legally take place either after the deaths of both parents or while one or both parents was still alive, provided the surviving parents agreed. The state had ceased to try to affect the timing of household division.

Other aspects of Tang inheritance law that would change involved the complex set of women's property rights. Perhaps most visibly, the Tang dynasty's Kaiyuan edict stated that unmarried daughters were entitled to dowries valued at one-half of a son's marriage expenses;

this legally specified right of women to a dowry would disappear by the Song and never be revived. The effect of this deletion should not be stressed overly, since dowries were well protected in customary practices; but neither should it be considered unimportant, since it did deny legal recourse to those women, and perhaps their husbands, who felt their dowries had been too meager.

Another significant change in women's property rights was a decline in the wife's legal property rights over her dowry. The Tang and Song codes both stated that a wife's dowry property was kept separate from her husband's and his brother's property, and at division time was not included in the devolution to the brothers. By the Ming, this language was gone. Again, the change in law may not have been significant in practice, but such a change did close off one avenue of legal relief to women.

A further loss of legal rights over dowry property was, at least in part, due to the rule of the Mongols. As explained above, the Mongol systems of residence and inheritance differed considerably from the Chinese. The clash between the two was most severe in the case of widows and their property. A Chinese widow of the Tang-Song period could and often did return to her natal home with her dowry property and her children. If a Mongol widow were to remarry out of her husband's clan, the clan would stand to lose considerable property, not just the dowry, but also the husband's property, which was under the widow's control. The traditional Mongol solution to this problem was the levirate, a practice by which the widow remarried a male relative in her husband's clan, thus keeping the wealth within the clan.

To the Chinese, with the common practice of coresidence of parents and married sons under one roof, the levirate was anathema, because it established the possibility of a brother marrying his deceased brother's widow and all the tensions such a legal right might entail. The solution to the contradictions between these two systems, one that allowed free widow remarriage with control over dowry property and the other that used the levirate, was a compromise: widow chastity, enforced by loss of dowry property if she remarried (Holmgren 1986:127–192). In 1303 a statute was enacted that was subsequently incorporated into the *Yuan dianzhang*, the *Compendium of Statues and Substatutes* for the Mongol dynasty, which read as follows:

> Regarding dowry lands and other goods that a woman brings into her marriage: from now on if a woman who has once been married wishes to marry again to someone else, whether she is divorced while her [first] husband is alive or is living as a widow after her husband has died, her dowry property and other belongings that she brought into her marriage should all be taken over by the family of her former husband. It is absolutely not permitted for her to take them away with herself, as was formerly done. (quoted in Birge 1992:262–263)

Thus, while the Mongols did not tinker with the equal-male side of Chinese inheritance, their influence would be felt in the realm of women's property rights, significantly weakening widows' rights over dowry property. The *Great Ming Commandment* would incorporate the 1303 Yuan statute, and this prohibition would be carried over into the Qing Code as well.

Tang law regarding the inheritance of property in extinct families, defined as families with no male heirs either natural or adopted, would change as well. In the Tang, provided the father had made no disposition in a will, the property of extinct families would go first to daughters either married or single; failing daughters, it went to close agnatic kin; and failing close agnatic kin, it went to the state (Bernhardt 1995:273).

The Song state would make an attempt and possibly succeed at changing this dramatically. The historian must temporize when discussing the Song period, which was one of great intellectual, social, economic, and military ferment. As just the most famous example, in 1127, the Northern Song was defeated militarily by the Jin dynasty and was driven south to Hangzhou, where it survived until 1279 as the Southern Song. Philosophical, practical, and military debates raged among scholars, the emperor, and his advisors. During this dynasty of upheaval, thousands of laws, rules, and rescripts were established, only a small fraction of which are extant. Thus the degree that these laws actually changed is unclear and a subject of much debate among specialists.

One line of argumentation runs that owing to the massive military expenditures associated with resisting the invasions of the Jin and the Mongols, the Song state was forced to increase the land and contract taxes (Hansen 1995:86–92). In this vein, the Song may have attempted, for the first and possibly the only time in imperial Chinese history, to impose an inheritance tax. The tax would occur in those cases in which the household was becoming extinct. For these families, the state introduced several new rules and distinctions and made what for the Tang had been a simple undertaking into a process of considerable complexity.[6]

The new set of rules stated that in the case of an extinct household, the state could take a percentage of the property, the percentage varying with the particular family situation. In an extinct household that further lacked any daughters, in Tang law close agnatic kin acquired the property. New Song law denied close agnatic kin this right, and the property was confiscated by the state (Bernhardt 1995:275). The Song also imposed a somewhat progressive inheritance tax on the amounts received by daughters and postmortem heirs (heirs appointed after the deaths of the parents) of extinct families. For amounts of less that 500 *guan,* there was no tax, and the daughters and the heir received the full amount. For amounts ranging from 500 to 1,500 *guan,* the heirs received only 500 *guan.* If the property was valued above 1,500 *guan,* the heirs could receive only one-third, up to a total of 3,000 *guan.* If the property totaled 20,000 *guan,* the heirs could receive 2,000 *guan* more, for a maximum of 5,000 *guan.* All amounts above these maximums were to revert to the state (ibid.).

The argument suggests that the Song state extended its reach even further. Another rule distinguished among daughters: while in the Tang all daughters, regardless of marital status, inherited extinct household property equally, in the Song unmarried, married, and "returned" daughters would inherit differently.[7] The Song also contrived a new distinction between premortem and postmortem heirs. In the Tang an heir could be adopted either before (premortem) or after (postmortem) the deaths of the parents, and he would receive the entire family property (Burns 1973:268). In the Song, while the premortem heir still inherited fully, postmortem heirs received only a portion, at most one-third, of the property.

The inheritance of the property of extinct households thus became a complex, three-way interplay between the state, the daughters, and the postmortem heir. Table 1 shows the details. One significant effect of this new extinct family inheritance regime was, quite surprisingly, to expand the rights of the daughters in relationship to the postmortem heir. In the Tang, the postmortem heir would have received the property in full, while in the Song he received at most one-third,

Table 1
Extinct Family Inheritance in the Song Dynasty

In an Extinct Family with No Postmortem Heir Plus . . .	The Daughter(s) Receive(s)	The State Takes	
Unmarried daughter(s)	1	0	
Unmarried and returned daughter(s)	1	0	
Returned daughter(s)	1/2	1/2	
Married daughter(s)	1/3	2/3	
In an Extinct Family with a Postmortem Heir Plus . . .	The Post-mortem Heir Receives	The Daughter(s) Receive(s)	The State Takes
Unmarried daughter(s) at home	1/4	3/4	0
Unmarried daughter(s) and returned daughter(s) at home	1/5	4/5	0
Returned daughter(s) at home	1/4	1/2	1/4
Daughter(s) who have married out	1/3	1/3	1/3
No daughter either returned or married out	1/3		2/3

Source: Bernhardt 1995:274.

while the daughter or daughters received anywhere from one-third to four-fifths.

If this Song pattern of extinct family property distribution was actually mandated by the state and subsequently enforced empire-wide, it represents considerable change from the inheritance law of both the pre- and post-Song periods. The problems with this argument, however, are several. Most important, questions of how widespread the enforcement of the law was and how much local resistance the new laws aroused are simply impossible to answer; in addition, some Song scholars are known to have advocated that the state take no taxes from extinct families and distribute the property even more widely, including more distant kin and tenants. Resolution of the question of what changed in Song inheritance must be left to the Song specialists, but to my mind the changes described above deserve strong consideration.

Legal Changes: From Yuan to Qing

During the Yuan (and holding constant through the Ming and Qing), the Song's extinct family inheritance tax disappeared along with its legal distinctions between premortem and postmortem heirs. Any male heir, appointed pre- or postmortem, received the property in full, which in effect scaled back daughters' property rights in relationship to the postmortem heir. Ming law mandated that extinct family property go first to a postmortem male heir (if one could be found), then to daughters (equally and regardless of marital status), and then to the state (Farmer 1995:93, 159–160). Ming law further narrowed women's property rights by mandating that, when widowed, women were legally required to have an heir appointed, which effectively shrank their daughters' rights to extinct family property. This legal requirement to have an heir appointed meant that if any male heir, at first within the five grades of mourning (meaning agnatic males out to fourth cousins) and later no matter how distantly related (meaning those who shared a surname), could be found, daughters could not inherit. Daughters' rights were thus highly conditional: they inherited from their natal home if, and only if, there were no male heirs, either born or appointed (Bernhardt 1995:298).

The Qing Code, as opposed to the Tang and Song codes, further limited the rights of daughters when the state allowed a practice called "combined succession," in which one son was allowed to be heir to his father and to one or more of his father's brothers as well. Combined succession thus denied property to daughters who had no brothers but did have one male cousin (Bernhardt 1995:299–300). In these subtle ways, women's inheritance rights were diminished over time.

Another change from Ming to Qing was an addition to the order of property ultimately confiscated by the state from truly intestate families. In the Ming, the order was, first, an appropriate heir; second, daughters; and third, the state. The Qing Code specified that if there were no legal male heirs, no daughters, and no close agnatic kin, only then did the property revert to the state. This addition of close agnatic kin before state confiscation was a Qing addition to the Ming sequence (Bernhardt 1995:298).

In sum, the overall pattern for Chinese inheritance law from the Tang to the Qing is one of continuity. The rule—all family property was to be divided equally among the sons—remained unchanged and was in fact clarified over time. Several elements that did change over time, culminating in the Ming and carried through the Qing, were the cessation of the state's attempt to control the timing of division, the elimination of daughters' legal rights to a dowry, a diminution of daughters' rights to extinct family property, and a weakening of wives' and widows' rights of control over their dowry property.

Early Household Division Practices: Han to Qing
Continuities: Equal Division among Brothers

Inheritance practices of the pre-Qing period were considerably more complex than what the law prescribed. There are extant scattered household division documents,[8] which are few in number, terse, and vague as to the size and value of the property being divided. A more extensive and nuanced source is a series of legal case decisions compiled in the Southern Song dynasty (1127–1279) called the *Minggong shupan qingmingji*, or the *Famous Judges' Collection of Clear and Lucid Cases* (hereafter *Qingmingji* or QMJ).[9] Further legal evidence can be found in Robert Van Gulik's *T'ang-Yin-Pi-Shih* (1956), an annotated translation of court cases from as early as the Han dynasty. These varied sources afford a necessarily quick and perhaps too simple view of the continuities and changes in Chinese inheritance practices over a period of 1,700 years, but they do establish a baseline from which to view inheritance practices during the Qing dynasty.

The basic principle of Chinese inheritance—equal division of family property among sons—emerges from virtually all of the sources. Stories from Sima Qian's *Shiji* and Ban Gu's *Hanshu* have led scholars to conclude that the equal-male inheritance system was a generally accepted rule in the Han dynasty, though will makers had some flexibility in dividing property (Ch'u 1972:16–17, 262, 299).

The earliest extant household division document is dated 909 and was discovered in the grottoes of Dunhuang in dry northwest China. Three brothers, Jiaying, Huaizi, and Huaijia had been orphaned when young, and they asked their relatives and neighbors to oversee the division of the family property, consisting of two plots of land, housing, trees, and farm animals. The plots of land were each divided into three pieces: Jiaying received two plots totaling 10.5 *mu*,[10] and he would share the use of an ox with Huaizi. Huaizi received two plots of land totaling 9.5 *mu,* the shared use of the ox, and the shared use of two trees with Huaijia. Finally Huaijia received his two plots totaling 9.5 *mu,* his shared use of the trees, and one unspecified farm animal. Thus Jiaying's extra *mu* of land was balanced by the other two brothers' extra trees and, in Huaijia's case, an extra animal (Zhongguo kexueyuan lishi yanjiusuo ziliaoshi 1961:405).

A second division document, dated 948, concerns a division that took place in Fuzhou and Nanfeng in Jiangxi in southeast China. The father, known as Ancestor Xuan, and his wife née Meng were seventy-three *sui*.[11] They had three sons—Lun, Jing, and Shao—and eighteen grandsons. Lun and Shao had moved to Nanfeng, leaving the parents and second brother Jing in Fuzhou. The parents state that they are no longer able to manage the property, which totals more than 1,700 *shi*[12] of income and includes irrigated land, dry land, tea lands, ponds for fish, ducks, and geese, and ancestral temples. Though the property is located in the two locations of Fuzhou and Nanfeng, the division is simple. Jing will receive all the property in Fuzhou, where he lives, and Lun and Shao will divide equally the property in Nanfeng, where they live (Wu Zuoxi 1917, 5:4–6). For the Southern Song dynasty, the *Qingmingji* case titled "Brothers Falsify Information on Property" illustrates an arithmetically simple division between two brothers. In 1185, father Weng Zongyu divided his fifty-eight *zhong*[13] of land between his two sons, Weng Hua and Weng Xian. Each received twenty-nine *zhong* (QMJ 1987:373).

A complex case titled "Individually Selling Undivided Property" illustrates the equal rights of the son of a concubine. Father Fang Wenliang had three sons, two by his deceased wife née Huang and one by his concubine née Li. Father Fang died, and the management of the family property passed to his eldest son, Yande. The second brother died leaving a son, Zhongyi. Third brother Yunlao, the son of concubine Li, was only two *sui*. A dispute over Zhongyi's gambling debts brought the family to court. Zhongyi had illegally sold and pawned family property in order to pay these debts, and his uncle Yande went to court to reclaim the property. Yande made his claim in an illegal manner, however, by stating Zhongyi was his son, rather than his nephew, in order to lay claim to even more of the family property. The court sorted out the various family relationships and competing claims and, in order to resolve the problem, decided to divide the household. Some land was given to concubine Li as her *yangshan* property.[14] The court then ordered that the "remaining land and other property will be divided into three equal shares, and each will establish his own household." Thus Yunlao, the son of a concubine, inherited equally (QMJ 1987:303).

In the above case the position of Zhongyi, the son of a deceased brother, illustrates the dispensation of property when one brother is dead: his son or sons take his share. A 1481 division from Yongchun county, Fujian, is further evidence. The Kang family had had three brothers, Fucheng, Furui, and Fuqing, but the eldest, Fucheng, died, leaving his widow née Wu and one son, Kuanyang. The division therefore took place between Kuanyang and his two uncles. Kuanyang received one *suo*[15] of land, one fish pond, and the attached mountain land. The two uncles were going to continue to work together, and they took one *suo* of sugarcane land, a pond, and the attached mountain land. They would manage the lands and pond jointly but would build separate houses. The family was liable for one *shi* of grain corvée tax, and after division each branch would pay one-third of a *shi*. Thus if a brother died before household division but after giving birth to a son, that brother's share went to his son (Yang 1990:80).

An exceptional case titled "A Son Married In with His Mother Plots to Take the Property of Father and Son" shows the state actively upholding the principle of equal division, despite the wishes of the father. Tan Nianhua had an unspecified number of sons by a first wife. She most likely died (the details are not given), and in 1208 Tan married the widow A Wei, who had a son, Li Ziqin, from her previous marriage. Tan Nianhua became so infatuated with his new wife that she was able to convince him to expel his blood sons from the household and, over time, turn over all his property to her son, Li Ziqin. Some property was turned over legally, and even more was taken illegally through the use of forged contracts.

Tan Youji and the other blood sons waited until their father died

and then brought the case to court. The court ordered burned all
the contracts and deeds, both the legal and the illegal, that gave the
property to Li Ziqin. Next, all Tan Nianhua's former property and
all the property Li Ziqin had bought in his own name with his ill-
gotten gains was divided equally among all of the sons. Even Li Ziqin
got a share, though he also received one hundred strokes of the light
bamboo for his crime. Thus father Tan's wishes, which entailed an
unequal division of property, were overturned by the state in the
interests of equal division (QMJ 1987:124).

There are only scattered household division documents extant for
the Yuan and Ming dynasties. The Yuan documents share the same
form as those of the previous and later dynasties but lack sufficient
details of property distribution for analysis. For the Ming, the most
complete is dated 1374, and it reveals that sons born to women other
than the wife also inherited. In this case, the household division document demonstrates that sons born to women outside the household
could share equally at household division time. The document is for
the Guo family division of 1374. Father Guo, known as Ancestor
Yuanxian, resided in Fuzhou and had married the woman Yang, who
had given birth to two sons, Guiqing and Zigui. Father Guo's business often took him some distance to Jianningfu, where he began a
relationship with a woman named Wu Foxiao, who gave birth to a
son, Jianlang, in 1351. In 1363 Wu Foxiao died, and father Guo
brought their son Jianlang back to his home in Fuzhou. At some point
between 1363 and 1374, father Guo died, without paying back a
debt to his first son and daughter-in-law.[16]

At the point of household division in 1374, the family's land provided 25.4 *shi* of income. First, 3.5 *shi* was awarded to eldest son Guiqing as repayment for the loan to his father. The remaining income
was divided into equal shares of 7.3 *shi,* one for each of the three
sons. The family further had two houses. One was divided in half,
the east side going to Guiqing, the west to Zigui. Jianlang received
the second house. Thus while Jianlang was not the son of the first
wife and was born outside of the household, he shared equally in the
division of the property (Guo Jiechang 1892, 7:1–2).

A later and much simpler Ming document, dated 1481, shows a
nephew and two Kang brothers dividing their property. Each received
one fish pond and was required to pay .333 *shi* in taxes (Yang 1990:
256). The much wealthier family of Xu Xiake, a noted Ming scholar

and official, divided its extensive and varied property in 1514. Despite the complexity of the division, which had to make arrangements for a daughter's dowry, parental sacrifices, and a brother's marriage expenses, each of the three brothers received exactly 12,598.761 *mu* of land (Lü 1988:111–120).

The foregoing evidence illustrates that the basic principle of household division, equal division among all sons, was standard practice for the period from at least 900 to 1644. Blood sons, sons born outside the home, and concubines' sons were all entitled to an equal share of the family property.

Continuities: *Yangshan, Dowries, and Marriage Expenses*

The *Qingmingji* cases and other evidence suggest two other inheritance practices as well. One is the setting aside of *yangshan* property for support of aging parents. In the case "The Buyer Forges a Contract to Engross Land," two ponds and one plot of dry land were given to mother A Song as her *yangshan* support (QMJ 1987:305). In the above-mentioned "Individually Selling Undivided Property," concubine Li is specifically awarded land as a *yangshan* portion (QMJ 1987:303). In another case, the widow Ye is allowed to keep fifty-seven *dan* of land as her *yangshan*, even though the conspiracy into which she entered to get it was probably illegal (QMJ 1987:141). In Xu Xiake's 1514 division mentioned above, the widowed mother, née Yang, kept 1,700 *mu* of land as her *yangshan* (Lü 1988:111–120).

Another inheritance principle that emerges from the evidence is that of a daughter's right to a dowry and most likely an unmarried son's rights to marriage expenses. *Hanshu* and *Shiji* stories reveal that as early as the Han dynasty daughters might receive a dowry as large as a brother's share (Ch'u 1972:17–18). The Southern Song evidence concurs. In "A Remarried Wife Wants Her Previous Husband's Property," the Wei family had three sons, Jingmo, Jingxuan, and Jinglie. The second, Jingxuan, married in succession two women, both née Zhao. Jingxuan and his second wife had a daughter, Rongjie. Jingxuan died, and his second wife Zhao remarried Liu Youguang, who, to the horror of the court, came to live in the Wei household. The court decided that Zhao and Liu should leave the Wei household and go live in the Liu household. Even though Zhao's daughter Rongjie accompanied them to the Liu residence, the two surviving Wei brothers, Jingmo and Jinglie, were required to pay for her dowry because she was their blood niece, and the family property had never been divided (QMJ 1987:353).

In a simpler case, widow Ye had a daughter Guiniang, possibly from a previous marriage. Widow Ye entered into a conspiracy with her brother, Ye Shiyi, part of which allotted thirty-one *dan* to Guiniang as a dowry. The court allowed this property to remain with Guiniang (QMJ 1987:141). In Xu Xiake's 1514 division mentioned above, the family set aside a total of twelve *qing* of land for the dowries of two daughters. Marriage expenses were also set aside for the third brother, who was engaged but not fully married (Lü 1988:111–120). Thus the evidence suggests that three fundamental principles—equal division among sons, *yangshan* support for parents, and dowries or marriage expenses for unmarried siblings—lie at the core of Chinese household division in the seven centuries preceding the Qing dynasty. As we shall see, these principles form a line of continuity through the Qing period.

Detecting and Periodizing Complex Changes in Inheritance

But while the continuities are strong, some noticeable differences in inheritance rights do emerge in a pre-Qing to Qing comparison. These differences lie primarily in two related areas: adoption of heirs and women's property rights. As to adoption, families without sons were considered heirless, even if they had a daughter. This legal situation was known in Chinese as *hujue* or *juehu,* and meant the family line was becoming extinct. If a son was adopted before the deaths of the parents, he received the family property in full. But if the parents died heirless, there were two possibilities: the daughter(s) inherited or a boy within (or in some situations from outside) the lineage was appointed a postmortem heir.

One legal dispute suggests that this pattern may have been in place as early as the Western Han dynasty. In the reign of Emperor Xuan (73–49 B.C.), a wealthy old man named Chenliu had no sons. He had one married daughter from his deceased first wife, but he remarried and his second wife gave birth to a son. When Chenliu died, his daughter by his first wife claimed the family property by arguing that Chenliu was not the real father of the son. The case was decided by Bing Ji, a famous Han official, who said: "I have heard that a son begotten by an aged father cannot bear cold and that in the sun his body will cast no shadow." So Bing Ji called in a group of similarly aged children and had them stand in the cold: only Chenliu's son showed the effects. Then Bing Ji made the group stand in the sun: only Chenliu's son cast no shadow. Based on this evidence, the daughter was punished, and the property went to the son (Van Gulik 1956:78–79).

Though the evidence used to decide may be unbelievable, the case does suggest strongly that the daughter's claim would have been legal had there been no son. In other words, in extinct families, daughters inherited the family property.

Another early legal dispute, dated about 1050, provides similar evidence. This was a case of murder in which a thief killed an entire family, the husband and wife dying immediately, the son the following day. The authorities at the prefectural level followed the rules of property disposition in extinct families and awarded all the property to the family's married daughters. But there was opposition, and one official said: "At the time when the father and mother died the son was still alive; therefore the property belongs to the son. The married daughter and her married sisters are not entitled to a share" (Van Gulik 1956:170).

The story demonstrates that in cases in which a family had no male heir, daughters, even those already married into other families, inherited the property. On this general principle, there was no disagreement. In this particular case, however, the daughters were denied the property because, after their parents died, their only brother lived one more day. For that day he was the legal owner of the property, and when he died, the property passed by law to his heirs, not to his sisters. If he had no heirs and if none was appointed, as is probable in this case, the property would revert to the state (Burns 1973:xiii).

Though the evidence is scarce, it is generally agreed that in the Tang the postmortem heir was treated no differently than the premortem heir, that he inherited fully and the daughters inherited nothing (Bernhardt 1995:274; Burns 1973:268). In the Southern Song this would change, as the state imposed its inheritance tax and related three-way property division scheme. Under this changed inheritance regime, in extinct families the property was variously divided between the state, the postmortem heir, and the daughters, depending on the family's particular structure. Some of the *Qingmingji* evidence sug-

Figure 1
The Tian Family Structure at Division Time

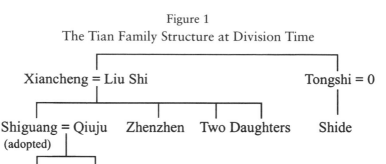

gests that the law was enforced at least some of the time. In the Xiong family dispute over a deceased daughter's dowry property, the decision states that an appointed heir "should only receive one-fourth of the property" (QMJ 1987:110). In the Luo family dispute, third brother Ren was trying to appoint an heir to his deceased second brother, Zong. In this case, since there were no women in the household, one-third went to the heir, and two-thirds went to the state (QMJ 1987:107).

In a complex case suitably titled "The Appointed Heir Receives Only One-Fourth of the Property,"[17] the Tian family was involved in a complex dispute about naming an heir. The first generation of the Tian family had two brothers, Xiancheng and Tongshi. Both were married, Xiancheng to a woman née Liu. Xiancheng and Liu had an elder adopted son, Shiguang, and a younger blood son, Zhenzhen. Shiguang was married to a woman named Qiuju, and they had two daughters, both very young.[18] Zhenzhen was still single. Younger brother Tongshi also had a son, Shide. Figure 1 represents the Tian family's extended family structure at the time of the dispute. The document states that when Xiancheng died, his property was divided equally between Shiguang and Zhenzhen. Subsequently Shiguang died, and the document states that the law allows Shiguang's property to go to his daughters, one-half to each.

The case comes to court because Tongshi tries to appoint his son, Shide, as postmortem heir to Shiguang. Though there are some technical problems with the appointment, the court allows it. Shide therefore receives one-fourth of the property as posthumous heir, and the remaining three-fourths is divided between the two daughters. Because the girls are young, the property goes to their mother, Qiuju, to manage, but she is not allowed to sell it. Thus the case is illustrative of daughters' changed, and slightly expanded, property rights in the Southern Song: if an heir was not appointed, the daughters divided all the family property equally; but if a postmortem heir was appointed, the daughters still divided a percentage based upon their marital and residential status (QMJ 1987:251).

Changes in property rights also occurred for women who were widowed. The Song sources suggest that, by contrast with the Qing, the rate of widow remarriage was relatively high. In the Xiong family dispute, the deceased third brother's widow, A Gan, remarried and for good measure claimed property in the Xiong household (QMJ 1987:110). In the Tan family dispute, the widow A Wei had married into the Tan family, and she brought in her son Li Ziqin from her previous marriage (QMJ 1987:124). In the Xu family dispute, the widow A Feng married the elder Xu and brought her son, Chen Baisi, from her previous marriage (QMJ 1987:304–305). In the Wei family dispute, widow Zhao not only married Liu Youguang, but tried to bring him into the Wei household (QMJ 1987:353). And in the Wu family dispute over father Wu's property, the widow Wang remarried out (QMJ 1987:365). While statistical comparisons are impossible and while many widows of the pre-Qing period certainly did not remarry, the evidence strongly suggests that Southern Song women had considerably more latitude in deciding whether to remarry than did women of the Qing.

Related to widow remarriage was a woman's right to take her dowry property and property acquired using the dowry as investment when she remarried. In the Wu family dispute, widow Wang "originally had twenty-three *zhong*[19] of land when she married in, and with this dowry she acquired up to forty-seven *zhong*, and when she packed her boxes and remarried, she took it all with her." She is allowed to do this, even though there is a son in the family by a previous wife (QMJ 1987:366). In the Wei family dispute, widow Zhao claimed a section of the Wei house on the basis that she built it with her own dowry money. The court ruled against her, not because such a claim was inherently illegal, but because she was lying: the house had been built before she married into the family (QMJ 1987:353).

Analysis of inheritance practices in the following Yuan and early Ming dynasties is severely hampered because there are no sources equivalent in quality to those of the *Qingmingji*. Thus, it is hard to determine exactly when and how women's property rights changed between the Southern Song and the Qing, although such changes clearly occurred, as the situation for women in the Qing was quite different.

It should first be noted that women had clearly defined property rights from at least as early as the Han dynasty. An *yizhu*[20] document from the year A.D. 5 unearthed in Jiangsu province, though not dealing directly with household division, confirms that women had rights over property in certain circumstances. The document was written by the woman Yu and was signed by witnesses, making it legal. It states that she had three husbands in succession, and that she had four children by her first (three sons and one daughter)[21], one by her second (a son), and one by her third (a daughter). Gongwen, the son by her second husband, had run off at age fifteen *sui* and committed a crime; he was sentenced to four years of labor service and presumably had his property confiscated by the state. The woman Yu goes on to say that she had previously given several pieces of land to her daughters, but now Gongwen has returned from his punishment. Therefore, she is having her daughters return the land to her, and she will turn it over to Gongwen, who may manage it but not sell it (Chen and Wang 1987:20–25, 36). The suggestions are tantalizing: a woman married three times giving land to her daughters and then recalling it to give to a son? While the document does demonstrate that women had property rights, the case is too isolated to further define what those rights might have been.

By the Tang and Song the picture becomes more clear. Tang dynasty women had clearly defined legal property rights to a dowry and to family property in those cases where the family had no male heirs.[22] In the late Song there may have been a slight increase in property rights in those rare cases of extinct households that appointed a postmortem heir. But by the Qing, women's property rights had narrowed considerably.

The right of widows to remarry and remove dowry property upon remarriage, so strong in the Southern Song, had disappeared completely in the Qing. If a Qing widow remarried, she not only left behind her dowry property but also, as a general rule, her children, especially sons. And in the Qing, the rights of the postmortem heir had expanded at the expense of daughters. The postmortem heir most frequently received one hundred percent of the family property,[23] while the daughters received nothing. Daughters could inherit their natal family's property only in those instances in which no male heir could be found. Qing women's only two remaining rights were to a dowry at marriage and to a share of the family property (only if there was no male heir of any type).

When did these changes occur? A traditional interpretation associates the narrowing of women's propety rights with the Southern Song. After all, it was in the Southern Song that a revitalized and more misogynist form of Confucian philosophy, Neo-Confucianism, emerged and came to dominate the examination system so central to the formation of elite ideals and philosphy. Neo-Confucianism placed much greater emphasis on widow chastity, for instance, considering a widow who remarried (and thus removed her dowry property) to be an immoral betrayer of her husband. And the Song dynasty was the period in which foot binding for women became commonplace. Zhu Xi (1130–1200) himself, the architect of the Neo-Confucianist canon, was an ardent exponent of foot binding. He and his son-in-law, Huang Gan, were also quite pointed in their desire to limit women's rights over dowry property. Thus it was often assumed that the narrowing of property rights came hand in hand with the emergence of Neo-Confucianism and foot binding during the Southern Song.

This traditional view has recently been severely challenged. It is now argued that the Southern Song was in fact the high-water mark for women's property rights, with women enjoying not only rights to remarry and to remove dowry property, but also to direct inheritance of family property valued at one-half the share that a brother received (Birge 1992). In this view, the narrowing of women's property rights must have occurred later, probably in the Yuan.

My sense of the *Qingmingji* evidence, however, is more in tune with the traditional view. The two or three scattered references to a daughter's direct inheritance of one-half of a brother's share are insufficient and in too stark a contrast to the rest of the *Qingmingji* evidence to prove that such a law or practice ever existed (Bernhardt 1995). As to women's rights over dowry property, one illustrative *Qingmingji* case written by Huang Gan reads as follows:

> The lady Ch'en in becoming the wife of Hsü Meng-i, should treat the family of Hsü Meng-i as her family. . . . Even though she had had

no children, it still would not have been fitting for her to return [to her natal family]. How much more so when she has three daughters and a son? . . . The land that her father gave her for her marriage is the land of the Hsü name. If her husband has acquired land, it is land of the Hsü name even though it goes under the name of trousseau. How can the lady Ch'en hold it? Suppose that there were no children in the Hsü name. Then if the lady Ch'en were to take the land and treat it as what she held herself, it would be fitting. But having four children, she should take the land and divide it among all her children.[24] (quoted in Burns 1973:188)

This judgment indicates that the lady Chen is indeed taking her dowry property, and possibly some property generated by the dowry, with her back to her natal home; it also indicates that the author of the judgment, Huang Gan, the son-in-law of Zhu Xi, finds this deplorable. Since this is a *Qingmingji* case from the Southern Song, and it is written by an official so close to the icon of Neo-Confucianism, it would be feasible to conclude that it represents the beginning of the attempt to narrow a remarried woman's rights to her dowry property.

Evidence of a consolidation of this loss of rights over dowry property can be found in the 1303 Yuan law quoted above. The law's denial of widows' rights over dowry property suggests a harmony between the rising Neo-Confucian views on the Chinese side and the sense that freely remarrying widows with property were a threat to the levirate on the Mongol side. But it is too much to expect the evidence to confirm exactly when and how the new philosophy and law worked their way through the society and did, in practice, deny widows their right to dowry property upon remarriage; it is also too much to ask exactly when their rights to property in extinct families narrowed owing to the increased use of adoption of heirs, both pre- and postmortem. The best guess is that the practice began in the Southern Song with the advent of Neo-Confucianism and was consolidated and codified in the Yuan and early Ming.

A final possible change in Chinese inheritance processes was a narrowing of the power of the family head to devolve his or her property through the use of a will. The power to make a will was well established by Han times (Ch'u 1972:17). Scholars generally agree that, from the Han through the Tang and possibly into the Song, the family head had wider freedoms to use a will to devolve property, at least in those cases where a family line was becoming extinct (Bernhardt 1995:276; Burns 1973:261; Ch'u 1972:17, 299). A well-known early legal case from the Western Han Dynasty (206 B.C. to A.D. 24) suggests the wider power of the will.

A widowed man, whose total wealth came to over two hundred thousand strings of cash, had a three-year-old son and a married daughter. The daughter was described as "wicked" and her husband as "greedy and low-minded." Fearing the power of his daughter, the father called together the members of his clan and made a will giving all his property to his daughter. To his son, he gave only a sword, which was to be given to the boy upon his fifteenth birthday. When the boy turned fifteen, the daughter refused to turn over the sword, and the son went to court. The judge, He Wu, examined the case and realized that the father had given the property to the daughter only out of fear of what she might do to the young son. The sword was the symbol of the father's real desire to give all the property to his son, and He Wu ordered all the propety returned to the son (Van Gulik 1956:176–177).

The striking note in the story is the earlier use of the will to give the property to the daughter, an act agreed to by the clan members. This right to devolve property by will to a daughter in the presence of a living son, if it ever actually existed, is lost by the Ming at the latest. By the Qing, as we shall see, parents who chose to use a will, usually called an *yizhu*, had to follow the same principles of equal-male division as applied in all cases of household division. The power to devolve property by a will according to one's desires had been narrowed to the power to follow the rules of equal division.

Whatever changes in inheritance practices took place from the Han to the Qing, it is the continuities that stand out. Despite the adjustments in the rights of widows, daughters, postmortem heirs, and possibly testators, Chinese inheritance law and custom can best be summarized in three phrases: parents received support; unmarried siblings received marriage expenses or dowries; and all sons inherited equally. This pattern remained constant from at least the Tang through the Qing, a period of about one thousand years. It is also fair to say that, over this extended period, there is a remarkable harmony between code and practice in the area of inheritance.

Chapter 3

Qing Household Division:
Why, When, and How?

F ROM the vantage point of three thousand years of history, let us now turn to household division in the Qing period. When households divided, they did so for a variety of reasons and with a variety of outcomes in mind, but they did so through a fairly universal process. I propose to view this procedure from three perspectives, looking at the reasons why, the timing of, and the process through which household division occurred.

Why Did Households Divide? The External Factors

The reasons why and when households divided varied, with all aspects of family experience playing roles. As Maurice Freedman so well put it: "The problem is to find out at what point partition took place and why—a problem which is economic, legal, moral, religious, and, in a restricted sense, psychological" (Freedman 1979:236).

Franz Schurmann argues that no legal or community pressures mandated division, and he further suggests that division was caused by internal family dissension and possibly external economic pressures (Schurmann 1956:512). Schurmann has the balance right, but the definition of external economic pressures should be refined to include the forces of taxation, warfare, and banditry, which may have played roles in the timing of division at various points in Chinese history. As presented in Chapter 2, Lord Shang of Qin used tax policy to force families to divide early, and increased taxes on families with several males likely caused early division. Conversely, for the Song period, Burns has argued that the state sought to delay division (technically separation of registration) because it often resulted in the loss of tax revenue or duty-service. He states: "The splitting of one registered household into several very likely meant that those newly created came into a lesser category than the ancestor, or even into an exempt category, so that the state impositions became lighter or disappeared" (Burns 1973:113). While illegal or unreported division was undoubtedly widespread, the *Qingmingji* cases contain noticeably few cases of *yangshan* property, particularly for living fathers. It may well be that the Song state's prohibition of early division was effective.

For the late Yuan and early Ming, Zheng Zhenman has argued that the endemic violence of dynastic change pressured families into dividing early, splitting up property so as to present a less tempting target to bandits or marauding armies. Once order was reestablished in the early Ming dynasty, the government's attempts at population registration, corvée extraction, and other assaults on rich families continued to force these families to divide early. Finally, by the mid- to late Ming, when registration was relaxed and corvée was fixed, division could at last be delayed, and big families reemerged (Zheng 1992). By the second half of the Qing dynasty and the Republican era, all remaining taxation on individuals had disappeared in the early Qing tax reforms known as the *tan ding ru di*. These policies incorporated the head tax on individuals into the land tax, left no tax on individuals, and therefore eliminated tax policy as a factor affecting the timing of household division.

There is evidence that the external pressures of the endemic banditry occasioned by the fall of the Qing dynasty, the emergence of the warlords, and the Japanese invasion affected the timing of division. The bandit threat to property caused families to divide early. In the interviews recorded in the *Chūgoku nōson kankō chōsa* (hereafter *Kankō chōsa* or KC), North China peasants suggest that the banditry that arose following the 1937 Marco Polo Bridge Incident increased the occurrence of household division. When asked by Japanese investigators if the incident and ensuing disorder had had any effects on household division, many peasants stated that the danger had increased the number of divisions. The families reasoned that, by dividing their property into smaller portions, they presented less tempting targets to bandits (KC 1:8, 25, 33, 44).

Why Did Households Divide? The Internal Factors

Whatever roles taxation and banditry played in causing household division were secondary, however, to the roles of internal family tensions. Scholars have long debated the sources of these tensions, but the main lines of interpretation are two. The dominant school of thought, best exemplified by Maurice Freedman, has emphasized the inevitable disagreements among brothers as the main cause of household division. A second interpretation is represented by Margery Wolf, who has argued that disagreements between the brothers' wives was a main, if not the main, cause of division (Freedman 1966:46; Wolf 1972:164).

The peasants interviewed in the *Kankō chōsa* confirm that such intragenerational disputes were the main causes of division. When asked why division occurred, Hao Guoliang of Sibeichai in Hebei province responded, "If there are brothers and the feelings between them go bad, they divide the house" (KC 3:67). When asked for the most common reasons for division, Wang Qingchang of Houxiazhai in Shandong province responded, "The brothers don't get along, the brother's wives don't get along, and economic difficulties. That's all" (KC 4:443). An exchange with Hao Xiaohong and Hao Gouni of Sibeichai went this way:

Q: When does household division happen?
A: Most frequently when the brothers get married and the wives do not get along. It's called "bad feelings between the daughters-in-law." (KC 3:149)

But disputes between the elder and junior generations could cause division as well. The following exchange with Ren Fuyu of Lengshuigou, Shandong, makes the point well.

Q: Of the four [causes of division], which is the most common?
A: Bad feelings between the brothers' wives.
Q: The next?
A: Bad feelings between the mother-in-law and the daughter-in-law.
Q: The next?
A: Disputes between the brothers.
Q: The next?
A: Father and son not getting along. (KC 4:92–93)

As the above conversations suggest, the reasons for division varied, the most common being disputes between brothers and between sisters-in-law. But disputes between members of different generations, such as the stereotypical tension between the mean mother-in-law and her powerless daughter-in-law, also caused division.

The Deeper Causes of Household Division

What were these family disputes about? The *Kankō chōsa* interviews reveal that the often related problems of poverty, growing families, and fear of the wastrel son precipitated most instances of household division. Li Yunjie of Shajing, Hebei province, and Hou Ruiwen and Liu Zixin of Houjiaying, also in Hebei, all stated that divisions sprang from poverty (KC 1:79; 5:66, 74). By this logic, in hard times the brothers wanted to remove their individual portions of property before things got worse (KC 1:242).

In addition to and often connected with poverty, an increase in the number of family members could cause division. Liu Zixin states:

A: In my own case our family got large and my father discussed it with everybody and divided the house.
Q: Does this happen often?
A: Yes. (KC 5:74)

An interview with Hou Shupan of Houjiaying went this way:

Q: After you went to Manchuria, did your brothers divide the house?
A: Of course. Twenty-three years ago.
Q: Why did they divide the house?
A: There were too many people, more than twenty, and the land was poor. Their lives were getting worse, so our parents wanted to divide the house. (KC 5:69)

As if to symbolize the problem of increasing family size, many household division documents contain the stock phrase *sheng chi ri fan* (teeth emerging, days troublesome), meaning that the number of mouths is increasing, making daily affairs more difficult to manage.

The increase in family size had several effects on family life. As the number of brothers increased and as they married and had children of their own, just the numerical increase in family members complicated the daily accounting and work routines. Given the difficulties in assigning value to the different types of family labor and the inevitable differences in individual consumption needs and labor capabilities, the perception that one family member was being favored or slighted inevitably multiplied as family size grew. As these possible sources of conflict increased in number, so too did the difficulty of maintaining family harmony. With conflicts increasing and harmony decreasing, the likelihood of household division grew.

The essential economic tension of Chinese family life was the contradiction between the per capita distribution of daily necessities and the equal-male *(per stirpes)* nature of the inheritance system. As a hypothetical example of this tension, consider a family with three sons, the first married with four children, the second married with one child, and the third still single. In this family, the first son's conjugal unit is consuming for six people on a daily basis; the second unit is consuming for three; and the third is consuming for only one. Thus the consumption ratio is roughly 6:3:1.

But if the brothers divide the house, the size of the conjugal units is not considered, and each brother receives an equal-sized share. Thus, all other things being equal, while brother number one benefits from keeping the family together, brothers two and three would benefit from dividing the house. They have a direct economic interest in division.

Since the brothers have been raised together and have adjusted to each new sibling as he or she has come into the family, they may be less sensitive to or concerned about the implicit unfairness of the situation than the sisters-in-law who have married into the family. Sisters-in-law, such as the woman married to brother number two in the example above, have not been as socialized into the family structure and thus may be more sensitive to the tensions inherent in family economics. They may thus be the motive force for many divisions (Wolf 1972:64).

A final reason for household division was the fear of economic losses associated with a lazy, wastrel, or dishonest son. When asked why he had divided his family, fifty-six-*sui* Li Xinting of Houxiazhai responded, "Because my son was spending too much money" (KC 4: 445). In Sibeichai, Liu Yude and Zhang Zhongyin responded, "Because among the brothers there was one who did not work very hard, so it was becoming unfair" (KC 3:121). Perhaps the clearest response in this regard is from Li Liangfu of Lengshuigou: "For example, if there are three brothers, and one is not honest, the relations between the brothers will go bad, things will not go well. In that case the brothers will discuss it and then call in family, friends, and neighbors to be the witnesses, divide the land equally, and decide to live separately" (KC 4:109). In the first case, the father Li Xinting is ridding himself of the destructive effects of a spendthrift son. In the next two, the hardworking brothers are divesting themselves of their lazy or dishonest sibling. By dividing early, the parents and hardworking siblings can keep future gains that, had division been delayed, would have had to be divided equally with the lazy and the spendthrift. As Olga Lang so well put it: "Loafers are not supported, and many peasant families split up because one brother has been accused of being a drone" (Lang 1946:160).

The Timing of Division: Three Strategies

Given that internal tensions inevitably increased as families grew, family heads had available to them three strategies for timing the point of household division: they could wait until the tensions flared and then divide, they could divide earlier in the family cycle as a means of forestalling the disputes and maintaining a postdivision harmony, or they could work strenuously to minimize the tensions and keep the family together for as many generations as possible. These strategies are only occasionally mentioned in household division documents, and therefore it is instructive to turn to popular literature to shed light on this aspect of the division process.[1]

Dividing When the Tensions Flare

The first two strategies are vividly illustrated in Feng Menglong's Ming dynasty short story "Old Bondservant Xu Righteously Establishes a Household." The Xu family has three brothers—Yan, Zhao, and Zhe. Yan and Zhao each have a wife and one son, and though Zhe is the youngest, he and his wife, née Yan, have a total of five children, two boys and three girls. Youngest brother Zhe dies suddenly and unexpectedly, and two months later the two elder brothers meet to discuss the situation. Yan says:

"While you and I each have one son, third brother has two sons and three daughters, so his one share is as large as our two combined. Even when brother was alive, the work situation couldn't be called equal, and now that he's dead it's even worse. We work and suffer day and night, just to support that nest of deadbeats. And it will be even worse in the future when our kids all grow up and marry, and we will have to come up with four extra marriage shares for them. We should divide immediately into three shares, get rid of those lazy snakes, and then whether they have food to eat or not will be no concern of ours." (Feng 1985:781–782)

The brothers then divide the property, keeping the best for themselves and giving to their widowed sister-in-law the old servant A Ji. Though the division of property is unfair and therefore illegal, the two brothers prevail.

This first division illustrates the strategy of dividing when the tensions flare. The death of third brother Zhe has brought to the fore the inherent tension between the brothers and their widowed sister-in-law based on the per capita nature of family consumption and *per stirpes* household division. The brothers even mention third brother's four "extra" children, three daughters and one son, who are entitled to marriage expenses that the two surviving brothers will have to pay if the family remains united. The brothers therefore pursue their interests and divide the household, divesting themselves of their larger and less productive third branch.

Dividing Early to Avoid Disputes

In the years that follow, however, the widow emerges the victor in the economic struggle. The old servant A Ji proves that despite his age he still has energy and ability. He leaves home and, through a series of successful merchant ventures, acquires a considerable amount of money. He returns and together with the widow buys one thousand *mu* of land, and thus the third branch of the Xu family prospers. All five of the children marry, and the sons are successful in their educations and the examination system.

By this time A Ji has aged, his health is failing, and he is concerned about the looming household division. His final words are these:

"The two young masters have now grown up, and soon they will divide the house. If by that time bad feelings have overcome the good, the brotherly relationship will be harmed. So this old servant has already divided the family land and property into two equal shares, which I now give you two young masters. You must now each manage your own property." (Feng 1985:780–796)

In this second instance, the wise A Ji is dividing the property early in order to avoid arguments later, when the two sons would divide their now considerable property. His action nicely illustrates the second possible strategy for timing household division: doing it early to forestall family disputes.

This same strategy can be detected in a few Qing dynasty division documents. One from 1826 reads as follows: "But worldly affairs are like a game of chess, and people's hearts are not like those of old. Our numbers are increasing and daily affairs becoming complex, and the fields and land are becoming thin, so to avoid conflicts in the future, we should divide to prevent them beforehand." (TS 1910, no. 10, p. 1537). Another dated 1873 states: "It is said that rather than first having disputes and then dividing, it is better to divide at an early and appropriate time, so that the sons and grandsons will not have disputes" (TS 1910, 7:1529).

Keeping It Together for As Long As Possible

The third possible strategy—minimizing family tensions to keep families together for four or more generations—can be illustrated by two examples, the first from a family of considerable wealth. The experience of the Wu family of Quanzhou, Fujian, suggests the ways in which money could allow families to stay together for up to ten generations, or indeed as long as external conditions such as social stability allowed.

The Wu family produced a medicinal wafer that was used in the treatment of ailments of the digestive system. In the mid-Qing period, the Qianlong emperor tried it, found it quite effective, and gave it his blessing. This imperial advertisement boosted sales, and the family became quite wealthy.

The secret recipe for the wafer was kept in a locked box that was passed to each successive family head. The head was the only person who knew the ingredients, and he had complete control over all aspects of the business. He varied his suppliers so the materials would remain a secret, and he divided production tasks among the twenty to thirty hired laborers so that no worker understood the entire process. The cheapness of the raw materials and the fame of the product resulted in high profits.

Within the extended Wu family, each conjugal unit was given a monthly allowance, and each time a daughter-in-law married in or a wife became pregnant, the allowance for that family was increased.

The family business provided all members with support from cradle to grave, and up to ten generations ultimately passed under one big roof in Quanzhou without a single instance of household division. Nobody needed to work, and their leisurely lifestyle, filled with mahjong playing, led city residents to refer to them as *"a lao,"* a pejorative term that translated roughly as "lazy people who rely on their elders." By 1949, when the family head fled the city, there were over one hundred people resident in the single ninety-nine-room house. The family broke up only under the pressures of the Communist Party–led revolution (Xie Tianxi and Wang Lianmao interviews).

The Wu family demonstrates that it was possible for families to stay together for many generations, but it further suggests that the economic conditions that allowed such longevity were rare. In this case the family enjoyed a monopoly on a highly profitable product, and the profits could provide support and living space for an ever-expanding family. Perhaps even more important, the essential family property—the secret ingredients of the wafer—was not divisible. To have divided the secret would have harmed the product's name recognition and been detrimental to business. Thus the source of Wu family longevity was a secret medicinal formula that was both indivisible and immensely profitable. Such a constellation of economic conditions was not available to most Chinese families.

At the opposite end of the economic spectrum was the Zou family of Dongtou village, Pucheng county, Fujian province. The Zous were an impoverished family of "shack people" *(pengmin)* who lived in a remote mountain village. Despite difficult economic conditions, this family managed to maintain itself intact from the late Qing period until 1969, a period of five generations and more than one hundred years, during which time it grew to contain ninety-seven members.

The Zou family's economic base was a mix of agricultural, handicraft, and sideline activities. In the years before liberation in 1949, they grew paddy rice, dry-cropped rice, sweet potatoes, wheat, beans, and corn, which gave them the rough annual equivalent of 43,000 *jin* of grain and met about 70 percent of their subsistence food requirements. Their handicraft and sideline commodities included paper, charcoal, bamboo products, firewood, and dried bamboo shoots, which provided an income of 4,700 yuan and allowed them to buy the remaining 30 percent of their food requirements and meet other living expenses. Beyond providing food and housing, there was little surplus, and the family remained quite poor, to the extent that in the fourth generation, just before division in 1969, the Zou sons were having trouble finding wives willing to marry into the family.

The factors that allowed the Zou family to remain intact for five generations were, first, a special constellation of economic and geographic factors. The available agricultural land and other resources in the Zous' immediate village were too sparse to provide a livelihood for the entire family. Their papermaking business was located a great distance from home, and papermaking plus the other sidelines provided cash income essential to making ends meet. These economic and geographic factors created an integrated family economy that mitigated against division, since breaking up the various production components would have left individual families unable to make ends meet.

A second factor was the regional importance of lineage. In this part of Fujian, powerful lineages were a potent social force, and it was simply assumed that strong lineages oppressed the weak and that individual nuclear families had little chance of survival. A third factor was the use of familial ideology by the parents in the first generation, father Zou Rongxiang and his wife, Chen Shuiying, who survived him. They consciously inculcated a filial and loyal attitude among their eight sons in order to minimize the boys' tendency toward division. They also taught the sons to respect hard work and sacrifice, honoring those who worked the hardest yet consumed the least. Finally, and perhaps most important, the Zous selected their daughters-in-law with great care. They chose young women only from poor families of a social-economic background similar to their own so that the adjustment period would go smoothly. They accepted only those who were physically strong, willing to work hard, and would accept the family's poverty. Furthermore, they insisted upon young women who were gentle and easygoing, and would therefore take no interest in household affairs. The young women were instructed not to calculate individual profit and loss (Chen and Zheng 1987).

Thus it was possible for a poor family to remain together for five generations. The Zou family's pattern of integrated agriculture and sidelines, the power of local lineages, and the parents' skillful use of their authority to select their daughters-in-law and influence their sons all combined to minimize family tensions and shape a family that stayed intact.

The contrast between the Wu and Zou families, coming from almost opposite ends of the economic spectrum, raises the critical issue of class. Freedman formulated the paradigmatic position on the relationship between class and the timing of household division: while division was inevitable, poor families tended to divide early, and rich families tended to divide late, thus contributing to continued dominance of the rich. Rich families had the ability to stay together longer because their investments in housing and land allowed them to do so, and their need for economic cooperation required them to do so. The increased economic and political influence that derived from being a large family and would be lost upon division was motivation for staying together. Greater acceptance of Confucian morality may also have played a role. Poor families, by contrast, lacking the economic resources to stay together, divided earlier (Freedman 1958:29–30; Baker 1979:25).

The Wu and Zou families offer evidence both for and against Freedman. Clearly, it was easier for the Wu family to stay together, given their wealth, which translated into the ability to add housing space as the family grew and to support new family members. Intuitively, then, poor families would divide earlier. But the Zou family suggests an alternative view: poor families could stay together and work for subsistence. The ability of the Zou family to stay together did not result in any significant upward mobility, and the family remained as poor as ever. The issue of class and its effect on the timing of household division is thus problematic. Freedman's basic argument makes intuitive sense, but, unfortunately, evidence beyond the above two anecdotal illustrations does not come in a form that allows us to test his insights.[2]

Some Patterns in the Timing of Household Division

Turning from the exceptional cases of the Wu and Zou families to the more general rule, it is instructive to analyze the times at which household division tended to occur. From one angle, division in the late Qing and Republican periods could take three forms: a division in which a single brother extracted his share of property and branched off, a division while one or both parents were still alive, and a division after the deaths of both parents. The three patterns are clear in the division documents.

The first form of division can be seen in two Houxiazhai documents, from 1936 and 1937.

> The creator of this document, Wang Qingchang, because he no longer desires to live together, now asks fellow villagers and lineage members to divide the old home. (KC 4:443)

> The creator of this document, Wang Jinluan, because he no longer desires to live together, now asks fellow villagers and lineage members to discuss the matter. (KC 4:456)

An 1863 division document illustrates that a single brother could take his property in Taiwan as well. The Xiao family had three brothers, the eldest of whom was deceased and survived by his two sons. In the property division, the second brother, Minggao, took his share, while his younger brother and his nephews by his elder brother continued to reside together (TWGS 1, 9:861).

Interviews from the *Kankō chōsa* reveal that, while such divisions were infrequent, they were possible. One exchange went as follows:

> Q: If the father is alive, and all his children are grown and can take care of their own land, can the eldest brother take his share?
> A: Yes. It can't be prevented.
> Q: Are there many cases in which one brother takes out his portion?
> A: Few. (KC 1:49)

In another instance, one brother wanted to divide the house and leave, while his brothers opposed the division. He prevailed and forced his brothers to go through the procedure, but they then ignored the division and lived as before, minus the portion of the departing brother. If at a later date the two brothers wished to divide the remaining property, they would divide formally once again and draw up new division documents (KC 1:241). Lu Xishou from Banqiaocun reports that his house divided in 1941 and that each brother received forty *mu* of land. But he further states that, in 1923, his eldest brother had taken his forty *mu* for himself (KC 1:49). Thus, in Qing Taiwan and Republican North China, it was possible for one brother to force household division and take his share of the family property while the other brothers remained together.

The second type of division occurred when one or both parents were still alive. If the parents were living at the time of division, the document generally stated that they were dividing the property among their sons. In the property settlement, provision for the parents is made in the form of land or payment to care for them for the remainder of their lives. The following introduction from a 1936 Houjiaying division document is typical.

> The creator of this document, Liu Hui, is sixty-three *sui* and has given birth to three sons, the eldest Wanxi, the second Wanchen, and the third Wannian. Each is now grown and married. As I am now too old to control things, we have all talked it over, and all desire to take our houses, land, money, records, household items, and so forth, and, except for support for this old couple, divide the rest into three equal portions and give them to the three bothers. (KC 5:97)

If the surviving parent was the mother, the document frequently reads like this one from an 1843 division in Taiwan.

> The creator of this division contract is Widow Zhang, née Zheng. In the days when my husband was alive, I gave birth to four sons. . . . I humbly respect the inherited tradition of living together for nine generations . . . but the family members are ever more numerous and the enmities grow, and it is difficult to avoid plans of division. So I have invited the relatives to come and discuss it and to take all the property we have inherited and acquired, and divide it completely into four equal shares and draw lots to settle the matter. (TS 1910, 48:1619)

In the third and final type of division, both parents were deceased and the document states that the brothers are dividing the family property among themselves. The following 1908 example is from Houjiaying in Hebei province.

> The creators of this document, who will keep it forever, are Hou Yuandong and Hou Yuanhui, two brothers from the same mother. Father and mother died long ago, and we have lived together for many years. Now, however, owing to economic difficulties, it is hard to continue to live together, and we have willingly asked people from the lineage to take our houses, land, money, records, animals, carts, household items, and so forth, and divide them into two equal portions. Then we will rely on luck and draw lots. (KC 5:141)

A four-way division document from Taiwan in 1825 reads: "The creators of this document are Yang Wenxian, Yang Wenzong, Yang Wenhui, Yang Wende, and so on. We have heard of nine generations

Table 2
The Timing of Household Division

Province	Single Brother		Parent(s) Alive		Parents Deceased		Total No.
	No.	%	No.	%	No.	%	
Anhui	1	3	18	62	10	34	29
Fujian	1	5	12	57	8	38	21
Hebei	1	4	14	58	9	38	24
Shandong	2	22	5	56	2	22	9
Taiwan	4	6	46	66	20	28	70
Zhejiang	0	0	5	38	8	62	13
Total	9	5	100	60	57	34	166

Sources: JJS, KC, TWGS, ZPM, ZZM.

living under one roof, and the old traditions are worthy of respect; however our household becomes ever more numerous, and in the end we must divide" (TS 1910, 17:1557). The relative frequencies of the three types of division, as indicated by documents from the Qing, are suggested in Table 2.

Of 166 documents that contain sufficient information, nine divisions are a single brother branching off, one hundred took place while one or both parents were still alive, and fifty-seven took place after both parents were dead. These figures suggest a plausible pattern of household division in most areas of China: 5 percent early and exceptional divisions with a brother branching off, 60 percent taking place with one or both parents alive, and 34 percent taking place after the death of both parents. The notable exception is Yanzhoufu, Zhejiang, the location for most of the Zhejiang documents. Here division seems to have occurred most frequently when both parents were dead, though the small size of the sample—thirteen documents—makes any conclusion speculative. The figures as a whole suggest that household division tended to occur early enough in the family cycle that one or more parents was still alive and needed support.

A second view on the timing of household division can be constructed from family form at the time of division. Adopting an

Table 3
Family Form at Household Division

Province	Nuclear	Stem	Joint	United
Anhui	1	0	19	12
New families	2	0	65	48
Fujian	0	1	10	4
New families	0	2	31	14
Hebei	0	0	11	8
New families	0	0	39	23
Shandong	0	1	3	1
New families	0	2	8	2
Taiwan	1	1	28	12
New families	3	3	115	36
Zhejiang	0	1	3	1
New families	0	3	9	2
Total	2	4	74	38
Total new families	5	10	267	125
Average new families	2.5	2.5	3.6	3.3

Sources: JJS, KC, TWGS, ZPM, ZZM.

Note: This table covers only 118 documents, rather than the 166 in Table 2, as the remaining documents lacked sufficient information on family form.

analytical scheme used by Zheng Zhenman, families are divided into four types: nuclear, stem, joint, and united. Nuclear is defined as a family of parent(s) and possibly children, all unmarried; stem as parent(s) plus a child or children, one of whom is married; joint as parent(s) plus children, two or more of whom are married; and united as a family of brothers without parents (Zheng 1988). Applying this scheme to the household division documents gives the statistics shown in Table 3.

Table 3 reveals the expected pattern of early division before the united stage. While relatively few families divided in the nuclear or stem stages, once into the joint stage, with two or more sons married and a parent or parents still living, the number of divisions increases dramatically, accounting for 64 percent of all divisions. The number of divisions in the united stage, when both parents are dead, drops to

Table 4
The Number of Unmarried Brothers during Household Division

Province	Total Divisions	Divisions with Unmarried Brothers		Total Brothers– Number Unmarried
		No.	%	
Anhui	35	8	23	3–1 (2),* 4–1, 5–2, 5–3, 5–4, 6–3, 9–1
Fujian	21	1	5	3–2
Hebei	24	1	4	4–1
Shandong	9	0		
Taiwan	75	15	20	3–1 (3), 3–2 (3), 4–1, 4–2, 4–3, 5–1, 6–1, 6–2, 7–2, 7–3, 10–5
Zhejiang	13	3	23	2–1 (2), 3–1
Total	177	28	16	

Sources: JJS, KC, TWGS, ZPM, ZZM.
*Digits in parentheses indicate the number of cases.

about 30 percent. The average number of new families created by each household division runs between 2.5 and 3.6. Thus these numbers confirm that household division tended to occur after the marriage of most or all of the sons, yet before the deaths of the parents.

A third quantifiable variable indicative of the timing of household division is the marital status of the brothers. Table 4 analyzes the number of divisions in which all brothers were married as opposed to those in which one or more brothers remained single. The numbers suggest strongly that most families, fully 83 percent, divided late enough in the family cycle that all of the brothers were married. Table 4 also suggests that divisions in Taiwan and Zhejiang were somewhat more likely to have unmarried sons than those in North China and Fujian. From the three tables it is reasonable to conclude that at the point of household division, most families were late enough in the family cycle that all sons were married, yet still early enough that at least one parent was still alive.

Table 5
Family Size and Form in Sui'an County, Zhejiang

Village	Total Families	Family Form	Total Population	Average Family Size
Wujiazhuang	9	N-5 S-1 J-1 U-1 O-1	45	5
Zhenfengzhuang	11	N-6 S-1 J-2 U-2 O-0	71	6.5
Shuangqizhuang	30	N-13 S-6 J-4 U-5 O-2	112	3.7
Nanchuanzhuang	23	N-7 S-4 J-6 U-6 O-0	140	6.1
Yangjiazhuang	4	N-1 S-1 J-2 U-0 O-0	24	6.0
Changtanzhuang	4	N-2 S-1 J-0 U-0 O-1	13	3.3
Taixiazhuang	47	N-20 S-15 J-3 U-6 O-3	185	3.9

Village	Total Families	Family Form	Total Population	Average Family Size
Huochuanzhuang	12	N-6 S-1 J-3 U-2 O-0	62	5.2
Totals	140	N-60 (43%) S-30 (21%) J-21 (15%) U 22 (16%) O-7 (5%)	652	4.7

Sources: ZPM.

Note: N = nuclear; S = stem; J – joint; U = united; O = single individual.

A fourth view on the timing of household division can be deduced from the extant tax registers of Sui'an county, Zhejiang province. The registers provide statistics on family size in several village communities, thus presenting a larger context than the division documents and a context in which it is possible to analyze the effects of household division on family size and form. Shen Bingyao of the Zhejiang Provincial Museum has dated the registers to the late Yongzheng or early Qianlong era, between 1728 and 1750 (Shen Bingyao personal communication). The registers list each individual resident in the household, the amount of land the family owned, and the family's tax liability. I have tabulated the totals for family size and form in Table 5.

In these eight villages, family form and size confirm that household division tended to occur early enough in the family cycle that large families were not very common. Families in the united form are only 16 percent of the total, a figure even lower than figures deduced from household division documents. Sixty-four percent of families are in either the nuclear or stem form, and the average family size is 4.7 persons per household. These figures suggest strongly that early and regular household division tended to keep families small.

A final question on the timing of division concerns the time of year at which families undertook the task of dividing the household.

Table 6
The Monthly Frequency of Household Division

Month	Divisions		Month	Divisions
1	19		7	12
2	19		8	10
3	13		9	13
4	9		10	19
5	14		11	20
6	8		12	17

Sources: JJS, KC, TWGS, ZPM, ZZM.

Table 6 shows the distribution based on 173 documents that contain a precise date. The data show a slight tendency for division to increase during the late fall and winter months, with the tenth, eleventh, twelfth, first, and second months accounting for 54 percent of the divisions.

The Process of Household Division

The household division process was a ritualized combination of informal practices and formal procedures that included prominent elements of Chinese customary law and were designed to ensure fairness, equal division, and legality. For analytical purposes, household division can be viewed as a five-stage process.

Making the Decision

Stage one was the informal period during which a family member or members decided to divide the house, initiated the process, and achieved family consensus that the house should in fact be divided. While the informal nature of this decision makes generalizations difficult, it is likely that the process differed based on which family member initiated the drive toward division and how much resistance there was from other family members and the community.

All family members had to reckon with community opinion, which was in general opposed to division, probably because division upset established village patterns of family, social, and even political relationships. Villagers often used mediation to try to prevent division, and at times they succeeded (KC 1:189, 252). As Yang Ze of Shajing states, "Initially the neighbors and lineage head will try to mediate and avoid division" (KC 1:141B). Yang Run states that the mediator could be any suitable person—a lineage member, a relative, or a neighbor. Four or five of the mediators would try to resolve the dispute, but if they could not, the family divided (KC 1:295B–C).

If the motive force for division was the father, his authority as the family head was paramount, and division followed. A deceased father's widow's power to initiate division was roughly the same, and she could divide the household when she felt it was necessary. Documents from divisions orchestrated by widows often contain the phrase *feng mu ling,* meaning "following mother's orders" (KC 3:93).

If the parents were alive and a son or sons initiated division, the process might become more complex. If the parents agreed with their son's desires, then the division proceeded; but if the parents were opposed and the son was adamant, he could begin by agitating within the family. The term frequently used to describe this process was *nao fenjia,* meaning to agitate or kick up a fuss in order to get the family to divide (Cohen 1976:202). If the internal agitation did not produce the desired result, the son had to seek outside support. He might first go to lineage members, then to more distant relatives, and finally to non-kin arbitrators or the village head. As a very last resort he might go to the county court, a tactic that could not result in a favorable ruling but would be a powerful attempt to embarrass his father into agreement. Thus a determined son could make it clear that family life would be one continuous quarrel if he did not get his way, and most fathers could be pushed into dividing their households. If a father was absolutely opposed, a son still might prevail if the lineage members and relatives agreed to the division (KC 1:115, 301A). The father still had to sign the division document, however.

If both parents were deceased, the eldest brother had somewhat greater authority than his younger brothers to initiate or resist division. But the eldest brother's authority was never as strong as a father's, and generally, as Yang Ze states, if a brother, any brother, wanted to divide, he could force division.

> Q: If there are four brothers and one wants to divide, and the others are all opposed, what happens?
> A: They divide. (KC 1:276B)

A daughter-in-law had no legal power to force household division, and therefore if and when she desired division, she had to work through her husband.[3]

The Role of Witnesses

Once the family had come to an agreement to proceed with division, the informality of stage one was left for the more clearly understood principles of stage two: calling in the witnesses. Twenty-two of thirty-three North China division documents state that witnesses were called in to watch over the process; in Taiwan fifty-nine of seventy-one documents make such a claim. In Zhejiang the numbers were three of thirteen; in Fujian eleven of twenty-one; and in Anhui twenty-four of thirty-five. A typical document from Shajing contains the following:

> The creator of this document and the divider of the property is Du Chun. Of his four sons, three are already married, and only the fourth is not. Now because I am getting old and my strength is declining and it is difficult to deal with daily affairs, I have invited lineage, family, villagers, and friends to divide all the land, gardens, houses, property, and so forth. (KC 1:291)

The *Kankō chōsa* interviews further demonstrate that the invitation of witnesses was not mere legal rhetoric. The witnesses were called in because their roles were essential to the process. Witnesses could be lineage members, relatives, neighbors, or friends, and the attendance of witnesses was required for the process to be legal (KC 1:80, 253, 295, 297). In North China, non-kin were often witnesses, while in Anhui and Taiwan lineage members predominated. Their main task was to oversee the division process to be sure it was done fairly (KC 1:253). If the division among the sons was unequal, they would not give their consent, and the division could not be completed, as revealed by this exchange:

> Q: If in a division three *mu* of land goes to the eldest brother, four *mu* to the second, and five to the youngest, and the eldest brother complains, can the division be done, ignoring him?

A: No, that cannot be done. Not the land. The land price may rise, and it's an important thing, so during a division the witnesses will not consent and take responsibility, so it's no good. (KC 1:297)

From among the witnesses, some, perhaps as few as one or as many as six, were then selected to serve as the formal guarantors who signed the division document. These guarantors were noted in the document by titles that varied by region. In Hebei they were often noted as *zhongbaoren* and *zhongren,* in Shandong as *jieyi* and *xiangren,* in Anhui as *pingqin* and *pingzu,* and in Taiwan as *weizhongren* and *zaijianren.*[4] The guarantors' signatures were required on the document, and virtually every household division document has these signatures. Guarantors might include the lineage head, lineage members, or, sometimes, the dividing sons' maternal uncle. The mother's brother's signature is on about 10 percent of the household division documents; he was brought in because his equal relationship to all the sons made him a fair mediator. The guarantors' roles were twofold: to guarantee equal division and to mediate disputes after the division (KC 1:6, 139, 229, 238, 297). This first duty is clarified in an interview with three peasants.

Q: [What are the duties of the lineage head in] household division?
A: To be the guarantor. In the case of household division, the lineage head's permission is normally obtained. But it is also all right if it isn't. If he opposes it, another relative can be the guarantor. The guarantor is to guarantee the equal division of the property. (KC 1:229)

As to the second duty, a talk with Li Guangzhi of Shajing went as follows:

Q: If the brothers have a dispute over land, do they ask for mediation from somebody in the lineage?
A: If it's after household division, the guarantor on the division document will be asked to mediate it.
Q: If you don't go to the guarantor, can you go immediately to the village head?
A: You can take the division document to the village head, but generally you go to the guarantor. (KC 1:139C)

Negotiating Family Property Division

Once the witnesses and guarantors were selected, the family entered stage three: negotiating the division of property. First the family had to distinguish between family property and any existing individual property, since the latter was exempt from division. Individual property most often had its genesis in a daughter-in-law's dowry. A woman marrying into her husband's family usually brought in as her dowry a variety of household items plus money (KC 1: 266B–C). This property did not go to the family head, usually her father-in-law, and it remained under her and/or her husband's control. The wife might or might not turn it over to her new husband, and the amount was kept secret (KC 1:29C, 1:317B). This money could be increased through sideline activities such as chicken raising or by saving unspent remainders from the family allowance (KC 1:317B, 1:272C). If a brother worked for wages in a city, he might hide some money as individual property under his wife's name (KC 1:217A). This accumulated individual money could be used to buy property, either land or housing; and, while the property belonged to both husband and wife, only his name went on the contract (KC 1:271C). At the woman's death, her individual property went to her husband (KC 1:272C). At the point of household division, this individual property of the wives and brothers remained in their possession, and it was not considered when calculating equal division of family property (KC 1:29C).

While individual property was theoretically possible within the property system, the amounts tended to be small. In a village such as Shajing, there was in fact little if any individual property, as this conversation with Yang Ze illustrates:

Q: What are the types of individual property?
A: Land, housing, money. Money and land mostly.
Q: When and how does individual property come about?
A: When the wife brings in money. She gives it to her husband, her husband buys land, and it is his own property.
Q: Is there anyone in the village with individual property?
A: No. (KC 1:269)

Once the individual property was defined, all the family property, including land, housing, household furniture, agricultural tools, draft animals, and kitchen items, was totaled up. Special arrangements were made for elderly parents, unmarried siblings, and trusts. Then the remaining property was divided equally among all the sons. The division could be done by discussion, if the sons and the guarantors could agree on an equitable division and each son accepted his share. But property was seldom absolutely equal. As one division document stated: "Land is never equal in fertility and stoniness; rooms differ in beauty and ugliness" (TS 1910, 65:1649).

If the discussion could not produce agreement, the brothers drew lots. When this technique was employed, first all or part of the family property was divided into equal portions, and then the brothers drew lots to determine who received which portion. Eight of the thirty-three North China division documents mention the drawing of lots, such as the following from Lujiazhuang in Shandong.

> The creators of this document are Xing Mingde and his brothers, Mingdao, Mingshan, and Jing. Because household affairs are difficult and support is insufficient, the four brothers have discussed it and have decided to divide the house and live separately. Therefore they have asked relatives, friends, lineage members, and neighbors to come. The house, land, animals, and household goods will all be mixed together and divided into four equal shares, which will be chosen by lot as a means of settlement. (KC 4:363)

In Taiwan fifty-three of seventy-one documents mention the drawing of lots, in Zhejiang four of thirteen, in Fujian ten of twenty-one, and in Anhui eighteen of thirty-five.

The *Kankō chōsa* interviewees corroborate the practice of drawing lots. One discussion went

Q: How are the portions of the brothers decided?
A: The house, the land, and the other property division is seldom done according to request. Generally the drawing of lots is relied on to decide. (KC 1:6)

An interview with Zhao Tingkui went

Q: When you divide the house, must the property be divided?
A: Yes it must.
Q: What about the house?
A: The old house must also be divided, and it's done by drawing lots. (KC 1:241)

Hao Yiqin of Sibeichai remembered his division this way:

> A: We divided the house into four areas—left, right, front, and
> back—and put them on lot-paper. We put the papers into a tea
> cup, lifted it up high, and drew. The lots were divided up by the
> witnesses. (KC 3:96)

The drawing of lots might be used for all the property or just
a portion of it, such as the household utensils. In any case, it en-
couraged equal division, as it was in the brothers' own interest to
see that each lot contained an equal amount of property. In some
parts of China such as Taiwan and Anhui, the drawing of lots
may have been done as part of a ceremony in front of the family altar
(TS 1910, 63:1646) In North China, there was no such ceremony
(KC 1:252B).

The Writing of the Household Division Document

Once the property had been defined and divided, the family entered
stage four: drawing up the household division document. Household
division documents carry a wide variety of names in Chinese, but for
analytical purposes they can be categorized as two types: *fendan* and
yizhu. A family drew up a *fendan* if the actual division of property
was to take place immediately; it drew up an *yizhu* if the division was
to go into effect later, usually after the deaths of the parents. Thus
the *yizhu* was similar to a will in Western societies; but given that
division of property generally occurred simultaneously with the writing of the document, the *fendan* was much more frequently used. The
terms for each of these documents varied with geography. In Taiwan
the *fendan* was known by at least fifteen names, the most common
being *jiushu;* in Fujian the most frequent was *jiushu;* in Zhejiang *fenguan* was most common; and in North China *fendan* and *fenjiadan*.
The *yizhu* also had many variant names.[5] In a *fendan* all surviving
parents and the brothers signed the document, while in an *yizhu* generally only the parents signed. Whatever the differences in the name
of the document and the numbers of signatures, the rules of equal
division applied in all cases, even in the case of a parent's deathbed
wishes (KC 1:277C, 278A, 317A).

The drawing up of the document was essential to legalizing
the division process. A talk with Yang Ze, Yang Run, and Zhang
Yongren of Shajing went

Q: Must it [the drawing up of a division document] be done?
A: If the document is not drawn up, the household cannot be divided. (KC 1:229C)

And another interview with Zhao Tingkui went

Q: Must it [the drawing up of a division document] be done?
A: Yes it must. If there is no document, the division is null and void. (KC 1:241B)

Household division documents follow a pattern that remained unchanged through the Qing and Republican periods and that was uniform in all areas of China. The first section is a prologue, which contains the title of the document, the name or names of the dividers, the names of the sons, and any details that affect the property division. Such details might include the adoption of a son, the existence of an unmarried sibling, or the existence of a widow of a deceased son, in other words, all the particulars of family structure that affected inheritance. The prologue might contain the general outlines of the property division. It might also contain short bits of family history, and it frequently contained stock legal phrases.

These legal phrases, terms, and references were designed to provide a touch of legality and "completeness" to the document (Longyan Local Gazetteer Committee interview). Some of these terms were used to stress the fairness of the division. One was *pin da jun fen*,[6] meaning that the property had been "divided equally among the sons." This was the most frequently used term, appearing in 135 of 191 division documents. Another was *zhi gong wu si,* meaning "the division has been done most fairly and without selfishness." Other phrases were designed to acknowledge the ideal of remaining together for many generations, yet to justify the need to divide early. A respectful reference is often made to Zhang Gongyi, a man of the Tang dynasty whose family stayed together for nine generations (TS 1910, 39:1593; Morohashi 1955, 4:744). But this reference is usually followed by the phrase *shu da fen zhi,* meaning that though we respect Zhang Gongyi, we must now divide, just like "the tree that becomes large and grows branches" (TS 1910, 6:1524; see also nos. 40, 41). Another common justification for division is the phrase *sheng chi ri fan,* meaning "we are dividing because the number of mouths is increasing and daily affairs are becoming more complex."

Another category of terms function as admonitions to the family members. One example, *ge wu fan hui,* means "none may later come back and dispute the division"; another, *zheng chang jing duan,* means that family members "must not dispute the values of the property after division." Some phrases stress the legality of the procedure, such as *kong kou wu ping,* meaning "since oral agreements are not reliable," we are writing this document for proof of the division.

The second section contains the details of the property division. Generally the surviving parents' *yangshan* property was written first, then any special set-asides for unmarried siblings or trusts, and then the equal shares for the sons. The property was described in detail, with land often described both in terms of location and by name. Housing was often described in terms of location and the number of rooms. Other property such as draft animals and farm tools was sometimes included. Each brother received a copy of the document, and in most cases the documents were exact copies. In other cases each brother's document listed only his own share of property.

The third section, located at the end of the document, includes the date of the division and the required signatures, which generally were those of any surviving parents, the brothers or their heirs, the witnesses, the guarantors, and the scribe. Figure 2 shows a typical household division document.

Concluding Ceremonies

Once the household division document had been drawn up and signed, the family entered stage five: the final ceremonies. These generally included a last supper at which the brothers and their families ate together for the final time. In North China the entire family plus those, such as witnesses, guarantors, the lineage head, and the village head, who helped in the division ate at this event called a *sanyifan,* "dissolution dinner" (KC 1:276C). In South China, there is often reference to a brief ceremony in front of the family altar. Lin Yueh-hwa has described one such ritual:

> The last part of the performance was an offering of two wooden kettles before the ancestral shrine. The kettle was heaped with steaming rice, the symbol of abundance. Dunglin and Eldest *Go,* now equal heads of two equal lineages, bowed down before their ancestors. Then each took a kettle to his respective kitchen. Thus as last the Hwang family was divided, and two "separate hearths" were set up. In the evening a feast was held, in which the arbiter and the guarantors were guests of honour. (Lin Yueh-hwa 1947:126)

In Fujian, the final ceremonies might be more drawn out. The parents started a fire in their stove and carried burning embers to start the fires in the stoves of each new family. *Zongzi,* sticky rice dumplings wrapped in bamboo leaves, might be given to the neighbors. And sometime in the two weeks or so following the last joint supper,

Figure 2
A Typical Household Division Document

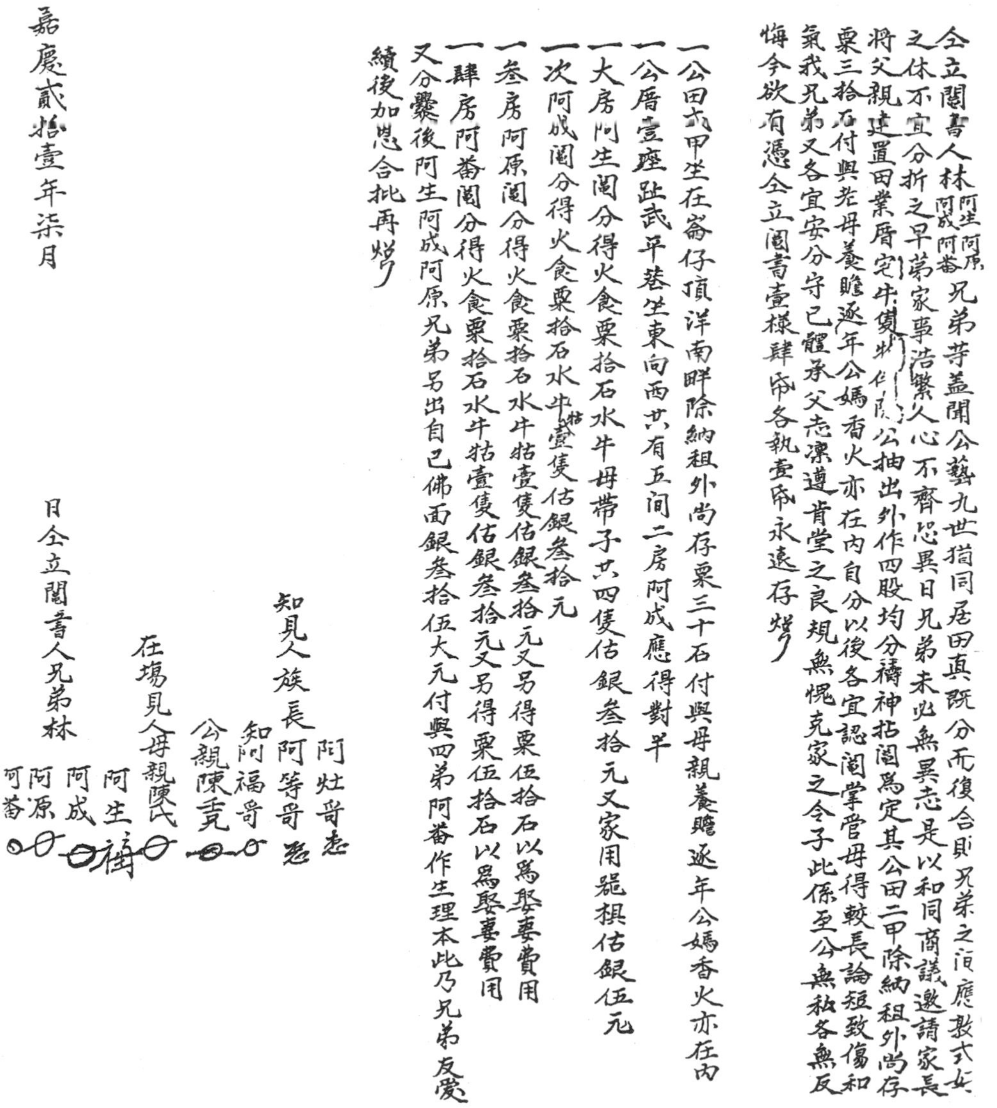

全立閬書人林阿壁阿原阿善兄弟芽蓋開公藝九世指同居田真既分芣復合則兄荣之情應散式女之休不宜分折之早弟家事浩繁人心不齊恐異日兄弟未必無異志是以和同商議邀請家長將父親遺置田業厝定牛奢料公抽出外作四股均分禱神扐閬掌為定其公田二甲除納租外尚存粟三拾石付與荖母養瞻逐年公媽香火亦在內自分以後各宜禱認閬掌管毋得較長論短致傷和氣我兄弟又各宜安守己體承父志凜遵肯堂之良規無愧克家之令子此係至公無私各無反悔今欲有憑全立閬書壹樣群庶各執壹帋永遠存炤

一公成六甲坐在崙仔頂洋南畔除納租外尚存粟三十石付與母親養瞻逐年公媽香火亦在內

一公厝壹座趾武平苓坐東向西廿六有五間二房阿成應得對半

一大房阿生閬分得火食粟拾石水牛母帶子共四隻佑銀叁拾元

一次阿成閬分得火食粟拾石水牛牯壹隻佑銀叁拾元

一叁房阿原閬分得火食粟拾石水牛牯壹隻佑銀叁拾元又得粟伍拾石以為娶妻費用

一肆房阿蕃閬分得火食粟拾石水牛牯壹隻佑銀叁拾元又得粟伍拾石以為娶妻費用

又分鑊後阿生阿成阿原兄弟另出自己佛面銀叁拾伍大元付與四弟阿蕃作生理本此乃兄弟反慶

續後加恩合批再炤

嘉慶貳拾壹年染月

日仝立閬書人兄弟林
阿成
阿生
阿原
阿蕃

在場見人母親陳氏
知見人族長阿等哥
知阿福哥
公親陳兌

阿灶哥

each daughter-in-law's natal family came to present gifts to their daughter's newly independent family. The gifts were household and kitchen items such as pots, bowls, cleavers, chopsticks, and wash basins. On the practical level, the gifts got the new family off to a good start, and on the symbolic level, they emphasized the family's continued support for their daughter.

The newly independent families generally lived around the same courtyard, and according to custom in some areas of Fujian, the gift-giving families had to enter in strict order of seniority, the family of the eldest son's wife first, the second son's wife second, and so on. Frequently the family of a younger wife tried to force their way in early, which resulted in much pushing and shoving at the main gate. As each family entered, firecrackers were set off. This day symbolized the end of the household division process in many parts of Fujian (Li Xingfang and Longyan Gazetteer Committee interviews).

Once these five stages were finished, the process of household division was complete. The new families were now legal entities in the eyes of the village, the lineage, and the state. The ritualized, public nature of the process, including the calling in of witnesses and the last supper, served to notify the village and the lineage of the formal existence of the new families.

Household Division and the State

In the normal course of events, household division was not reported to any state organ during the Qing dynasty. Not one of the Qing household division documents in my sample mentions the state, nor does any have a chop or other indication of regular state involvement.[7] The situation was the same in the North China villages of the *Kankō chōsa* during the Republican period (KC 1:303B). An interview with three Shajing peasants went like this:

Q: When you divide the household, do you register anywhere?
A: No, we don't report anywhere. (KC 1:229C)

Another exchange was revealing, because it suggests that the Republican government had been trying to impose some changes related to registration.

Q: And how is it [the postdivision situation] registered in the population register?

A: The population register has only recently come out, so we've
    never reported it. We don't know how to do it. (Uchida 1956:93)

But it is not accurate to say that the state was irrelevant to household
division. Household division disputes that proved unmanageable at
the community level or that resulted in violence could and did end up
in court, and these will be discussed in detail in Chapter 6.

To summarize, then, there were patterns regarding why, when, and
how families underwent household division. The reasons for household division were generally internal family schisms that arose from
poverty, increasing family size, or the destructive effects of a lazy,
dishonest, or incompetent son. The contradiction between the per
capita consumption regime and the *per stirpes* inheritance regime was
a major underlying factor. Although the troublesome relationship
between China's extended family form, its family property regime,
and the individual's rights to that property were at the core of
the decision to divide the household, external forces, such as war,
banditry, and taxation, could also affect the timing of division.

While household division could happen at any time following the
birth of two sons, it tended to occur following the marriages of the
sons but before the deaths of both of the parents. Thus the typical
development of family form in China was from the nuclear stage to
the stem stage with one son married. If the family had more than one
son, it proceeded to the joint stage, during which it would most likely
undergo household division. A smaller number of families would
remain in the joint stage long enough for the parents to die, enter the
united stage, and undergo household division in this form. While a
few families had the economic base or the internal discipline to stay
together for five or ten generations, they were rare, and thus family
size in Qing and Republican China tended to remain small.

Once the family reached the crisis point, the division process itself
was a ritualized five-stage procedure that was rooted in customary
law and normally took from two days to two weeks. Lineage and village members were called in as witnesses and guarantors. The property was analyzed and divided, and the necessary documents were
drawn up. In the concluding ceremonies, the newly independent
families took up their new residences and received their recognition
from the community. In the normal course of events, the state was
not involved in household division, making division primarily a
community-based process.

Chapter 4

The Rights of Individuals in Qing Taiwan

W ITH a basic understanding of the whys, whens, and hows of household division, let us now turn to a case study: Qing dynasty Taiwan. This chapter presents the principles and practices of household division in Qing Taiwan from 1730 to 1900. Rooted in ground-level materials such as family documents, it analyzes the rights of each individual in the family at the point of household division and in so doing creates a baseline from which to compare Qing Taiwan to Republican North China in Chapter 7.

The Rights of Sons: Basic Principles

Household division among the Chinese in Taiwan during the Qing dynasty followed the inheritance regime rooted in Chinese law and custom, even though Taiwan was a frontier society that included many recent settlers. Household division was guided by the property rights of the individuals in the household, the most prominent of which was the right of each son to an equal portion of the property. Thus at the point of household division the first critical question was, who was a son?

The simple answer was, all sons of the same father. If a father had only one son, household division was unnecessary, and the transfer of property to the son upon the parents' deaths was so natural there was no legal act to mark the transfer. The one son inherited all family property without legal process. Even assuming that a family had two or more sons, that household division had not occurred, and that both parents died, again the transfer of property to the sons was natural and required no legal procedure (Shiga 1978:124).

If the father had two or more sons, however, household division would occur at some point, either before or after the deaths of the parents, and the brothers would receive equal shares of the family property. A very simple and representative case occurred in 1836, when two brothers, Bitao and Bilan, divided their household.[1] After providing for their elderly mother and sacrifices to their ancestors, the family's two pieces of land were divided precisely in half. One plot was divided into equal halves of .45 *jia*,[2] and each brother assumed 82.5 of the 165 *jin*[3] sugar-tax responsibility. The second plot was divided into identical shares of .4 *jia*, and each brother assumed half of the four yuan rent responsibility (TS 1910:43). This first basic principle of household division is illustrated in Figure 3: Sons 2 and 3 inherit equal shares of father 1's property.

Figure 3
Basic Principle Number One

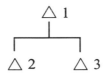

But household division was seldom so simple. It could frequently be complicated by the death of a son, such as in the Zhang family division of 1854. The family had originally included two brothers, the elder Qian and the younger Kun. Qian had died, leaving one son, Alian. The family property was therefore divided equally between uncle and nephew, Zhang Kun and Zhang Alian (TS 1910:61). This second basic principle of household division held that, if a son died, the deceased son's son (the father's grandson) inherited the son's portion of the property. It is illustrated in Figure 4: Son 3's portion passes to grandson 4, so division takes place between uncle 2 and nephew 4.

In the fifth month of 1893, the Wu family divided their house in a manner illustrative of a third basic principle that was a combination of the first and second principles. The family had included two

Figure 4
Basic Principle Number Two

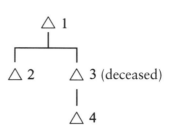

brothers, an elder brother whose name is not given and a younger brother, Xianyu. The elder brother had died leaving two sons, Shiqing and Shifeng. When division occurred, the property was divided into two equal shares, one going to uncle Xianyu and one going to his two nephews Shiqing and Shifeng. This is division on a *per stirpes* basis and can be illustrated as in Figure 5. In this case the share of property of surviving brother 2 would be the same as the combined share going to his nephews 4 and 5. The property that goes to the nephews is owned equally, and they can work and manage it jointly, or they can divide it into equal, though now reduced to one-fourth-sized, shares.

Figure 5
Basic Principle Number Three

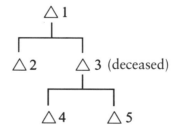

A factor that further complicated household division was the practice of polycoity, which in Chinese law meant a man could have a wife and concubines. In the Li family division of 1886, for instance, father Li had a total of six sons, the first four by his wife, née Lai, the last two by his concubine, whose name is not mentioned. Despite the slight to the concubine herself, the property was divided equally among all six of the sons, the concubine's two sons inheriting equally (TS 1910:6). This fourth principle held that all sons inherited equally regardless of which mother bore them, be she the first wife, a second wife, or a concubine. This principle is illustrated in Figure 6. Father 1 has a wife, a second wife he married after the death of the first wife, and a concubine. Each of the women has a son, and at the point of household division, each son (2, 3, and 4) inherits an equal share of property.

Figure 6
Basic Principle Number Four

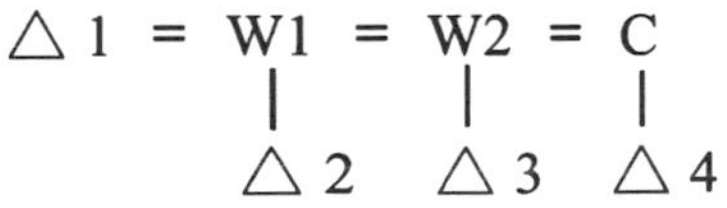

$$\triangle 1 = W1 = W2 = C$$
$$\triangle 2 \quad \triangle 3 \quad \triangle 4$$

The Rights of Sons: Special Cases

These four basic principles for defining father-to-son inheritance rights sufficed in most circumstances, but particular situations often required creative solutions. For example, a brother who was absent from the family presented a dilemma at division time. Thus in 1816 father Yang and his third son, Wenzong, quarreled, and father Yang sent Wenzong away. In 1818 father Yang died, and in 1822, after an appropriate mourning period, the remaining three brothers divided the house. They agonized over how to treat their missing brother, and in the end, since they were unsure if he was alive, they did not set aside property for him.

When Wenzong surprisingly returned in the sixth month of 1824, the family had to find a share for him. In the ninth month their unmarried sister Jinniang became seriously ill, and in the eleventh month she died. Her dowry property was sold off, providing the family with 150 yuan, and this was given to Wenzong as his share. Eldest brother Wenxian also paid Wenzong an additional 40 yuan for marriage expenses, bringing the total to 190 yuan. Though the three brothers' shares had originally averaged 268 yuan, the family fortune had declined in the intervening years. Wenzong accordingly accepted this as a share, and a new division document was drawn up (TS 1910:17).

Thus a son absent from the house at the time of division was entitled to a share of the property, even if he had been sent from the house by the father. In practice he probably had to return to claim his property.

Two legal cases from outside of Taiwan add further details on the rights of sons. The son of a remarried widow who followed his mother into her new household was entitled to a share of property in his natal home from his blood father's estate. Thus in a 1733 case from Jiangxi province, Gui Gaowan lost his father, and his mother remarried. Perhaps because he was only three, he followed his mother into the house of her new husband, while his elder brother Gaoqi remained and worked their .42 *mu* of land. In 1732, Gaowan married and returned to reclaim his half share—.21 *mu*—of inheritance land. Gaoqi resisted, and in the fight that ensued, Gaoqi died. At trial, Gaowan was sentenced to death, but his wife was specifically awarded her husband's inheritance land, confirming Gaowan's inheritance rights (Chang 1986:B31709–15).

Such sons were not, however, automatically entitled to property in the house of their stepfather. Thus in 1747, widow Fu remarried to Pan Jielang, and she brought into the marriage her son, Niansheng. When Jielang died, he left two pieces of sacrificial land, and a dispute arose as to their allocation. The court decided that part of the land could be used to support widow Fu in her old age but that, when she died, all the land was to go to Jielang's nephew, leaving Niansheng's heirs with nothing (Chang 1986:B81579–85). Thus sons brought in with a remarrying widow did not necessarily share in the property of their stepfather. If such a son was formally adopted by the stepfather, he would probably inherit as an adopted son.

Young, unmarried sons resident in the house also presented dilemmas. In the tenth month of 1770, the aged and sick Xiao Guanghe divided his house. He had had four sons, Yuncong, Yuncheng, Yunwu, and Yuncai. The eldest, Yuncong, had died young, but before dying he had had a son, Chuansheng. The document states that Chuansheng would temporarily reside with second brother Yuncheng, who was instructed to treat Chuansheng as a son. Third brother Yunwu was also "young and naive," and so he would temporarily reside with his stepmother, née Zeng, who was instructed to treat him as if she herself had given birth to him. It is probable that fourth brother Yuncai was also young, but since he was the son of Zeng, he would automatically reside with her and thus required no special arrangements.

Thus one grandson and one or two sons were young enough to require guardianship, but that did not diminish their shares of property. After making set-asides for sacrifices to ancestors, dowries for daughters, and an extra amount for the eldest grandson,[4] the remaining property was divided equally among the four branches. The three remaining brothers and the grandson received property so exactly even that they would each receive 19.44 *shi* in rent and be required to pay 1.72 taels in tax (TS 1910:63). Thus the ages of sons did not affect their rights to inherit equal shares of family property.

Physically or mentally disabled sons also presented dilemmas, as seen in the Chen lineage division of 1827. The five Chen branches jointly held some mountain land that was left as common property during a previous division.[5] They subsequently decided, for reasons that are unclear, to divide it up. One brother, Xiyuan, was head of a branch and was described as "lacking in his four limbs" (*siti you kui*). As a result, he was provided with a small, extra portion from which he could collect rent for his living expenses. The remainder of the land was divided equally among the five branches, including Xiyuan's. Thus Xiyuan's disability did not limit his right to inherit; in fact it entitled him to slightly more land in this case (TS 1910:54).

In another instance from the twelfth month of 1837, a certain Cheng Zong died, and his property went to his now orphaned son, Jiuying. Jiuying was described as "lacking in his four limbs, foolish, and ignorant." A variety of lineage, family, and village elders were concerned that he would waste the property—four tracts of dry land —and fail to provide sacrifices to his ancestors. They therefore drew up a document stipulating that, should Jiuying try to sell the land arbitrarily, he would be removed from ownership, and the land would be maintained intact. He was not, however, denied his right to inherit the land and would only be removed should he try to sell (TS 1910: 34). While not conclusive, the evidence does suggest strongly that physical and mental disability did not exclude a brother from receiving an equal share of property during division and in fact may have allowed him to receive a slightly larger share because of his disability.[6]

A final dilemma for families undergoing division was the treatment of a son who had died without leaving an heir. A particularly illustrative case occurred in the twelfth month of 1897. A deceased

Mr. Ye had had a total of five sons, probably by three different women. Two of the sons, brothers number three and four, had died, and the remaining three were dividing the house. Brother number three (whose name is not given) had been adopted out while young. The previous year he had married, his wife had given birth to a son, and then suddenly and unfortunately all three had died. Now his natal house was undergoing division, and the document states that, as an adopted out son, he "should not in principle get a share of property, but because of a mother's natural disposition to treat her sons equally," a house and a garden, valued at 570 yuan, was set aside for his, his wife's, and his son's sacrifices. His mother would manage the property until a grandson became available for adoption into the place of this deceased son. Brother number four had also died, apparently when quite young, but the family decided to pay for his sacrifices out of the common property and not to set aside any special amount for him (TS 1910:39).

The He family division of 1866 displays an alternative strategy to provide for a deceased son. The second brother, Liangui, had died without an heir, and the document states: "The property that should have gone to second brother Liangui will be divided equally among the three other branches, and afterwards whichever branch has a grandson to adopt into his place, Father [He] will provide twelve yuan to this grandson, and the branches may not complain" (TS 1910:69). Father He is allowing Liangui's share to be divided, but he is also providing an incentive to entice a son into allowing a grandson to take up the slot as an adoptive heir, presumably to carry on the sacrifices to Liangui.

This differing treatment suggests that a range of strategies were used by families with a deceased heirless son: at one extreme, the family could set aside an entire equal share and then adopt a son to manage it; at the other extreme, they could offer minimal sacrifices. The factors determining which strategy a family used were most likely, first, the availability of property and, second, the age and marital status of the son at the time of his death. The farther along in the life cycle the son was at his death, the more likely the family was to set aside a full share and adopt a son.

Thus in Qing Taiwan custom, all sons were entitled to an equal share of the household property, regardless of the status of their mother, regardless of whether they were physically present at the time of division, regardless of age, and regardless of whether they were mentally or physically healthy. Only by dying without issue could their share be diminished, though even in death, some sons still symbolically received a share via an adopted son. To receive an equal share, the status as son was the critical factor: fitness and need were not considered.[7]

Legal Disinheritance of a Son?

Regarding whether a son could be legally disinherited, the eminent Japanese scholar Shiga Shūzō has argued that disinheritance did not exist either in traditional China's law or in customary practice (1978:139). My research so far tends to confirm Shiga's conclusions to the extent that there was no regular, standardized, and frequent process of disinheritance. But an interesting case from Ba county in Sichuan suggests that something approaching disinheritance might have occurred during the Qing in rare instances.

In 1816 father Peng Anxiang wrote an *yizhu* document and had a copy deposited in the Ba county yamen for safekeeping. The document states that in 1813 Anxiang's son, Yingzhou, illegally brought into the house a concubine named Gong Ergu. The acquisition of the concubine was illegal not because Yingzhou was already married to a woman née Wang, but primarily because Yingzhou wanted to raise Ergu to the status of wife, a violation of Qing law. With his father, his wife, and his wife's brother in opposition, Yingzhou became violent and threatened to kick his father out of the house. Father Anxiang went to the neighborhood mediators to seek a solution, but they were unable to deal with Yingzhou. Thereupon Anxiang went to court.

The magistrate decided against Yingzhou, sentenced him to three months in the cangue, and ordered the concubine returned to her natal home. Yingzhou, however, was able to bribe his way out of the punishment. He returned home and assaulted his father and his wife. Father Anxiang went back to court, which this time increased the sentence and had Yingzhou struck thirty times across the face and then put in the cangue for another three months. Yingzhou managed to bribe his way out again, and the ensuing fight at home was worse than the previous one. Anxiang went screaming down the street, and when the case came to court again, Yingzhou had his sentence increased to forty strokes of the heavy bamboo and was locked to a stone. But the resourceful Yingzhou bribed his way out a third time and fled far away, but not before threatening to return and take revenge for the loss of his concubine.

Father Anxiang was terrified at the thought of having his son return, scared that Yingzhou would take and waste all the family property and also fearful that his daughter-in-law and his four grandchildren might be killed. Therefore he wrote up the *yizhu* turning all the property over to his daughter-in-law. The document was signed by the lineage elders, ensuring its legality, and a copy was deposited in the yamen. Thus the son, Peng Yingzhou, was denied his inheritance rights, though the property went to his wife and his children (BX 6–3–9748).

The extreme nature of Yingzhou's repeated violent behavior and his absolute refusal to bow to legal decisions and punishment suggests the extent to which a son had to go to be denied his inheritance rights. The facts that no legal term that equated to "disinheritance" was used in the case and that father Anxiang used an *yizhu* to resolve the matter suggest just how rare such legal actions must have been.

The Rights of Adopted Sons

Adoption was frequent in Taiwan, as the work of many anthropologists suggests.[8] If a father had adopted one son and the relationship between the two had gone smoothly, the rule relating to blood sons applied: the adopted son inherited the entire family property without legal process. Thus it is likely that in the majority of adoption cases, the adopted son inherited fully, although there is no legal paper trail available to test this hypothesis.

Fourteen percent of the inheritance documents I analyzed do contain references to adoption, and these documents suggest that the rights of an adopted son lacked the clarity of the equal rights of a son. While most often entitling him to an equal share, his rights could in some cases vary based on particular situations. The evidence further suggests that the most useful analytical framework is to divide adoption into two types—*baoyang* and *guoji*—though the terminology in the documents is not consistent. Within each type of adoption, the son's inheritance rights in his natal and adoptive homes might differ.

A third inheritance practice closely related to adoption was the appointment of an heir, a person appointed and provided with property in order to conduct sacrifices to a deceased individual. Such appointments were often made at household division time, and the language, documents, and property awards frequently appear similar to adoption.

The *Baoyang* Form of Adoption

The *baoyang* was the less frequent type of adoption. In the Lin family division of 1886, two of the four sons, the eldest and the third, had been adopted *(yang)*, and in the process of household division all four sons received equal shares of property. No mention is made of property rights in the two adopted brothers' natal homes (TS 1910:15). In 1892, when the Li family divided their house, father Li was dead, and he was survived by his wife, née Lin, and his three sons. The first two had been adopted *(baoyang)*, had no blood relationship to the family, and had already died. The third brother was born to father Li and his wife, was thus a blood son, and was still living. This third brother received lineage property valued at seven hundred yuan owing to his status as a natural son. But at division the household property was divided into three shares, one each for the sons of the deceased first and second brothers, and one for the surviving third brother. The descendants of the adopted brothers thus inherited family property equally, lineage property unequally, and no mention is made of any property in their natal homes (TS 1910:13).

It thus appears the *baoyang* form of adoption was adoption of a son with no relationship to his natal family. He may have been an orphan or from a family of a different surname. The adopted child had strong and possibly full inheritance rights in his adoptive home but apparently had no property rights in his natal home.

The *Guoji* Form of Adoption

The more common form of adoption was *guoji*, involving the moving of a son from one brother to another within the family, from one branch to another within the lineage, or from one family to another within the surname group. When widow Xu ordered family division in 1868, she demonstrated a classic *guoji* adoption within the family. Her first son, Tong, had died without issue. She had her second son, Xunzhi, send his second son, Laoma, to become the adopted son of Tong. Laoma not only inherited a full share, he also received extra land as an eldest grandson portion (TWGS 2, 8:921).

When *guoji* adoptions extended beyond the immediate family and involved sending a son to another branch of the lineage or the surname group, the son being adopted out could inherit property in both his natal and adoptive homes. Thus in 1838 four orphaned brothers divided their considerable household property. The two youngest brothers had been adopted out to relatives on their father's side. Despite their being adopted out, they received from their natal family full shares, including land, housing, garden, and bamboo groves (TWGS 1, 9:830).

In a similar case from 1828, the Cai family had six brothers, and the third, Masheng, had been adopted out as heir to a relative of his father. The original contract reads that the family will divide the property into five shares. But because Masheng's adoptive family was poor, they wished to help him, and thus the brothers reduced their portions, formed the property into six shares, and Masheng received one. He drew lot number four and inherited equally (TWGS 10, 7:555).

The Liu family division of 1897 illustrates an interesting cycle of *guoji* adoption. The Lius had three sons, the second of whom, Shenyu, had been adopted out to his uncle as a second son. When household division occurred in his adoptive home, he received half of the property, with which he apparently returned to his natal home. His natal home then underwent division, and his half share from the adoptive household's division was combined with the property in his natal home. This unified property was then divided among the three brothers, allowing each to inherit an increased amount (TS 1910, 65:1649).

Another division, this one from 1873, contains two *guoji* adoptions, one within the family, the other of a son adopted in, and suggests just how complex adoption inheritance rights could become. The family had three sons, two born to the first mother and one adopted by the second mother, née Lin. Brother number two had died young, and the now deceased father had had first brother's second son adopted as heir to brother number two. Widow Lin had adopted brother number three from within the same surname group.

This arrangement allowed all three branches to share equally in the division (TS 1910, 7:1529).

But sons who had been adopted out could also receive less than full shares of property from their natal homes. The Li family division of 1895 is illustrative. Widow Li, née Huang, was dividing her property between her two sons, Bingyu and Bingjun. Bingjun had been adopted out to the family of his father's younger brother, where he joined another adopted son, Bingyou. Since Bingjun would receive half of the property of his adoptive father, he received less than a full share in the division of his natal home, only 6.755 *shi* as opposed to Bingyu's 46.755 *shi*.

A division that involves two adoptions illustrates this same pattern. When widow Zheng divided her household among her six sons and stepsons, brother number four, Guangxu, had been adopted into the family of his father's elder brother. Brother number one, Guangbao, had died without issue, and subsequently brother number three's son, Zhentian, had been adopted as heir to Guangbao. In this case, Zhentian, as heir of the eldest brother, received a full share. But the adopted-out Guangxu received a set-aside of three plots of land to conduct sacrifices to his adoptive father, and he did not receive a full share, as the document states he will receive his adoptive father's property (TS 1910, 11:1540). Thus the son adopted within the family received a full share, while the son adopted out received only sacrificial property.

As an added complication to the patterns of adoption, some divisions had to deal with the rights of a son adopted into the family who was then followed by the birth of a blood son. In an 1870 division, father Xue Tiancong divided his property. Father Xue had two sons: the first, Sanyang, was adopted in from father Xue's eldest brother; the second, Kaisheng, was a blood son born after the adoption. Both had had their marriages arranged, and both inherited land, housing, household items, and debt equally. Thus in some cases, when a blood son was born following the adoption of a son, both could inherit equally (TWGS 5, 8:430).

This was not always the case, however. In an 1839 legal dispute from Ba county, Sichuan, an adopted son, Li Maofu, sued a younger blood son for being unwilling to divide the family property. The court decided against the adopted Maofu, primarily because he had been adopted from a family of a different surname (Liu) and thus was not entitled to inherit. But the court did allow him to retain the grain, a water buffalo, and fifty taels of silver (used to rent land) that his adoptive father, Li Chunyou, had given him by contract some years earlier (BX 6–3–9755).

A similar instance took place in Taiwan in 1871. Father Hu Yuanli had no sons by his first wife and so adopted two boys. He entered them into the lineage genealogy as *minglingzi*, the Taiwanese equivalent of *baoyang*-style adoption, even though the boys were in fact from a distant branch of the lineage. After the death of his first wife, father Hu married again, and his second wife proceeded to have five sons. He and his second wife then arranged marriages for the two adopted sons, sent them off to seek a livelihood, and thus the adopted sons did not inherit equally (Sung 1974:29).

In the pattern that emerges here, fathers such as Li Chunyou and Hu Yuanli, fearful of not having a son, adopted one or two. When a blood son or sons were subsequently born, the fathers provided money and capital to set up the adopted sons in separate homes, sent them off, and planned to allow the blood son or sons to inherit the remaining property fully. In the case of Li Maochang, the court essentially agreed with the practice, and thus an adopted son inherited less than a full share of the family property. The contrast between those adopted sons who, following the birth of a blood son, inherited fully and those who did not is most likely explained by the distinction between *baoyang* and *guoji* adoptions. Those who were adopted from within the family, lineage, or surname group inherited equally; those from outside the surname group could be sent off with less than an equal share.

The Appointment of an Heir

The appointment of heirs differed from adoption in that it involved different amounts of property and was designed to assure sacrifices after death, rather than to provide a share of family property to an adopted son. A complex appointment in 1866 suggests the variety of ways adopted heirs could be treated. Of three brothers, only one, Jingcheng, survived, and he was heirless. For his own heir, Jingcheng appointed a lineage relative (called a nephew), Pirui. For his eldest brother Jingtuan, three other "nephews" were appointed joint heirs. For his younger brother Jingwei, no specific heir was appointed, but Jingwei's land was to be divided equally between the two branches represented by Pirui and the three nephews, and both branches were to be heirs to Jingwei (TWGS 10, 7:584).

An adoption contract from 1899 also illustrates the appointment of an heir for sacrificial purposes. The Lan household had undergone division earlier, at which time the family's four sons were all deceased. Though three sons had heirs, one—brother number four— did not. The family set aside three pieces of rice land for the future heir of brother number four, and the adoption document now states that his place is being filled by Wangquan, second son of Lan Yuan-tang, heir to one of the original brothers. Wangquan accordingly receives the three pieces of land (TS 1910:27).

An 1817 division orchestrated by widow Yang contains an adoption that is neither purely adoption nor the appointment of an heir, but probably a combination of both. Widow Yang was a stepmother to three boys and the mother to one. At division, the three stepsons received equal shares. Her son, however, had been "half adopted" or "half appointed heir" *(banci)* to the Huang family. For this reason, he received only half a share in his natal home, probably because he would receive a share in his adoptive home (TWGS 8, 7:644).

Thus the property rights associated with adoption could vary and were subject to negotiations in many instances. It is likely that in most cases the one adopted son inherited the adoptive family property fully and received nothing from his natal home, but it was also possible for the adopted son to enjoy rights in both his adoptive and natal homes. In *baoyang* adoption, he received nothing from his natal home and up to as much as a full share in his adoptive home. If a blood son was born after the adoption, however, it was possible for the *baoyang* son to be sent off with less than a full share of the property. In the *guoji* form, he inherited a full share from his adoptive home; and he might inherit no property, a partial share, or a full share in his natal home. In the more frequent *guoji* scenario, therefore, the adopted son often benefited economically in that he inherited more than just an equal share of property in his adoptive or natal home. The appointment of an heir, while often similar to adoption, generally involved less property and was designed to assure that the heir would conduct the proper sacrifices after the death of the individual bestowing the property.

The Rights of Parents

Family members other than brothers had well-defined property rights at the time of household division, and these rights were provided in the form of set-asides or guaranteed payment rather than equal shares. The amount could be more or less than a brother's share, and the number and size of such set-asides depended primarily on the size, form, and wealth of the family.

Parents had legal and customary rights to continued support in their old age; they also had customary rights to a funeral when they died. These could be paid from one set-aside or funded separately. The most frequent set-aside for parents was termed *yangshan,* though other terms existed, and was designed to provide for the parents' economic support in their old age. Sixty-five percent of household divisions took place while at least one parent was still alive, but of these only 62 percent actually allocated property for a *yangshan.* This figure suggests that in 38 percent of household divisions, the surviving parents felt they could rely on their children for support, rather than needing to hold on to independent property.

For those who chose to keep a *yangshan,* land was often the first choice, as in 1837, when He Yuantong divided his 16.2 *jia* of land among his seven sons. To provide for himself and possibly his wife in old age, he kept 7.15 *jia* under his control (TS 1910, 37:1590). In 1773 four Lin brothers divided their total of 8.1 *jia* of land, and they set aside 2.9 *jia* for the support of their aging mother (TS 1910, 52:1626). In other cases the *yangshan* might take the form of rental income, as in 1893, when two Wu brothers set aside a total of 32.3 *shi* of grain rental income for the support of their stepmother (TS 1910, 45:1612). *Yangshan* could also be in the form of money, as in the Han family division of 1793. The surviving parents in this case were the senior Han's second wife and a concubine; of the family's total wealth of 64,280.952 taels of silver, 2,080.2 were set aside for support of the two women (TS 1910, 75:1667). Support might also come in the form of periodic guaranteed payment. Thus in 1825 three Yang brothers claimed they had insufficient property to create a formal *yangshan* for their father's surviving concubine, née Hong, but they agreed that each year in rotation one brother would pay sixty yuan for her living expenses (TS 1910, 17:1557). Finally, creative solutions could be found, as in the 1898 division in which the aging Chen Xunquan kept an unspecified number of tea bushes as his *yangshan* (TS 1910, 47:1616).

Funeral and burial expenses were most often assumed to be covered by the *yangshan,* and on occasion this assumption was made explicit. In the 1868 Jian family division, when widow Jian, née Huang, set aside two *jia* of land and a shop as her *yangshan,* the division document states: "Mother's land and shop, in the days after mother is one hundred years old,[9] after the burial expenses have been paid completely, all will be kept as common land, and the three branches will rotate their use" (TS 1910, 41:1601). If the *yangshan* was found insufficient to pay funeral and burial expenses, the brothers were expected to make up the shortfall. Thus in 1838 second mother Zheng set aside one plot of garden land "for my *yangshan* as long as I live and for my funeral after I die. If it is insufficient, the five shares[10] will pay equally" (TS 1910, 11:1542). If a *yangshan* did not exist, the brothers were expected to pay burial expenses. Therefore in 1853 the three Du brothers divided their house just after the death of their mother, and as part of the division, they pawned four plots of land and used the cash to pay for their mother's funeral (TS 1910, 46:1615).

Of the household division documents I have analyzed, in eighteen cases the numbers allow for a calculation of the relative amount of property set aside for *yangshan*. The evidence is presented chronologically in Table 7. Table 7 illustrates that the amounts given to parents for their support in old age could vary considerably in type, total, and relative percentage, from a low of 3 percent to a high of possibly 63 percent of the total family property. The figures suggest a plausible pattern as well. While wealthy families set aside more property in total terms than did middle or poor families, they often set aside less in percentage terms. This pattern is particularly striking among the wealthiest families, cases 1, 5, and 15, in which the *yangshan* was only 2 to 7 percent, while in the poorest families, cases 12, 13, 8, and 17, the range was from 16 to 68 percent. This pattern suggests that as class position declined and family property provided income at or closer to the subsistence level, parents claimed relatively more for themselves at division time. This finding in turn suggests that parents had claims to survival and support that were somewhat stronger than the claims of the brothers to their equal shares.

Table 7

Yangshan Support as a Percentage of the Family Estate

Case No.	Year	Total Estate	Yangshan	%	No. of Parents Alive	Source
1	1725	26,971 liang	500 liang	2	1[a]	JJS 117
2	1732	44.883 mu	13.985 mu	31	1[b]	JJS 332
3	1752	106.28 mu	4.816 mu	5	1[a]	ZPM 7:8666
4	1773	8.2 jia	2.9 jia	36	1[b]	TS 1910:52
5	1793	64,281 liang	2080 liang	3	2[c]	TS 1910:75
6	1796	3.005 jia	.975 jia	32	2[a]	TWGS 2, 8:863
7	1816	28 jia	3.8 jia	14	1[d]	TS 1910:36
8	1825	1381 yuan	352 yuan	25	1[e]	TS 1910:17
9	1831	33.4 mu	2.15 mu	6	1[b]	JJS 591
10	1833	442 ping	62.2 ping	14	1[b]	JJS 223
11	1837	16.2 jia	7.15 jia	44	1[d]	TS 1910:37
12	1857	2.69 jia	1.69 jia	63	1[d]	TWGS 2, 8:886
13	1863	6.71 mu	1.55 mu	23	1[b]	ZPM 13
14	1868	14.9 jia	2 jia	13	1[b]	TS 1910:41
15	1879	21,700 yuan	1600 yuan	7	2[a]	TWGS 1, 9:895

16	1893	210.4 shi	40 shi	19	1[b]	TS 1910:45
17	1895	63.5 shi	10 shi	16	1[b]	TS 1910:9
18	1897	3,636 yuan	774 yuan	21	3[f]	TS 1910:39

[a] Father and wife.

[b] Wife only.

[c] Wife and concubine.

[d] Father plus mother who may be alive, but she is not mentioned.

[e] Concubine.

[f] Three wives.

Unmarried Sons and Marriage Expenses

Ideally, household division took place after all sons were married, at which point marriage expenses were no longer a family concern. But 17 percent of divisions took place before all sons were married, and the unmarried brothers were entitled to some extra property, because their married brothers had already received this considerable expense. At the point of division, the set-aside for marriage expenses generally was in the form of cash. Thus in 1793, when the wealthy Han family divided its fortune, the family set aside 395.2 taels of silver so that their third brother, Gaoduan, whose wife had died, could marry for a second time. A further 1,840 taels was set aside to cover the marriages of sixth brother Gaolin and two sisters, though the specific amount for each sibling was not stated (TS 1910, 75:1667).

When the much less wealthy Yang family divided their property in 1818, five of ten brothers were unmarried. To fund marriage expenses, each of the five married brothers was required to pay 30 yuan annually to their father, who would provide 50 yuan to each unmarried son. Once the five younger sons were all married, the 30 yuan payments would cease (TS 1910, 42:1604). In 1825, when missing brother Yang Wenzong returned to his family after they had divided the family property, he was awarded 150 yuan as a brother's share and an additional 40 yuan as marriage expenses (TS 1910, 17:1557). In 1838, when widow née Zheng divided her household, her two unmarried sons, numbers five and six, and the adopted eldest grandson all received 50 yuan for future marriage expenses (TS 1910, 11: 1540). In the Ye family division of 1897, fifth brother Qisheng was still single and so was awarded 300 yuan for marriage expenses (TS 1910, 39:1593).

While marriage expenses were normally provided in cash, other types of settlements were possible. In the 1837 He family division, for instance, the youngest two sons, He Lu and He Tong, were unmarried. As a result, He Lu was given an extra .55 *jia* of land, and He Tong was given .65 *jia* specifically for marriage expenses (TS 1910, 37:1590). In an 1838 division, third brother Zhang was unmarried, and so in addition to his brother's portion, he was allowed to till and harvest the family's sacrificial lands for two years to cover his marriage expenses (TS 1910, 64:1647). In the 1896 Li family division, a plot of land was set aside to fund both widow Li's *yangshan* and the marriage expenses of her two sons, Weiji and Weide (TS 1910, 70:1659).

The Li family division of 1886 reveals some intriguing variations on marriage expenses that occurred as a result of the practice of minor marriage, or *tongyangxi*.[11] The family's third brother, Kaijin, was married, but his wife had been brought in as a *tongyangxi*, and so he was awarded 78 yuan as a "room dowry" *(fanglian)*. Fourth brother Pengshi was married, but his wife's dowry had apparently lacked "clothes," so he was awarded 12 yuan. Fifth brother Caisheng was married, but like third brother his wife had been a *tongyangxi*, so he was awarded 50 yuan as a "room dowry." Sixth brother Tiansheng was not yet married and so was awarded 110 yuan to cover complete marriage costs (TS 1910, 6:1524). Thus, while sixth brother Tiansheng received 110 yuan to cover complete marriage costs, Kaijin and Caisheng had married their fostered brides, and most likely their extra money was intended to make up for the missing dowry. Fourth brother Pengshi's 12 yuan probably made up for some perceived shortage in his wife's dowry.

A few household division documents allow for statistical calculation of the relative amounts of marriage expenses. The results appear in Table 8. To the extent that five examples from such utterly different families can demonstrate anything, they suggest that, while a son's marriage expenses were relatively small in terms of the total wealth of a family (1 to 4 percent), they could be very large in relationship to the portions that each brother received (6 to 57 percent). Examples four and five further suggest that marriage expenses were a greater burden for poorer families.

The Inheritance Rights of Daughters

During the process of household division, women in the household enjoyed property rights depending upon their status as daughters, wives, or widows. Since division ideally took place after the marriages of the children, unmarried daughters emerge in only 9 percent of the documents in this study. But these daughters did have rights, both to continued support and to dowries. Thus in 1770, when the Xiao family was undergoing division, two sisters were unmarried, and it was decided that their future dowries were to be paid in

Table 8

Marriage Expenses as a Percentage of the Estate and a Brother's Share

Case No.	Year	Total Property	Brother's Portion	Marriage Expenses	%*	Source
1	1725	26,971 liang	2807	500	2 (18)	JJS 117
2	1793	64,281 liang	7003	395	1 (6)	TS 1910:75
3	1825	1040 yuan	268	40	4 (15)	TS 1910:17
4	1837	16.2 jia	1.06	.6	4 (57)	TS 1910:37
5	1843	7.63 mu	2.7	1.33	17 (49)	JJS 375

* Marriage expenses of a single brother as a percentage of total family property, followed by, in parentheses, marriage expenses of a single brother as a percentage of a brother's portion.

cash from the family's trust of common property (TS 1910, 63:
1644). In another late-eighteenth-century division, the Zhuang family
had not yet married their third daughter. Second brother was to take
thirty *shi* of grain from the harvest of his land plus fifteen yuan from
a loan due to be repaid, and give both to third daughter as a dowry
(TS 1910, 12:1543).

In the 1793 Han family division, two younger sisters had not yet
been engaged, and a total of 1,840 taels of silver were set aside to
pay their and a brother's marriage expenses (TS 1910, 75:1667). In
1825 the Yang family had an unmarried sister, Jinniang. The family
agreed that Jinniang would live with their father's surviving concubine, née Hong, and that the brothers would provide 24 yuan per
year for their sister's living expenses. Another 200 yuan would be set
aside for her dowry. Given that the family's total property amounted
to about 1,040 yuan and that the three brothers' portions averaged
268 yuan in value, this expense for their sister was a considerable
percentage of the total (TS 1910, 17:1557). In another Yang family
division, this one from 1897, fourth sister remained unmarried, and
the family decided to store up the harvest from at least eleven plots of
commonly held land to fund their sister's living and dowry expenses
(TS 1910, 62:1643).

Since household division ideally occurred after the marriages of all
children, the evidence concerning unmarried daughters is sparse. But
what does exist suggests that unmarried daughters were entitled to
two things: living expenses and a dowry. Though quantifiable evidence is even sparser, it appears that the amounts for these two
expenses could be substantial. It is likely that living expenses and
dowries were generally in the form of movable property and cash,
seldom in land. Significantly, unmarried daughters never signed the
household division documents, suggesting that their rights to support
and dowries were more customary than legal and that they had little
power to influence the proceedings and property distribution.

The Inheritance Rights of Wives

Only rarely in the process of household division did women
emerge in the documents as wives of husbands who were living. In
one such occurrence—the He family division of 1866—father He
Guozhen and his wife, née You, were both alive and were both listed

as receiving the same *yangshan*. Father, wife, and wife's brother all signed the division document (TS 1910, 69:1656). In another instance, the Zhuang family division of 1778, two wives emerge even though their husbands were still alive. Father and grandfather Zhuang were both still living, as were grandfather's wife, née Lin, and father's second wife, née Zhuang. For reasons that are unclear, both father and grandfather received a joint *yangshan* piece of land. Wife Zhuang received a different piece as her *yangshan,* and wife Lin had received a *yangshan* piece of land previously. Thus both of these women held independent *yangshan* while their husbands were still alive (TS 1910, 12:1543). Generally, however, wives of living fathers and sons did not play official roles in division. Indeed it is often impossible to determine from the household division documents how many of the wives of living husbands were even alive, and thus it can be presumed that the property rights of a wife were incorporated into those of the husband as long as he lived.

The Inheritance Rights of Widows

Women most frequently emerged in the household division process as widows in one of several generational positions. They could emerge as the surviving head of the family after the death of the father. In this situation the widow might be the head of the family, she might control the division process, and she might retain a *yangshan* portion of property if she wanted one. In the 1770 Lin family division, father Lin was dead, and his widow, née Chen, was listed among the signatories as the mother of the dividers. She received 2.9 *jia* of land as her *yangshan,* which was 36 percent of the family's total land and was over five times the .55 *jia* each brother received (TS 1910, 52:1626). In the division of the wealthy Han family in 1793, father Han was dead, and he was survived by his second wife, née Guo, and his six sons. The document states that widow Guo was dividing the family property, and she reserved for herself 1,639.2 taels of silver as her *yangshan,* which was 3 percent of the family fortune and equaled 23 percent of each brother's share (TS 1910, 75: 1667). In 1836, when the two brothers Bilan and Bitao divided their household, though their widowed mother is not mentioned by name, she received 1.2 *jia* of land, which was more than the .85 *jia* that each brother received (TS 1910, 43:1607). In the Zhang family division of 1843, the widowed mother, née Zheng, took charge and divided the family property among her four sons, keeping the rental income from one piece of dry land as her *yangshan* (TS 1910, 48: 1619).

In 1868, widow Jian divided her household among her three sons. The document specifically states that she had "inherited her husband's land, housing, furniture, and household items" that were now being divided. Her brother, who had been a creditor, was repaid, and he signed the document. She kept two *jia* of land and a building as her *yangshan*. Widow Jian subsequently managed her property so well that in 1881 the family had to meet again to divide the three *jia* of land she had acquired (TS 1910, 41:1601). In 1895 widow Li divided the family property between two sons. Even though she was her husband's third wife and the two sons were from the first wife, she was apparently the only surviving widow. She took charge of the division, kept ten *shi* of income as a *yangshan*, divided the property between the two boys, and signed the document as the divider (TS 1910, 9:1535).

Widows also had rights to a funeral, and so in 1826 widow Wang divided her family property among her six sons. She kept for herself one piece of land as her *yangshan*, and she also made perfectly clear how the expenses of her burial, coffin, and burial clothes were to be paid (TS 1910, 10:1537).

Widows who were heads of families did not always stand in for their husbands, however. Thus in the 1893 Wu family division, the property was divided between two nephews and an uncle. A stepmother was still alive, and she received 32.3 *shi* of annual income, but she was not mentioned by name, she did not sign the document, and the three men were the formal dividers of the property (TS 1910, 45:1612). In the 1897 Ye family division, deceased father Ye was survived by three widows, yet the division was handled by his three sons, and though the widows received *yangshan*, they signed the document merely as witnesses (TS 1910, 39:1593).

Women frequently emerged and played roles in division as widows of brothers in the generation dividing the parents' property. For instance, in 1837 He Yuantong divided his property among his seven sons, and his first son, He Jia, had already died. He Jia's widow, née Wang, received a full share of land totaling 1.2 *jia*, and she signed the division document herself. Any children she may have had were not listed (TS 1910, 37:1590). In 1857, when the Zhang family divided their property, the first brother and his parents were already dead. As a result, the first brother's widow, née Gu, not only received a full share of the property and signed the document, she was formally in charge of the entire division process (TS 1910, 40:1599).

But like fathers' widows, brothers' widows did not always stand in for their deceased husbands. In an 1868 division, the first two of four brothers had passed away and were survived by their widows and sons. In this case, the sons stood in for their deceased fathers, and the widows signed the document as merely being present rather than as heads of their branches (TS 1910, 8:1531). And in an 1896 division, the deceased third brother's widow, née Cai, and her son together received their share of property and signed the document (TS 1910, 44:1609). It seems fair to conclude that a brother's widow's position was related to whether she had a son. If she had no son, she inherited her deceased husband's share of the property; if she had a son, her branch received an equal share, but control could go either to her or to her son.

The Inheritance Rights of Second Wives and Concubines

As we have seen, a woman who married into a family as a second or third wife, or came in as a concubine also had certain rights at the point of division, and those rights were in part related to her status as wife or concubine. Qing law allowed males only one legal wife at a time, though they could take in as many concubines as they wished or could afford to support. If a man's wife died, he was allowed to take another wife or to raise a concubine to the status of wife. It is clear from the household division documents, however, that the legal distinctions between wife and concubine, and the laws against having more than one wife at a time were not strictly maintained. The relative rights of wives and concubines are, therefore, somewhat unclear, though it is most likely that, while wives received equal consideration, concubines could receive less property than wives.

Thus in the Ye family division of 1897, father Ye's three wives, née Lu, Wu, and Lin, all survived him. They each signed the document as a "witness mother," and the *yangshan* set-aside of house, rice land, and garden went to all three as a group. Later adjustments of the *yangshan* to pay for funeral expenses were made so as to guarantee and equalize the future payments (TS 1910, 39:1593).

If we focus on those women specifically labeled as concubines *(shu, ceshi)* in the documents, the picture of equal treatment shifts. Concubines did receive *yangshan* property, as illustrated in the 1825 Yang family division. The brothers divided the family property, and their deceased father's surviving concubine, née Hong, was first promised 60 yuan per year in *yangshan*. A year later these arrangements were changed, and she was given a flat 250 yuan to invest and a servant girl valued at 102 yuan (TS 1910, 17:1557).

In instances where both a wife and a concubine survived, the *yangshan* of the concubine might not be of equal value. In the 1793 division of the wealthy Han family, for instance, Han Guoshi was survived by his second wife, née Guo, and a concubine, née Hua. Guo was formally in charge of the division process, and she set aside 1,639.2 taels of silver for her own *yangshan;* she gave the concubine 441 taels for the same purpose (TS 1910, 75:1667). In the 1886 division of the Li family, the first wife, née Lai, had given birth to four sons, and a concubine who is not named had given birth to two sons. Both women received independent *yangshan* property, the first wife receiving 83 *shi* of grain income plus an unspecified amount of money for her burial, while the concubine received only 32 *shi*. The wife signed the document, while the concubine did not (TS 1910, 6: 1524). Thus, while wives received equal treatment during household division, the status of concubine entailed receiving less property than a wife.

To sum up, the basic property rights embodied in the process of household division in Qing Taiwan were three: each son had a right to an equal share of the property, though adopted sons' rights were sometimes negotiable; all unmarried sons had rights to marriage expenses and unmarried daughters to continued support and dowries; and parents, including husbands, wives, and concubines, had rights to continued support and a funeral. If family property was minimal, the rights of the parents took precedence over the rights of the other members of the family. And if a poor family had unmarried children, providing their marriage-related costs might have taken precedence over providing shares for each son, though the evidence does not clearly resolve this issue. The interaction of these three rights determined the basic pattern of Qing Taiwan household division, and these basic rights were the rules around which individuals and families adopted strategies in pursuit of their interests.

Chapter 5

Dividing Different Types of Property in Qing Taiwan

HAVING illustrated the rights of individuals in Qing Taiwan, let us now turn to the objects that these rights pertained to: property in its various forms. The major forms of property divided at division time were housing, land, and debt, but each form had myriad variations in the Qing Taiwan context.

Equality of Living Space

As to the division of living space, the primary concern when dividing housing was to provide each brother with an equal amount of space, regardless of the present size of his conjugal unit. Though equality of space was the salient concern, two other factors operated as well. First, the dividers tried to keep the newly independent families intact by providing them with rooms that were close together if not contiguous; and second, they tried to place the eldest son in the favored location to the right of the central ancestral hall.[1]

As a measure of equal division, one pattern was to divide the housing into exactly equal parts by the number of rooms. In an 1842 division, for example, the eldest of three brothers was dead, so the division took place between his son and the two surviving brothers. Each of the men received the same amount of space: four rooms of tiled-roof housing and two rooms of thatched-roof housing (TWGS 1, 9: 841). In a Wu family division of 1894, five brothers drew lots specifically for housing, and each received one of the five available rooms

(TWGS 1, 9:894). And in an 1898 three-way division between an uncle and two nephews, each received exactly four rooms of housing (TS 1910, 1:1515).

In other situations, the equal division of living space was expressed in less precise terms. In the Xiao family division of 1770, the house was being divided into two sections, so the family divided it down the middle: brother Yuncheng received the left side, brother Yunwu the right (TS 1910, 63:1645). In the Lin family division of 1773, the housing and the land it stood upon were divided into "four shares" for the four brothers (TS 1910, 52:1626). And finally, in the Cai family division of 1862, the four brothers each received one building and the vegetable garden land adjacent to it (TWGS 1, 9:859).

The division of housing space was not always so easy to accomplish, however. The rooms that compose a house are not always of equal size and value, with the type of roof—thatched or tiled—often representing the difference. Also, the total number of rooms might not have been divisible by the number of brothers. In such cases, a brother receiving an unequal share of housing could be compensated with other property. The 1826 division guided by widow Wang stands as a good example. Widow Wang had six sons, who in order of age received housing as follows:

Yupan

Left side of new building	2 rooms
Cross room (small)	1 room
Central hall	one-half
Inner west side	1 piece

Yubi

East side of old building	1 section
Miscellaneous housing	2 pieces
Cash to build housing	80 yuan
One water buffalo	

Yuqing

Right side of old building	2 rooms
Central hall	one-half
Land next to old building	1 piece
East side of back house	1 piece

Yushen
Right side of new building   2 rooms
Central hall   one-half
West side of back house   1 piece

Yutai
Left side of old building   2 rooms
Central hall   one-half
Land next to old building   1 piece

Yubin
Miscellaneous housing   1 piece
West half of old building   1 section
Cash to build housing   80 yuan

The above list suggests that each brother was entitled to roughly two full rooms, one half of a hall, plus a bit more. Four of the brothers —Yupan, Yuqing, Yushen, and Yutai—had shares roughly equal to this amount, depending upon the values of the vaguely defined "pieces" that they received. Yubi and Yubin fared less well, so they were reimbursed in cash specifically earmarked for housing construction, and Yubi obtained a water buffalo in addition. Thus, when rooms could not be divided into exactly equal shares, other property or cash could be used to equalize the distribution (TS 1910, 10: 1538).

Equality was not the only principle families employed when dividing living space. Most dividers also tried to keep each newly independent family residing as a unit, with their rooms and kitchen in one area, ideally adjacent to each other; and in those cases in which the parents had already died, the families tried to place the eldest brother and his family in the rooms to the right of the central ancestral hall. The Yang family division formalized in 1873 displays this pattern. The eldest brother's adopted son, Youde, received rooms on the right side of the central hall, second brother Chaolai received the rooms on the left side of the central hall, and third brother Fu received housing to the right of Youde (TS 1910, 50:1623).

Another example can be gleaned from an 1838 division among four heirs. Chengchang, the eldest, received the big room to the right of the central hall and the seven rooms extending in front of it. Baochuan, the fourth brother, received the set of nine rooms to the right of Chengchang. Yuxi, the third son, received the big room to the left of the central hall and the seven rooms in front of it, while Baoqing received the nine rooms to the left of Yuxi. This division embodies all three principles: equality, integrity of the conjugal units, and the traditional positioning of the eldest son (TWGS 1, 9:830).

There was a serious hazard latent in such a pattern of housing division. Since the new families assumed legal ownership of the rooms in which they resided, they could subsequently sell those rooms, perhaps even to non–family members. Such a sale would raise the disturbing prospect of family members and outsiders residing around the same courtyard, and this concern was expressed in a number of division documents. In the division just mentioned, a clause reads: "As to the share each has received of Ancestor Peng Fu's home, if at a future date any of the four shares move to another location, they may not allow outsiders to live in the building" (TWGS 1, 9:830). And the document from the 1892 Li family division reads in part: "If there is anybody who desires to move to another location, [their] foundation land, bamboo garden, and the house will revert to those who remain for management" (TS 1910, 13:1546). And after a six-way division in 1886, the document's section on housing read: "If any branch wishes to move away, they cannot sell to outsiders" (TS 1910, 6:1527). Thus families tried to offset the centrifugal effects of equal housing division by limiting the new families' power to rent or sell to outsiders.

Equality of Land

Land and the rights and responsibilities inherent in landownership were of the greatest importance at the point of household division. Its disposition occupies by far the most space in the household division documents. This extended treatment of land division was necessitated by three sources of complexity inherent in landownership: land was possessed in a variety of ways because of the *dazuxiaozu* system of divided landownership in Taiwan; no two plots of land were of exactly equal agricultural quality or market value; and the land transfer process known as the *dian*, or pawn transaction, made future ownership uncertain. The household division documents reflect all of these concerns to varying degrees. For analytical purposes, I propose to look at the division of land from several angles:

first, at the division of land in its various forms of ownership; next at the division of land of differing values; third, at land involved in a pawn transaction; fourth, at the division of land taxes; and, finally, at the division of the legal documentation related to land.

Land Division among Owner-Cultivators

As to the various forms of landownership, the Zhuang family division of 1778 is illustrative of division among wealthier owner-cultivators. Grandfather Zhuang had personally opened up forty-one *qiu*[2] of rice land to cultivation, and since he had only one son, no division was necessary in the second generation. His son in turn gave him three grandsons, and when the time came to divide the house, the land was simply divided among these three grandsons: ten *qiu* to the eldest, fifteen to the second, and sixteen to the third. (TS 1910, 12: 1543).[3]

In the 1838 division orchestrated by widow Zheng, there were fourteen plots to divide among six brothers. The eldest, Guangbao, had died young, and his adopted heir received two plots. The second, Guangyan, received four plots, while the third, Guang'an, received two. Fourth brother, Guangxu, had been adopted out to his uncle, but he received three plots anyway, while the fifth, Guangyin, and the sixth, Guanglüe, received one and two plots, respectively (TS 1910, 11:1540). In 1816 the Fu family divided their holdings of 117 individual plots totaling twenty-eight *jia* among three sons. After providing for the parents and the eldest grandson, the eldest brother received 4.6 *jia* of rice land (plus some rental income from other land) and the second brother 5.4 *jia* of rice land. The third brother had died without issue, and subsequently each of his elder brothers appointed one son as his heir. These two adopted sons received a total of 9.6 *jia* of both dry and rice land. More revealing is the fact that the eldest brother's portion totaled twenty-nine individual pieces of land in seven locations, the second brother's twenty-three pieces in three locations, and the adopted heirs' forty plots in eight places (TS 1910:36).

Thus equal division among wealthier owner-cultivators with many individual plots of land could take into account several factors: agricultural productivity of the plots, location of the plots in relationship to home, and the location of the plots in relationship to each other. These families could arrange the large number of plots so as to provide each brother with equal value and, ideally, with plots located so as to make walking to them and working them efficient.

Owner-cultivators with less property could not so easily arrange equal division, since the smaller number of plots allowed less flexibility when matching value. If the plots were divided intact—that is to say, they were not split into smaller plots—one or more of the brothers' shares was going to be unequal. Two strategies used to resolve this dilemma were to compensate with money or property those brothers whose land was of lesser value or to divide each plot by the number of brothers. In 1862 the Cai family divided their household, and after providing for sacrifices, four plots of differing sizes remained to go to four sons. The elder two brothers split the largest plot into two pieces of exactly 1.90349 *jia,* while the third brother received two plots, and the fourth brother received the remaining one. The problem was, however, that third brother's two plots were of greater value than that of the elder two brothers, and the fourth brother's single plot was of lesser value. The solution was to have third brother pay 100 yuan, 60 yuan of which went to fourth brother (TWGS 1, 9:859).[4]

The Lin family division of 1880 stands as another example of plot splitting among poorer owner-cultivators. The two sons, Juexian and Jinli, had inherited .55 *jia* of rice land. To simplify the division, the brothers just divided the plot into two equal shares of .275 *jia* (TS 1910, 51:1624). In another instance, in 1874, three brothers—Youde, Chaolai, and Fu—faced a more complex situation as they owned three significant pieces of land, one piece of vegetable garden in front of the house, and two plots of dry crop land. The brothers divided each plot carefully into three, marked the first two with stones to clarify the new boundaries, and awarded a one-third section of each plot to each brother. Chaolai received the middle sections, Youde the western sections, and Fu the eastern sections (TS 1910, 50:1622). Thus, in order to adhere to the principle of equal division, poorer owner-cultivators often had to resort to strategies of compensation or plot splitting.

A final detail for owner-cultivators dividing land, rice land in particular, was to ensure that irrigation water would continue to be available to the new families. Division documents covering the dispensation of irrigated land often contain phrases such as this one from the Xu family division of 1873: "The water that flows from

the upper reaches to irrigate below must not be selfishly diverted"
(TWGS 3, 10:911).

Land Division by Tenants and Landlords

Division of land by tenant families was a somewhat different
affair, since it involved the rights of the landlord. Tenants had to
ensure that the rent they owed would continue to be paid by the newly
independent families. In the 1773 division among the Lin brothers,
two plots were divided between four brothers. Each plot was divided
into four pieces, netting each brother two plots .25 *jia* and .3 *jia* in
size. In addition, each brother had to pay .4 *shi* of rent. The lands
awarded to the surviving mother and set aside for sacrifices were also
saddled with rental payments of .06 *shi* and .03 *shi,* respectively (TS
1910, 52:1627). In 1836, the brothers Bitao and Bilan divided a
rented piece of dry land into eastern and western halves, each brother
assuming two yuan of the rental payment (TS 1910, 43:1608).

Landlords receiving rental income did not need to consider the
interests of the tenant when household division occurred, because
they divided merely the rental income, not the land itself. Thus, in
the 1879 Chen family division, a piece of land inherited from an
ancestor provided the family with thirty *shi* of income a year. The
three Chen brothers agreed to take ten *shi* each (TS 1910, 24:1571).

A Taiwan Peculiarity: The *Dazu-Xiaozu* System

Landlord-tenant relations in Qing Taiwan were usually more complex than the above examples suggest, because of a two-tiered landownership pattern known by the two forms of rent that typified the
system: *dazu* and *xiaozu.*[5] This *dazu-xiaozu* ownership pattern predominated in the central and northern regions of the island, and its
origins lie in the Qing state's attempts to guide settlement on Taiwan.
On the Taoyuan plain, for instance, the Qing state issued to a petitioner (either an individual or a group) a patent granting ownership
of a poorly defined tract of land. This person or group then had ten
years (six years after 1723) to bring the land under cultivation and
was given a three-year exemption from the land tax. If the patent
holder failed to make progress, the land could be awarded to another
petitioner.

The patent holder, who was quite often an absentee investor,
recruited peasants from the more densely populated areas of Taiwan

or Fujian and settled these men as tenants on the land. The tenants paid a rent known as *dazu* (big rent) to the patent holder, who in turn paid the land tax. Because of the difficult work of reclamation associated with wet rice agriculture, such as construction of rice paddies and irrigation systems, the tenant was considered to have invested at least his labor and perhaps some capital as well, and for this he acquired a form of ownership of the land. He could sell or lease his cultivation rights independently of the patent holder. If he rented out the land, he collected a rent called *xiaozu* (small rent). The second tenant, or subtenant, was provided with a small parcel of land and a hut, in return for which he paid the *xiaozu*, which could approach 60 percent of the crop. In this way the patent settlement system created a two-tiered system of rent payment and landownership in much of Taiwan (Knapp 1980:60–63; Zhou 1991:20–55)

The first common pattern of *dazu* payment was essentially no different from a pure landlord-tenant relationship, in that the tenant-cultivator paid *dazu* to a landlord. The Huang family division of 1819 stands as a nice example. The four Huang brothers had four plots of land, each of which they divided into sections. Each brother was required to pay 2.28 *shi* of *dazu* to an unnamed landlord (TS 1910, 23:1567). When the two Yang brothers, Shangbang and Shangpeng, divided in 1827, Shangbang received three plots, on two of which he had to pay *dazu*. The amount on the first plot was specified in another contract, and the amount on the second was 1.23 *shi*. Shangpeng received three plots, all of which were liable for *dazu*. The amounts on two were unspecified, while for the third he had to pay 1.33 *shi* annually (TS 1910, 66:1651). In 1853 the Du family divided their relatively small amount of property. The elder brother, Du Lao, received one plot on which he paid 1 *shi* of *dazu;* the second, Du Qian, received two plots and paid 1 *shi;* the third, Du Chang, received five plots and was liable for 2.25 *shi* (TS 1910, 46:1615). And as a final illustration, in 1817 the two brothers Sihui and Zhiping decided to set aside a plot of dry land for sacrificial purposes. The plot would rotate yearly, and the brother who cultivated it would pay the .5 *shi* of *dazu* (TS 1910, 49:1622). Thus tenants who owed landlords *dazu* rent faced similar pressures as other tenants: they could divide the land in any manner they desired, but they had to ensure continued payment of rent.

A more complex situation in household division occurred when families collected *xiaozu* from a tenant but also paid *dazu* to another landlord. Sometimes, as in the Li family division of 1896, the amount of *dazu* payment could be left unclear, though payment was required. In this case the second and third brothers received twenty and ten *shi* of *xiaozu* income, respectively, from which they were required to pay unspecified amounts of *dazu* (TS 1910, 70:1659). In other cases, both *dazu* and *xiaozu* amounts were specified. When the Zhuang family divided their household in 1871, they owned *xiaozu* rights to 1.2 *jia* of land that they divided three ways. A common sacrificial trust was endowed with 12.5 *shi* of *xiaozu* and was liable for 3.08 *shi* of *dazu;* and third brother Zhuye received 15.1 *shi* of *xiaozu,* from which he had to pay 3.6 *shi* of *dazu* (TS 1910, 67:1652). In the 1893 Wu family division, the dividing uncle and nephews set aside 40 *shi* of *xiaozu* income for a stepmother, from which she had to pay 7.7 *shi* of *dazu*. Another plot, which was possibly set aside for sacrificial purposes, generated 14 *shi* of *xiaozu* and was liable for 2.2 *shi* of *dazu* (TS 1910, 45:1613).

The already difficult proceedings in the 1886 Li family division orchestrated by widow Li, née Lai, were further complicated by the *dazu-xiaozu* system. The family owned a piece of rice land that generated 210 *shi* of *xiaozu* income, from which they in turn paid 6.4 *shi* of *dazu* and 1.6 *shi* for irrigation water (called "water rent"). At division time, 4 *shi* was awarded to the eldest grandson, and the remainder was divided equally between four of the six brothers. A second plot, from which the family derived 98 *shi* of *xiaozu* and paid 5.6 *shi* of *dazu,* was divided equally between two of the six brothers. A third plot that provided 44 *shi* of *xiaozu* from which they paid 4.236 *shi* of *dazu* and a fourth plot that provided 45 *shi* of *xiaozu* from which they paid 1.7 *shi* of *dazu* were initially given to the first wife as her *yangshan* portion, but they were subsequently divided among her four sons (TS 1910, 6:1524).

Thus families that held rights to *xiaozu* income could freely divide the rent they received, and the recipient of the income was then liable for the related *dazu* rental payment. At the time of household division, the most likely basis for calculating the division was the net income after subtracting the *dazu* payment, though other considerations, such as the reliability of the tenant and the consistency of production from the land, must also have been taken into account.

It was also possible for landlords to receive *xiaozu* and not be liable for *dazu* payment, in which case *xiaozu* simply was a synonym for rent. Thus, in the Lin family division of 1886, the family had received in pawn land that gave them 110 *shi* of *xiaozu* annually. They awarded 15 *shi* to their mother as her *yangshan* support and 15 *shi* to the second brother as a special reward.[6] A further 52.4 *shi* was used to repay interest on a loan, and the remaining 27.6 was divided equally between the four brothers. No *dazu* payment was mentioned (TS 1910, 15:1553). When the Li family redivided their property in 1890, they owned rights to 122 *shi* of *xiaozu* and 40.89 of *dazu*. Thirty *shi* of *xiaozu* went to each of three sons, 20 *shi* went to the eldest grandson, and 12 *shi* went to the widowed concubine as her *yangshan* support. The 40.89 *shi* of *dazu* went to a sacrificial trust (TWGS 1, 9:898). And in another Li family division, this one in 1892, the family owned rights to 1,180 *shi* of *xiaozu*. The eldest son had died, so his son received 420 *shi;* the second son had also died, so his four sons received 380 *shi;* and the third son, the sole survivor of his generation, received 380 *shi* as well. Again, no *dazu* payment was mentioned (TS 1910, 13:1547).

Families who received *dazu* were equally free to divide it as they pleased. Thus in 1868 the Jian family owned rights to seven *shi* of *dazu*. They awarded this income to the eldest grandson, Linjiao, for two years as part of his eldest grandson portion. Thereafter it would be collected in turn by the three brothers and used for sacrificial purposes (TS 1910, 41:1603). In the 1898 Yang family division, the two brothers Wenbing and Wenqing had inherited rights to 207.894 *shi* of *dazu*. The sum of 31.708 *shi* was set aside for a lineage trust, 98.06 went to Wenbing, and 78.0414 went to Wenqing. The *dazu* was to be paid by specific tenants, who were listed by name in the division document (TWGS 1, 9:909). And in 1895 the two Li brothers Bingyu and Bingjun split equally the family's right to 3.51 *shi* of *dazu* (TS 1910, 9:1536).

Since both *dazu* and *xiaozu* rights could be bought and sold, in rare instances a family owned both the *dazu* and *xiaozu* rights to the same piece of land. Thus, in a three-way division in 1842, each brother received .3 *jia* of land, from which each received 2.4 *shi* of *dazu*, 20 *shi* of *xiaozu*, and .8125 *shi* of irrigation water rent, in total 23.215 *shi* for each brother (TWGS 1, 9:841).

Thus, in Qing Taiwan, tenant and landlord families undergoing household division had to take into account the various forms of possession that the two-tiered ownership system created and to ensure that the differing rights and responsibilities were carried into the next generation.

Some Tendencies in Land Division

An interesting tendency in the evidence suggests that families who owned both land that they worked themselves and rights to rental income, either *dazu* or *xiaozu,* tended strongly to use the income to fund set-asides such as *yangshan* portions. The Zhang division of 1843 is illustrative. The Zhangs owned about five plots of land that they worked themselves and, in addition, rights to an unspecified amount of *xiaozu* income. The land was divided among the four brothers, and the *xiaozu* was given to their mother as her *yangshan* portion (TS 1910, 48:1622). Twenty years later, the Xiao family division would reveal a similar pattern. The land was divided among the heirs, but the *dazu* was turned over to their widowed mother as her *yangshan* portion and was later to be used for her funeral expenses (TWGS 1, 9:861). In 1866 the Lin family owned unspecified amounts of land, which they divided among the three surviving brothers. Their rights to *dazu* and other rental income, the amounts also unspecified, went to their parents as *yangshan* support (TS 1910, 69:1656).

Families also tended to use rental income to fund sacrifices. In 1770 the Xiaos distributed the land that they worked to four heirs equally, while their *dazu* income, which totaled at least 40 *shi,* was kept as common property to fund sacrifices (TS 1910, 63:1645). When the Chen family divided in 1879, the land was distributed among the three sons, while 45 *shi* of *xiaozu* went to fund sacrifices (TS 1910, 24:1571). And in a 1901 Xiao family division, the three sons received housing, land, and tea bushes, while 25 *shi* of *dazu* income went to fund both sacrifices and the *yangshan* support of their widowed mother (TWGS 1, 9:911).

Factors to Be Considered in Land Division

Overall, then, the method of division of land was determined by the relationship a family held to the land: owner-cultivator, tenant, *xiaozu* landlord, or *dazu* landlord. For the two types of landlords, the critical factors in the calculation were simple: the amount of rent and, probably, the dependability of the tenant.

But what of the cultivator? The cultivator's chief concern would have been that the land he received provided his family with an equal harvest for equal labor as compared to the land of his brothers. Thus land quality must have been a crucial and complicating factor in household division. Which plot produced the highest or lowest return per unit of area or per unit of labor? Which plot was easiest to irrigate? Which plot was liable to flooding? Which plot was closest or farthest away? How all these factors were balanced is not recorded in the division documents, most likely because it was so fundamental to the process it did not require explanation. The documents record only the results: so many *jia* for elder brother, so many *jia* for second brother, and so on.

But the problem of land quality does often emerge in the distinction between irrigated rice land and dry land. Most division documents clearly distinguish between dry land (*di* or *yuandi*) and rice land (*tian* or *shuitian*).[7] The higher returns to rice land meant that the two types could not simply be divided on the basis of area. Furthermore, rice land, and dry land as well, varied in quality from one plot to the next. A particularly suggestive example of the division of lands of varied quality is the He family division that took place in the fourth month of 1837. The He family owned a total of 16.2 *jia* of land, 4.25 *jia* of rice land and 11.95 *jia* dry. Of the rice land, 1.8 *jia* was of "middle" (*zhong*) quality. The family consisted of father He, most likely his wife, and seven sons. The two youngest boys were unmarried, and there was at least one grandson. Table 9 shows how the land was divided.

After allowing for the set-asides, the brothers were awarded an average of 1.06 *jia* of land each. But such an average, while it provides an analytical center point, misses the critical problem of land quality. Brothers three and four received less than the average amount because of their larger amounts of rice land; brothers five and six received more than the average because they received less valuable "middle"-quality rice land. The less than average 1.0 *jia* shares of dry land awarded to brothers two and seven are harder to explain. Perhaps the land was particularly fertile and convenient; or perhaps the brothers received other property not mentioned in the division document. Whatever the explanation, it is clear that quality and type of land were critical issues at the point of household division.

Table 9
Division of Land of Differing Use and Value

Recipient	Dry Land	Rice Land	Middle Rice	Total
Parents	7.15			7.15
Eldest Grandson	.4			.4
Marriage Expense*	1.2			1.2
Brother 1	.9	.3		1.2
Brother 2	1.0			1.0
Brother 3	.2	.75		.95
Brother 4	.1	.75		.85
Brother 5		.45	.8	1.25
Brother 6		.2	1.0	1.20
Brother 7	1.00			1.00
Average per brother				1.06

Source: TS 1910, 37:1590.
* For brothers 6 and 7.

The Division of Pawned Land

The *dazu-xiaozu* ownership pattern and the differing value of land were not the only factors that complicated the process of dividing land. The pawn (or *dian*) transaction was often another knotty issue. In a land pawn transaction, a person who owned land would turn it over to a second party in return for an amount of cash, usually about half the market value of the land.[8] The second party then had use rights to the land, usually for a stated minimum amount of time. After this time, the first party had two options: to reclaim the land for the amount of money originally paid or to sell the land rights completely to the second party for the remaining portion of the full market value of the land. The pawn transaction thus created two parties with two related sets of rights: one with rights to reclaim or sell off the land pawned out, and one with temporary use rights on land that might be reclaimed or might become available for final purchase. For these reasons, land held as part of a pawn transaction could not be valued just like land held outright. If one brother received one *jia* of land owned outright and one brother received one *jia* of land held in pawn, such a division was unequal, since the latter was liable to lose his land. Thus the division of land enmeshed in a pawn transaction required special treatment at household division time.

In 1773 the Lin family encountered such a situation. They held one piece of land in pawn, in addition to other lands held outright. This pawned land and the rent and tax responsibilities that came with it were divided equally among the four brothers. Thus the danger of losing the land and the possibility of buying it later were assumed equally by all the heirs (TS 1910, 52:1627). In 1816 the Fu family held 28 *jia* of land in 117 plots. Six of these plots were held in pawn and were clearly noted as such in the division document. In the division settlement, none of the pawned land went to the *yangshan* portion. Five of the six plots went to the eldest grandson's special share, and the remaining one became part of the large share that went to the deceased third brother's two adopted heirs. In this way the danger of loss was assumed essentially by the eldest grandson, whose portion is discretionary and does not have to provide him complete sustenance (TS 1910, 36:1588). When the Chens divided their household in 1879, they held, in addition to much other land, one plot of rice land in pawn. They opted to keep the pawned land as common property, work it in rotation, and use the proceeds for sacrificial purposes. If the land was later reclaimed, the three brothers would split the reclamation money equally (TS 1910, 24:1571).

The Ye family division differed from the foregoing, because most of their property was held in pawn. The family had nine plots of land, six of which they held as part of a pawn transaction. One plot of rice land held outright and one plot of garden held in pawn went to the three mothers as their *yangshan* portion. The eldest brother received one plot held outright and one held in pawn; the second brother received one plot held in pawn; and the fifth brother received three lots, all held in pawn. The eldest grandson received one plot held outright. This distribution of risk is difficult to explain, though a hint does emerge in the division document. The three mothers' garden land held in pawn and the eldest grandson's portion were all in fact going into the share of the second brother, who would presumably be living with them and/or supporting them. Therefore, the distribution of land held outright and in pawn was roughly equal, though no simple and completely equitable solution was possible in this case. The third brother, whose land was entirely held in pawn, was most at risk (TS 1910, 39:1593).[9]

In 1886 the Li family met to write up a division document and formalize a division that had in fact taken place some years earlier, probably in 1875. In the initial division, the deceased husband's concubine had been awarded as a *yangshan* portion one piece of pawned in land that generated 32 *shi* of *xiaozu* annually. In the intervening period, the concubine had died and the land had been redeemed. Her two sons used the money to pay for her funeral and had 600 silver yuan left over. They took 100 yuan and lent it out at interest to buy their mother a burial plot in the future, and the remainder was divided equally, 250 yuan to each brother (TS 1910, 6:1526).

In the opposite situation, families who were undergoing household division and who had pawned land out had to find an equitable mode of distributing the rights to reclamation or final sale. One pattern was to treat the pawns as joint property in which all brothers shared equally. The 1893 Wu family division document has the following clause: "As to the property we have pawned to others, two account books will be made, elder and second brother will each keep one, and later when this common property is sold off or reclaimed, the two branches will discuss it and divide equally" (TS 1910, 45: 1614). In 1836 when Bilan and Bitao divided their property, the prologue to the division document contained this clause: "As to all our previously pawned property and land, the brothers must jointly sell out or jointly reclaim, they cannot do so individually" (TS 1910, 43:1606). And in a three-way division in 1898, the first and third brothers would split the benefits of the land pawned out. The clause reads: "The rice land that grandfather bought from Lin Deshan, plus a piece of mountain land, are now pawned out to Lin Biao, and when the time is completed, if we reclaim or sell out, brothers Nian and Long will divide equally" (TS 1910, 1:1515).

Another possible strategy was to allow any brother to reclaim the land individually, which probably acted as an incentive to bring the land back into the possession of the extended family. The 1871 Zhuang family division between three brothers contains this clause:

"And as to the 1.2 *jia* of land we bought from Jian Bozhi in the twelfth month of 1871, we pawned it for 200 yuan of silver; if there is any individual branch that can save up the money to reclaim the land, it may be considered as its own property" (TS 1910, 67:1654).

A family could combine joint and individual resolutions to the problem of pawned property. Thus in 1853 the Du family had to pawn out land to obtain cash to bury their mother. They decided to include in their division document a clause that read:

> As for the land at Matoujue, totaling twelve plots both big and little, we will first take out four plots from the southwest half to pawn to Wu Cai, and the money will pay for mother's burial. The remaining eight plots will be divided equally. As for the land that is pawned to Wu Cai, if at a later date the three brothers can pay the money, it will be common property; if one person can save up the money, it will be his individual property, and nobody is to interfere or create difficulties. (TS 1910, 46:1615)

The Division of Land Tax Liability

Another task related to the division of land was the clear allocation of responsibility for the land tax. The pattern of tax payment was complex, and for purposes of analysis I will discuss owner-cultivators first, then tenants, and finally landlords of all types. Owner-cultivators might be liable for taxes on their lands, and such tax liability was divisible. Thus in a two-way division in 1817, brothers Sihui and Zhiping received land for which each was liable for .7 *shi* of tax (TS 1910, 49:1622). And in an 1896 division of *yangshan* property, each of three sons received land, cash, debt, and tax responsibilities: Yangji was to pay 1.573 taels per year, Shuji 1.599 taels, and Danran 1.537 taels (TS 1910, 44:1609).

Tenants could be liable for tax payments as well. In the Lin family division of 1773, each of four brothers received two equal-sized plots of land for which they each had to pay .4 *shi* of rent and 65 *jin* of tax. The land given to the eldest grandson, the *yangshan* support for their mother, and the sacrificial trust were also required to make the same types of rent and tax payments (TS 1910, 52:1627). In a three-way division in 1896, each brother received land and was required to pay unspecified amounts of *dazu* rent and taxes (TS 1910, 70:1660). And in another three-way division, this one in 1898, the second brother received land on which he had to pay an unspecified amount of three types of rent and one type of tax. The son of the eldest brother received rice land on which he was to pay .873396 taels of tax and two types of rent (TS 1910, 1:1513). Thus tenants were not necessarily exempt from the burden of paying taxes, but they could divide these tax responsibilities at the time of household division.

Landlords were taxpayers as well. In the Xiao family division of 1770, each of four brothers received 19.44 *shi* of rental income and was required to pay 1.72 taels of tax (TS 1910, 63:1646). When the Wu family divided in 1893, the two heirs of the first son received 4.4389 *jia* of land on which they were to receive 65.2 *shi* of *xiaozu* rent and were required to pay 8.3885 taels of tax (TS 1910, 45:1613). In the Zhang family division of 1843, the *xiaozu* income from one piece of common land was awarded to the widowed mother as her *yangshan* support, from which she would pay the annual taxes (TS 1910, 48:1622).

In Qing Taiwan, an individual's relationship to the land did not automatically determine if he or she had to pay taxes. Owner-cultivators, tenants, and both *dazu* and *xiaozu* landlords could be responsible for one or more of the taxes related to a particular piece of property. At the time of household division, this tax liability was divisible along with the land to which it was attached.

The Division of the Documents

The final element in the division of land was the division of the various documents—deeds, sales contracts, pawn contracts, redemption contracts, and household division documents—that proved two things: that the family did indeed own the property it was dividing and, by extension, that the newly independent families were the new legal owners. These legal documents were divided among the new families in one of three ways.

The ideal pattern was to match precisely the division of documentation with the division of property. A three-way division from 1873 stands as a good illustration. The eldest grandson received one plot of land and the set of contracts associated with it; the eldest brother received land in three locations and the documentation that went with those plots; the second brother received land in one location and its documentation; and finally the third brother received land in four locations, a shop, and the documentation that went with them

(TS 1910, 7:1529). The Yang family, in its 1898 division between the two brothers Wenbing and Wenqing, was equally fortunate to be able to match property with documentation. The eldest grandson portion and its documentation went to Wenbing; Wenbing's rights to rental income and housing came with the eight related documents; Wenqing's land and housing came with at least nine different documents (TWGS 1, 9:909).

But divisions that allowed such a neat distribution of documentation were few. Land was divided according to value, and value seldom accorded with the pattern of legal documentation. Thus the act of household division created an ownership pattern that diverged from the written record. In these situations, there were two possible ways to divide the deeds: give all the documents to one person or divide them among the heirs. In either case the recipient was required to allow the other heirs to view and use the documents at any time. On occasion the heirs allowed one person to keep all the documents, such as in the 1866 Lin family division. In this instance, the three brothers divided land among themselves, and they appended the following to the division document: "The land documents total eight in all, are not divided, and will go temporarily to third brother Lianying. If they are needed at some time, they must be taken out and shown. He cannot refuse, and in the future when we divide them, each will receive his own share" (TS 1910, 69:1657). In 1861, when four heirs, two uncles and two nephews, divided their property, they decided to allow the eldest uncle, Yuanpei, to keep the documentation: "All the old contracts we have on hand and the documents to open the mountain land will go to Uncle Yuanpei to keep" (TS 1910, 14:1550).

More frequently, however, the deeds and contracts were divided among the heirs, even though the relationship between land and documents did not match precisely. In the 1819 Huang family division, at least four of the family's plots of land were split into smaller portions in order to make equal shares for the four brothers. Five deeds were distributed as well: the two deeds to the common land and the *yangshan* portion went to the first brother; the deed to the land bought from the Liao family went to second brother; the deed to the land bought from the Guo family went to third brother; and the pawn contract to the Wang family land went to fourth brother. The final sentence of this section reads: "If [these documents] are ever needed, they must all be taken out for public viewing, and each branch's sons and grandsons cannot make trouble in this regard" (TS 1910, 23:1568).

In the 1863 Lai family division, the family had a total of eight documents related to property, and they simply divided them by the number of brothers, each of the four siblings receiving two (TWGS 1, 9:860). The 1879 Chen family division was much more intricate in the matter of division of documentation. Guanfang, the eldest, received two contracts, one land deed, and one land pawn contract. Shuchun, the second brother, received five land deeds, a household division document, and eight other various documents relating to property the brothers would hold jointly. Qiufeng, the third heir, received two sale contracts, a household division document, a loan contract, and a pawn sell-out contract. After each brother's share of documentation was written out in detail, the following phrase was added: "If hereafter anyone wants to use the documents, they must be shown, and no refusal is allowed" (TS 1910, 24:1571).

Thus, except for those cases where property and documentation were perfectly divisible, the act of household division meant that the paper record no longer accurately reflected ownership. Though the old documents were kept in case of future disputes and transactions, they no longer testified to the pattern of actual ownership. This inaccuracy in the written record was adjusted, however, by the writing up of the household division document itself, which brought up to date the relationship between ownership and the written record. The division document was equivalent to a land deed or a contract of sale in that it legalized ownership of property, and it was the critical document in the resolution of later disputes relating to the divided property. As detailed in Chapter 3, the document was drawn up at the end of the division process, one copy for each heir. In the text, usually toward the end of the prologue and family history but before the actual listing of the property, clauses such as the following were appended: "We now draw up four exact copies of the division contract, and each branch will receive one to keep forever" (TS 1910, 23:1568); "In order to have proof, we now draw up six exact copies, one for each branch, for the sons and grandsons to keep forever" (TS 1910, 10:1537). Thus each branch received a new legal document that conferred on them title to their new property and represented the new pattern of ownership.

The Division of Debt

Family debts were a final issue that might complicate the process of household division. Ideally, debts were paid off before dividing, but in those cases where repayment was not possible, the debt was assumed by the heirs. The pattern of debt distribution varied between two basic poles: dividing the debt equally or pairing the debt with property and giving both to one brother.

If a debt could be repaid before or at the point of division, it effectively and equally reduced the shares of each heir. Thus the Yang family household division document records that in 1820 the family decided to sell a fishing boat and pawn some property in order to raise cash to repay a debt of 1,465 "big yuan." After the debt was cleared up, the remaining property was divided among the family members in 1825 (TS 1910, 17:1557). In 1893 the Wus took out more than three hundred *shi* of grain to repay debts, though the two brothers would be liable for any shortfall (TS 1910, 45:1614).

A debt that could not be repaid immediately was distributed among the heirs, often equally or close to it. Thus in 1827 the two Yang brothers divided their six pieces of land. The previous year their father had taken out a loan of an unspecified amount. To finance repayment of both principal and interest, elder brother Shangbang would contribute 34 *shi* and second brother Shangpeng would contribute 40 *shi*. If this 74 *shi* were to prove insufficient, the remainder would come from the common-sacrificial lands the two held jointly (TS 1910, 66:1652).[10] In 1886 the Lin family underwent a four-way division. The Lins had a total of three debts on which they owed 520 big yuan in principal and 200 big yuan in interest. The interest would be paid from grain rental income, but the principal would be repaid equally by the four brothers (TS 1910, 15:1554). In the Li family division of 1886, the six brothers were each required to repay 184.48 yuan of debt. Each son was to establish an individual debt repayment booklet in which to record his progress on repayment (TS 1910, 6:1528).

An alternative method of handling family debt was to have it partly or entirely assumed by one brother, if it was paired with property of value equal to the debt. In 1842 three brothers divided their land and rental income into four equal shares, the extra share going to Tianxi, the second brother, for which he assumed repayment of an unspecified amount of debt (TWGS 1, 9:841). In 1856 the Zhang family came together to rewrite a household division document. The division had taken place in 1848, at which point the *dazu* income from common land had been divided equally among the three sons. Subsequently all the records relating to the division had been destroyed in a flood, and there were now many debts associated with the common property. The solution was to draw up a new division document restating the basics of the 1848 division, but in addition changing the dispensation of the *dazu* income by giving it all to the second brother, who would undertake to pay the debts (TS 1910, 55:1632). In a three-way division in 1873, the eldest brother, Pengsheng, was given 810 *shi* of rental income to repay a debt of 10,500 yuan. Any surplus or shortfall was his alone (TS 1910, 7:1530).

Families could also combine methods for dividing debt. The Jian family division of 1868 stands as a good illustration. The Jians had such a large amount of debt that one sentence in the prologue of their division document reads: "Therefore I [widow Huang] invite the relatives and the lineage head, and taking all the property I inherited from my husband—land, housing, household items, and tools—and after first removing some to repay debts and some to maintain in common, the remainder will be divided into three equal shares for the three branches" (TS 1910, 41:1601). The family agreed to use three pieces of land totaling 3.1 *jia* to repay three separate debts. Three pieces of "house land" were used to repay another inherited debt. A shop and its furniture were added to some land, forming a total value of 264 yuan, which was used to repay a debt owed to widow Huang's brother. All this property would be sold off, and the cash generated would be used to repay the debts. If the money thus raised totaled more than the debts, the surplus was to be divided equally, but if the total was insufficient for complete repayment, the three brothers would equally make up the shortfall. This did not, however, end the debt problems of the family. Five more outstanding debts were given to Lianxing, the eldest brother, but these were paired with an extra 2.25 *jia* of rice land for him. He would assume sole responsibility for these, and any surplus or shortfall would be his alone (TS 1910, 41:1601).

Families that had debts owed to them also had to arrange how to divide the interest income and the future repayment of the principal. In these cases, a strategy of simple equal division was most frequently adopted. In the Lin family division of 1886, the Lins had lent 300 big yuan to Zhan Shuangmei. The interest—33.8 *shi*—was divided into four equal shares each year, and when the principal was repaid, it would be divided equally as well. The same arrangements were made for a loan of 100 yuan to Jia Qinghe (TS 1910, 15:1553). In 1893 the Wus were owed an unspecified amount of money, and in their division document they stated: "As to anyone who has borrowed money from us, both branches will see to repayment, and the income will be divided equally. Secret or individual collection to fatten oneself is not allowed" (TS 1910, 45:1614).

A Summary Example

In 1898 the Lin family met to divide their household. The Lin family structure and their property allowed for a division that was just complex enough to reveal many of the workings detailed above, yet simple enough to describe in a few paragraphs. Father Lin, known as Ancestor Wansheng, had died much earlier and had left two sons. The sons had both married, the eldest to a woman née Chen, the second to a woman née Liao. Chen subsequently gave birth to two sons, Ronghua and Laohou; Liao gave birth to Shikeng and Weizheng. Both women's husbands died before division, and thus the division took place between two conjugal units: widow Chen and her two sons and widow Liao and her two sons. In this case the property formally went to the widows' sons, and the mothers signed the division document as "witness mothers" rather than as heads of their branches.

The first line of the property settlement section of the household division document awards a piece of land that provides 12 *shi* of *xiaozu* income to the eldest grandson, who was most likely Ronghua. This eldest grandson portion was to go to him personally. The rest of the property was divided into two, and the branches drew lots.

The next section details the property awarded to Ronghua and Laohou, who had drawn lot one. This lot included a piece of rice land with its boundaries clearly recorded. It was .75235 *jia* in size, provided 19.1 *shi* of *xiaozu* income, was saddled with 2.65416 of *dazu* rent and 1.252235 silver taels of tax, and came with two related deeds. A second piece of rice land provided 60 *shi* of *xiaozu* income and came with a set of old documents that detailed the *dazu* and tax payments as well as the location. Lot one also included the northern half of a section of mountain land that contained stands of bamboo and tea plants, for which the boundaries were clearly recorded. The documents and deeds associated with this mountain property were to go to Ronghua and Laohou, but they were to be produced on demand. As to housing, lot one contained four rooms on the northern side of the tiled house, the northern half of the threshing ground, the northern half of the vegetable garden, and the northern half of the bamboo garden, which was marked off with a stone.

The second conjugal unit, composed of widow Liao, Shikeng, and Weizheng, drew lot two. This portion included a plot of rice land with boundaries clearly recorded, which provided 38.9 *shi* of *xiaozu* income and was required to pay 3.319842 *shi* of *dazu*. A second piece of rice land produced 40.2 *shi* of *xiaozu* income, and the *dazu* payment was recorded in the accompanying documents. Total tax payment on both pieces of land was 3.1849459 taels. Lot two further included the southern half of the mountain land, with bamboo trees and tea plants, and with boundaries recorded. The documents for this mountain land were to go to lot one, but widow Liao and sons could see them upon request. As to housing, lot two included four rooms, the southern part of the threshing ground, the southern half of the vegetable garden, and the southern half of the bamboo grove.

In sum, the two new families received housing and property that were mirror images of each other. Each family received approximately 78 *shi* of income, though a precise calculation is not possible; each had to pay *dazu* rent and taxes; each received one-half of the mountain land, bamboo trees, and tea bushes; each received one-half of the house and its surroundings. There was no debt to be divided among the heirs. The old family's unit of property had been simply split down the middle with half awarded to each new family. In Taiwan during the Qing dynasty, this was the ideal form of household division, and in most instances peasant, tenant, and landlord families divided their property in ways that closely approximated the ideal (TWGS 1, 9:907).

Chapter 6

Household Division Disputes in Qing Courts

T HE normal process of household division did not involve the Qing state or the courts. But a small percentage of inheritance-related disputes did go to court, and given China's large population, they represent a significant number of cases. In particular, the cases from Baxian in Sichuan are so rich in detail that they can be used to illustrate several inheritance-related issues at the same time. This chapter seeks to analyze how the community-based process of household division interacted with the Qing court system and how Qing magistrates adjudicated household division–related disputes.

Getting the Case into Court

Family quarrels, including inheritance disputes, generally involved great energy and expense, and magistrates were reluctant to become involved in such time-consuming and, from their point of view, unimportant cases (van der Sprenkel 1966:86; Macauley 1994: 176–183). Therefore, the first and most frequent response of a Qing magistrate to a household division dispute that involved nothing more serious was to refer the case back to the family, village, or lineage for resolution. In an 1861 case from Baxian, two Chen brothers and their widowed sister-in-law went to court in a dispute over dividing the household property. Upon receipt of the complaint, the magistrate dismissed it with this typical response: "It is ordered that the lineage resolve this; do not bring these [types of cases] to court." Household division disputes, in and of themselves, were not serious enough to require the magistrate's involvement (BX 6-4-2276).

But Qing officials had latitude and could become more involved if they chose to do so. In his book of advice to other magistrates on how to administer justice, Huang Liu-hung suggests a slightly more active role:

> In case of controversy [over dividing the family estate] the magistrate should order the head of the clan and the village elders to make an inventory of the family estate and present it to him. The magistrate then orders the family property divided equally among the brothers. The head of the clan and village elders are to be punished if they practice partiality and present an inaccurate inventory. (Huang Liu-hung 1984:451)

Thus, in a case dated 1839, adopted brother Li Maofu sued younger brother Maochang, who had been born after the adoption, for equal division of the household. There were no extenuating circumstances, but the magistrate agreed to hear the case anyway. And though the case was ultimately settled by mediation, two complaints were lodged, a hearing was held, and testimony was taken before it was resolved. Thus, while they tended to reject household division disputes, magistrates could choose to accept them (BX 6-3-9755).

A case from 1819 suggests one strategy that might succeed in bringing a case to the attention of the magistrate. On the sixteenth day of the ninth month, third brother Wan Yongkui stood outside the yamen door and screamed out his grievance. He claimed that his two elder brothers were denying him his one-third of their father's inheritance. The clerk at the door took down the complaint, and on the twenty-fourth of the same month, the magistrate agreed to take the case. Though Yongkui succeeded in getting his case heard, he lost his claim to the inheritance when the documents revealed he had been bought as a slave, not adopted as a son. But his example does suggest that "screaming the grievance" at the yamen door may well have been a way to seek legal redress (BX 6-2-4584).

One way to force the local magistrate to accept a household division dispute was to have it presented by a family member who held a Qing civil service degree, assuming a family was fortunate enough to contain such an individual. Thus the Tian family's three-year battle, from 1841 to 1843, over dividing the family property came to court immediately, and repeatedly, because the claimant was eldest brother Tian Shimei, holder of the *jiansheng* degree (BX 6-3-9759). A similar case is dated 1798. Two Zhao brothers, Fanghui and Fangshu, were arguing that a division had been done unequally. Though there were no extenuating circumstances such as violence, the court accepted the case, most likely because Fanghui held a *gongsheng* degree and Fangshu was a yamen official in charge of four runners (BX 6-2-4579).

Another way to force the magistrate to become involved was to claim that the household division dispute led to violence and injury. Cases that actually came to blows became cases of assault, or worse, and these required the government to become involved. Thus in 1851 Li Daicai presented a postdivision dispute over a vegetable garden boundary to the Baxian court. Daicai claimed his younger brother and sister-in-law had encroached on his land and beat him around the head and shoulders with a stick, and that he had suffered injuries. The magistrate's first response was that such family disputes should not disturb familial harmony and that the case should be returned to the family and lineage for resolution. But, because the younger brother and his wife may have injured Daicai, the claim of injury had to be investigated. An order was issued to send a runner to check the validity of Daicai's claim. The runner in turn reported that Daicai had indeed suffered some injuries, and the case was therefore accepted for adjudication. Testimony was taken, the younger brother was punished for his crime, a new garden border was mapped out, and a new contract was drawn up that would be left with the government for security. Thus the magistrate could adjudicate the assault charge and resolve the underlying household division dispute if he chose to do so (BX 6-4-1684).

Another more serious example occurred in 1733 in De'an county, Jiangxi province. In this instance, the dispute between two Gui brothers, Gaoqi and Gaowan, resulted in murder. The case had its roots in 1699, when three-year-old Gaowan's father died and his mother remarried. Gaowan was taken with his mother to the home of his stepfather, Yang Zecheng, leaving behind his inheritance rights to half of .42 *mu* of land. In 1732 Gaowan married, and in the next year he returned to his natal home to take possession of his .21 *mu* of inheritance land. Brother Gaoqi, who had been cultivating the land in the intervening years, initially agreed to turn over the land, but for some reason later resisted. A violent fight ensued, and Gaoqi died of his wounds. The court finally decided that Gaowan was guilty of killing his brother and that he was to be executed by immediate strangulation, but the court also mandated that the .21 *mu* of land go to his wife, confirming Gaowan's claim to the land. Thus, even in murder cases, the courts could decide to resolve the underlying household division dispute (Chang 1986:A55-100 [7-1]).

Not all household division–related cases that included a claim of injury were adjudicated, however. The magistrates were well aware that claims of injury could be fabricated, and they rejected some cases with rulings like this: "Immediately return this to the lineage for resolution; do not at year's end use false claims of injury to bring lawsuits and disrupt family harmony" (BX 6-4-1832).

Or the magistrate could simply adjudicate the assault claim and leave the underlying household division dispute unresolved. Thus in 1854 a household division dispute between uncle Huang Guoming and nephew Huang Tianhua escalated into violence, and uncle Guoming brought the case to court, claiming that he had been viciously assaulted and injured. The magistrate dispatched an investigator, who determined that uncle Guoming had not suffered any injury, and therefore no crime had been committed. The case ended there, leaving the household division dispute untouched (BX 6-4-1810).[1]

Adjudicating Household Division Disputes: The Rights of Sons

For those cases that he chose, or was forced, to accept, the essential task of the Qing magistrate was the defense of individual property rights embedded in the law and customary practice. Thus, in the key area of the property rights of sons, the court might choose to hear a case based on a claim of unequal division. Such a case occurred in 1798. The Zhao family had considerable property and debt, and had undergone three divisions in 1770, 1785, and 1795.[2] Third brother Fangshu was away during some of the proceedings, and following the last division, he became convinced that second brother Fanghui had kept more than his fair share. Fangshu went to court claiming unequal division, and the court agreed to hear the case. Before the magistrate ruled, however, the family and relatives came to mediate; the magistrate agreed to allow the mediation and he made no decision (BX 6-2-4579). Thus claims to unequal division could be heard in Qing courts, but given the guarantees of equality rooted in the household division process and the tendency of magistrates to push such cases back to the lineage or family for mediation, the relative percentage of such cases was probably small.

The Qing courts might also agree to hear cases based on the claim to the status of a son and the related right to an equal share of family property at household division time. One such case occurred in 1819, when Wan Yongkui went to court and claimed a one-third share of his deceased father's property, to be shared with his two brothers, Yongzhao and Yongfu. The two brothers countered Yongkui's claim, however, with documents that proved that Yongkui was not a brother at all. Their father Wan Zuocai had been an innkeeper, and one of his guests had run up a bill he could not pay. The guest "sold" Yongkui to Zuocai to settle the account. Father Zuocai had preserved the sale contract and had written an *yizhu* document specifically denying Yongkui a share of the property. The court took note of the documents and ruled that, since Yongkui was not even of the same surname, he had no rights. His claim was dismissed, but he was awarded the small amount of five thousand coppers as a face-saving measure, a common practice in civil disputes (BX 6-2-4584).

The Rights of Adopted Sons: Code versus Practice

Perhaps more frequent than cases involving the rights of sons to equal shares were those involving the rights of adopted sons. A case involving the family of Li Huibai is illustrative of how complex the adoption question could become. Li Huibai had both a wife and a concubine, but not a son. He therefore adopted Li Yuzhen, the second son of his elder brother. Yuzhen turned out to be a lazy good-for-nothing, and so Huibai went to court and had him expelled from the house. Huibai thereupon adopted Li Siye, who, though he had the same surname, was of no actual relationship to Huibai and family. Siye was a good student who earned a civil service degree, and his adoptive father was happy with the situation. When Huibai died, however, his wife became jealous of Siye's favoritism toward the concubine. She went to court to bar Siye from the succession and to have Li Longjian, the son of Yuzhen, appointed instead. The court held that neither Siye nor Longjian could succeed, Siye because he was not of the same Li family and Longjian because he was the son of the already barred Yuzhen. A search was made among all the relatives, and finally an appropriate heir, Li Yuanliang, was found. He was appointed heir to all the family property (Jamieson 1921:132).

This case is illustrative in several ways. First it reveals the relative freedom that the father, Li Huibai, had in adopting a son. Unhappy with Yuzhen, his first and legal choice, he dismissed him and adopted instead Siye, the son of a friend. That adoption, technically speaking, was illegal (unless Siye was under three, which was clearly not the case). This "illegal" adoption would have held, had it not been for the dispute between the wife and the concubine. Once this dispute reached the courts, the law was enforced, the illegal adoption disallowed, and a legal heir found. Hence the case also suggests that the customary practice of adoption was more freewheeling than the law demanded.

Disputes involving adopted sons who were followed by the birth of a blood son could also end up in court. Such a case occurred in 1839, a dispute between the two sons of the deceased Li Chunyou. The first son, Maofu, had been adopted, had had his marriage arranged, and now claimed that second brother, Maochang, was unwilling to divide the family property with him. The court decided that because Maofu's original surname was Liu, the adoption was not legal, and he was not entitled to inherit. He was, however, allowed to keep the fifty taels of silver, some grain, and a water buffalo that his father had contractually provided him earlier. Thus the court enforced the Qing statute that made inheritance illegal for those adopted from outside of the surname group over age three (BX 6-3-9755).

A somewhat similar case took place in 1850, but this time the son of an adopted son claimed an equal share of his grandfather's property. Father Li Shifeng and his wife adopted a boy, Li Yuxun, who was from the same surname group. They arranged a wife for him, and she gave birth to a son, Youde. Later, father Shifeng and his concubine, née Liu, finally succeeded in having a blood son, whom they named Yutian. Thereupon, father Li arranged forty *shi* of land for adopted son Yuxun and family, and the three went to live separately. But then both father Shifeng and adopted son Yuxun died. Grandson Youde may have wasted the forty *shi* of land he inherited, and so he occupied Yutian's home, demanding equal division of the now increased Li family property. The court decided that Youde had no claim to the property. He was punished for occupying the house and ordered to vacate. The reasoning for the decision either is not given or has not survived, but it is most likely that, because Youde's father had accepted the forty *shi* and moved out, and the increased property was acquired after the separation, Youde had no further claim (BX 6-3-9762).

Another form of adoption is illustrated in a Baxian case from 1861. Two Xu brothers had already divided the family property, and elder brother Wenzhong had a son, Xueyuan. The second brother, Wenyong, died, leaving his concubine, née Zheng, a widow. In this case, the son Xueyuan was declared the heir of both brothers. Concubine Zheng's property (over which there was a dispute to be discussed below) would remain under her management for the time being but would in the future be inherited by Xueyuan. This type of adoption in which one son inherits from two brothers was commonly called *jiantiao* (BX 6-4-2292).

While adopted sons had specified rights, they could also become targets of extortion, because law and custom required them to take good care of their adoptive parents. In the Ran family case of 1851, eldest brother Weijun had adopted out his son, Zhirong, to third brother Weixuan in a classic *guoji* adoption. After Weixuan died, all three surviving brothers accused Zhirong of not having taken good care of Weixuan and demanded money from him. In the mediated and compromise resolution arranged by the lineage, Zhirong was found innocent of any wrongdoing, but he paid his father and uncles 54,000 coppers anyway (BX 6-4-1717).

The Rights of Stepsons

Another class of sons, those who followed their widowed mothers into new marriages, could have their inheritance rights resolved in the courts as well. It is clear that the law did not give such sons inheritance rights in their new homes. This point is illustrated well in a case dated 1861, though it took about five years to resolve. In the Chen family, the three surviving brothers were all long-term laborers. Only the eldest brother, Daifa, was able to marry, and his wife was a widow who had one son, Jiarun, and two daughters from her previous marriage. Eldest brother Daifa died, and his wife wanted her son to be adopted as heir. The two other brothers opposed this, and the dispute resulted in a fight and an injury. The court therefore ordered that, though the property would remain in the hands of the widow, it could not go to her son, and the lineage must arrange a legal heir (BX 6-4-2276).

Where, then, did sons who followed their remarrying mothers have property rights? The court evidence suggests that they retained inheritance rights in their natal homes. Thus in 1860, after the death of widow Chen, née Chuan, a dispute arose over the disposition of her property, some rental income and household items. Widow Chen's one unmarried daughter wanted it, while her deceased son's widow, who had remarried and taken her son Guangwen with her, also claimed the property. The court decided that the unmarried daughter could temporarily retain the household items, but the rental income and later the household items as well would go to the grandson, Guangwen. Thus a son who followed his widowed mother into a new marriage retained his inheritance rights in his natal home (BX 6-4-2442).

Orphans, Parents, and Widows

Orphans too could use the courts. In 1854 four Sun children presented their case by hollering at the yamen door. Their parents had died, and a slave girl, née Huang, who had been owned by the family but had been married out to a man named Wang, was returned to manage the property and take care of the children. But the slave girl became involved in illicit sex with a nephew, and the children feared the two were plotting to deprive them of their property.[3] The magistrate investigated, ordered the slave girl to leave the house, and then had the neighbors select an honorable person to oversee the children and manage the property. Thus even orphans could defend their inheritance in courts (BX 6-4-1834).

The right of parents to support and a funeral also emerges from court cases. In 1857 six Long brothers came to court in a dispute over a plot of land. They had previously divided their household and had set aside a plot for their father's grave. When their father died, one brother, Xuetong, occupied the grave land. His claim was disputed by the others, and some violence, including the burning down of a house, ensued. In the end it was decided to draw new, clear boundaries and to bury father Long on the plot, ensuring him of a resting place (BX 6-4-2000).

Widows were also entitled to support and a funeral, a fact that emerges forcefully from a case dated 1858. Widow Zhao, née Liu, was eighty-three *sui* and lived off of 1.2 *shi* of grain that three brothers were required to provide in rotation. In 1858 brother Mingtai refused to continue paying his share and sold his mother's grave plot. Widow Zhao went to court to sue Mingtai, and the magistrate decided in her favor, ordering Mingtai to provide his fair share and not to sell the grave plot. He humbly agreed to do as ordered (BX 6-4-2084).

A widow's right to manage her deceased husband's property was consistently supported by the magistrates. The above-mentioned case of Chen Daifa's marriage to a widow stands as a good example. Though she brings in three children from her previous marriage and two surviving brothers contest her rights to the property, the magistrate decides that, because household division had already taken place, widow Chen is allowed to retain control of the property (BX 6-4-2276). A case from 1854 demonstrates that a widow had rights even if challenged by her father-in-law. Chen Shenhe had already divided his property among his four sons. His second son had died and was survived by his widow, née Yin. Father Chen then rented out some land adjacent to the widow's. He rented it to the Zhou family to mine coal, and the mine went under the widow's land, harming her irrigation, house, land, graves, and good geomantic position. For this she sued the Zhou family, but the court found the father-in-law guilty instead, because he had entered into the rental agreement. The court decided he should be beaten but suspended his punishment because of his advanced age and declared his rental agreement with the Zhou family null and void. Thus a widow could prevail, even against her own father-in-law (BX 6-4-1817).

As to whether remarrying widows had rights to their children from the first marriage, the record is mixed. In some cases widows took their children with them into the new marriage. Thus in 1861 when the above-mentioned widow Chen, née Zhang, married Chen Daifa, she brought with her one son and two daughters from her previous marriage to a Mr. Wu (BX 6-4-2276). And in 1860 when widow Chen, née He, remarried to Wang Songting, she took her son Chen Guangwen with her (BX 6-4-2442). But remarrying widows could also be denied rights to their children. In 1867 a widow, whose name is not given, was residing in Canton with some property, her son, and her daughter. She decided to return to her natal family in North China but was stopped when she arrived in Shanghai because of a lawsuit from her husband's family demanding the return of both the property and the children. Though the magistrate sympathized with the widow, he followed the law and ordered the property and children back to the husband's family (Jamieson 1921:150). Thus it would seem that a remarrying widow could take her children only if her deceased husband's family agreed and did not contest it in court. The record also suggests that, in practice and contrary to the law, widows often did take children with them, either into their new marriages or back to their natal homes.

If a widow had no son, the law specified that the lineage or family would choose an heir or an adopted son for her. But in some cases, widows themselves chose an adopted son. A case from popular literature is a good example. The Yan family had two brothers. The elder held the senior licentiate civil service degree *(gongsheng)* and had five sons. The second was Dayou, who had a wife, a concubine, née Zhao, and a son by his concubine. When Dayou's wife lay dying, he, with his wife's agreement, formally and publicly promoted his concubine to the status of wife. Senior Licentiate Yan and his family pointedly did not attend the ceremony.

Second brother Dayou then died, as did his son, leaving concubine-now-wife Zhao alone and in charge of her husband's property. Widow Zhao wanted to adopt her elder brother-in-law's fifth son, who was not yet twelve, probably thinking that she could win the youngest son's affection. But Senior Licentiate Yan not only insisted on appointing his second son as "heir" to his brother (meaning all the property would revert to Senior Licentiate Yan), he even refused to recognize Zhao as his brother's wife (which was why he did not attend the ceremony). Widow Zhao was a fighter, however, and she went to court. After a series of legal maneuvers, the magistrate ruled in her favor, stating that if Senior Licentiate Yan did not want to have his fifth son adopted out, widow Zhao could adopt somebody else. Again, a widow's rights were protected in court, including sometimes the right to select an adopted son (Wu Ching-tzu 1973:52–75).

The fact that widows had such strong legal rights to their deceased husbands' property had a negative side, however. Since the law stated that they had to leave such property if they remarried, they were often targets of their in-laws in plots to force them to remarry. In one case, the pressure drove the widow Guo, née Fu, to suicide. Guo Shina was an elder cousin of Guo Shilou, who had died leaving widow

Guo, a son, nine *mu* of land, and some housing. Guo Shina was poor and wished to get his hand on his cousin's property, but for this to happen, widow Guo would have to remarry. So Shina went to the widow's house, and in the conversation that followed, he became angry and threatened to "force her to remarry." Widow Guo became very upset at the threat, and though she apparently settled down for a while, later that night she killed herself. Guo Shina was found guilty of forcing her to remarry and was sentenced to banishment for life (Jamieson 1921:139–140).

A much earlier case from 1654 has a similar theme. Zhang Zhimei was a spendthrift and a playboy, so his father and uncles had long since split with him. He had one widowed aunt, née Jia, who had some property but no heir, so Zhimei decided to obtain her property by forcing her to remarry. First he tried to entice his brother into a plot to tell the Qing authorities that she was harboring a thief, which would likely result in her losing the property to Zhimei. But the brother refused to go along. So Zhimei himself, claiming to be a Manchu soldier looking for a thief, broke into her house. But upon seeing that his aunt was quite pretty, he raped her. The grandmother, née Li, who lived in the same courtyard, ran to the authorities. Zhimei was arrested and sentenced to death by strangulation. Though Zhimei forfeits his life, the story demonstrates just how the status of widow and its related property rights could result in victimization (Chang 1986:B11459-60).

Concubines, Divorces, and Unmarried Daughters in the Courts

Concubines had much the same rights and problems as wives. First and foremost, they were entitled to continued support. In a case from 1830, widow Zhan, née Qi, was a concubine and head of a family with four sons, two from her husband's wife and two of her own. After her husband died, the two sets of brothers argued over the property division that had been arranged by their father some years earlier. The magistrate asked the lineage to arrange a resolution, and it was decided to have each son pay 150 taels of silver for widow Zhan's support, her funeral, and the dowries for her two unmarried daughters (BX 6-3-9747).

Another case suggests that widowed concubines may have had

other rights as well. In 1831 widow Long, née Wang, came to court with a claim against her sister-in-law, who was a concubine. The sister-in-law was also a widow, both Long brothers and their father having died. Before dying, father Long had written an *yizhu* stating that both widows should stay together and work together to find a wife for the only son, Changgeng, that had been born to the elder sister-in-law, née Wang. But the younger widow did not wish to abide by her father-in-law's *yizhu,* and she instead found her own legal heir from within the lineage. Then she demanded division of the property. The case was never adjudicated, but the complaint does suggest that concubines may have had some freedom to select their own adopted sons or appointed heirs (BX 6-3-9749).

Another legal complaint, from 1833, suggests the limits on property rights that a widowed concubine enjoyed. One such widow, née Yang, survived both her husband and his wife. Neither the wife nor the concubine had had a son, so they had adopted a son, but the concubine maintained control of the family property. She began, however, to sell it off and give it to various friends and relatives, rather than to manage and maintain it for the future inheritance of the adopted son. The adopted son thereupon went to court to defend his inheritance. The case implies that a concubine could keep and manage a deceased husband's property, but if there was a son or an adopted son to inherit, she had to conserve it for him (BX 6-3-9752).

A case mentioned previously, in which the two Xu brothers used the *jiantiao* adoption strategy, illustrates both the rights concubines enjoyed and that such rights might lead to victimization, as in the case of widowed wives. Widow Xu, née Zheng, had managerial rights over 580 *shi* of grain and 60,000 coppers of income. But because Xueyuan, the son of her deceased husband's elder brother Wenzhong, had been appointed as her heir, Wenzhong tried to get rid of widow Xu in order to obtain control of her property. To do this he falsely accused her of entering into an illicit sexual relationship, which would, under Qing law, deprive her of her property. After a mediation attempt in which she was offered the right to maintain control over half of the property, she went to court demanding control of it all. The court sided with her, deciding that the accusation of illicit sex was fraudulent and that she could retain control over the entire property. She could not pawn or sell it, however, and when Xueyuan came of age, he would take control of it. Thus widowed concubines had definite property rights that were defensible in court, but their status as widows could make them targets of their deceased husbands' families (BX 6-4-2292).

Divorced women may have had property rights as well. Divorce was relatively rare in Qing China, and my sample contains only one such reference. The law, and custom probably as well, assumed that divorced women had no property and further assumed that they either remarried or returned to their natal families. But in one case from 1910, a divorced woman died, leaving behind a son (not from her previous husband and therefore probably illegitimate) and considerable property. Both the former husband and the widow's brother claimed the property, but the magistrate ruled that neither had a legal claim. In the end he ordered the property divided into shares among the woman's natural son, her brother, and a "charity." This dispensation may have been decided upon by the woman herself and written up in a will. Thus it is possible that divorced women with property had rights to decide on its disposition (Jamieson 1921:151–152).

One legal case further illustrates the rights of unmarried daughters to dowries. In the above-mentioned case of the widowed concubine Zhan, the four brothers were to pay the 150 taels not only to support widow Zhan, but also to fund the dowries of her two unmarried daughters. Thus, at household division time, brothers had the duty to fund their sisters' dowries (BX 6-3-9747).

Court Enforcement of Household Division Documents

In some cases the court was asked to play a slightly different role from that of defending the rights of individuals and to uphold special language in the household division documents. Thus, when the five Zhou brothers divided their household, they stipulated that whoever could reclaim the land they had previously pawned out could keep it. In 1825 brothers number two and four managed to accumulate the 1,100 taels of silver required to reclaim some of the land and keep it for themselves. The other brothers protested, and the case went to court. The magistrate upheld the rights of second and fourth brothers because of the language in the household division document (BX 6-3-9962).

The previously detailed case in which Wan Yongkui made his false claim to the status of son can also be seen in this light. Father Wan had left behind an *yizhu* clearly stating how the property was to be divided and specifically stating that Yongkui was not a son, that he was in fact accepted as payment for a debt, and that he therefore had no inheritance rights. The court here upheld the language of the *yizhu* (BX 6-2-4584).

The court could also use court-mandated household division as a method of settling disputes. In a very complex and lengthy case, six Tian branches were involved in a dispute over their family property. The property was extensive, including land, mines, lineage lands, and a lineage hall. There was also considerable debt involved. The eldest brother was attempting to keep the property undivided and to make himself manager. The other brothers opposed this plan, accusing him of being unfair, and demanded various forms of division of the property and the debt. The case became so convoluted that the magistrate finally just ruled against the eldest brother and ordered the entire property divided equally among the six branches (BX 6-3-9759).

A final role the local yamen could play was that of a safe deposit box for inheritance-related documents, usually in cases where the family felt that having a copy on file would avoid future disputes. The government was not obliged to accept such documents, however. The case of the widow Zhan again serves as a good illustration. Before her husband died, he wrote up an *yizhu* document that mandated how the property was to be divided among his four sons. It was a division complicated by two factors: his fifth son had died young, and he and concubine Zhan needed continued support. Father Zhan divided the property into six shares, one for each of his surviving sons, one to be kept jointly in honor of the deceased fifth son, and one for *yangshan* purposes. The first son wanted the joint property, however, so being fearful that the son might take it, father Zhan sent a copy of the *yizhu* to the yamen for safekeeping. The government refused to take it, however, stating that if the sons did not abide by the agreement, his concubine could bring it to court.

When, just as father Zhan expected, a dispute broke out after he died, the government asked the lineage to broker an agreement, which was done and has been detailed above. But this time concubine Zhan took a copy of the contract to the yamen for safekeeping, arguing that because her sons were young, they might have trouble in any future dispute. This time, the yamen agreed to keep a copy on file to guarantee the sons' property rights (BX 6-3-9747).

Household Division in Court: The Civil Law Process

Thus the relationship between inheritance law, practice, and the courts was one of relative harmony. The rights of sons to equal shares, of parents to support and a funeral, and of unmarried siblings to marriage expenses or dowries were well understood in practice and strongly enforced in the courts. Only in the area of adoption does there seem to be some dissonance, with adoption practices sometimes at odds with the letter of the law.

The evidence also strongly suggests that household division disputes were handled in a manner different from the penal form in which the Qing Code was written. Punishments were imposed only in cases that escalated into violence or theft. When the magistrate chose to hear a purely inheritance-related dispute, he ruled for one side or the other, or allowed a mediated settlement to resolve the problem. Thus, as Philip Huang and others have argued, there were recognized civil law procedures in Qing China, and household division disputes were adjudicated in that civil law manner (Philip Huang 1994).

Chapter 7

Republican Rural North China

L ET us now shift focus from Sichuan northward to the North China Plain and from the Qing forward to the Republican period of the 1930s and 1940s, allowing comparisons over both place and time. The differences in geography are essentially three: rural North China is characterized by a dry, less productive agriculture, simpler patterns of land tenure, and a closer proximity to the traditional center of political authority in Beijing. The differences in time are punctuated by three crucial political events: the destruction of the Qing state by the Chinese revolution of 1911, the establishment of a partially effective Republican government in 1927, and the conquest of North China by Japanese imperialist armies in 1937.

For purposes of inheritance, the critical change was the founding of the new Republican government, which passed a set of new laws that suggested radical transformations were in store for Chinese inheritance practices. This complex series of statutes attempted to bring Chinese inheritance law into accordance with major traditions in European law and simultaneously keep it linked to Chinese reality (Chang Tao Hsing 1935; Riasanovsky 1976:278–303; van der Valk 1969). Promulgated on January 24, 1931, and made effective on May 5, 1931, the laws totaled 171 statutes on family law, eighty-eight on succession and inheritance, and eleven on application (LRPG 1961: 338–360).

As a system, they embodied many radical departures from Qing law and practice, and space dictates that only the most salient changes

128

be mentioned here. The laws tied property more closely to the individual and inheritance more closely to the death of the parent, though household division did not have to occur immediately after the death of the parents (Articles 1147, 1151–1152).[1] The maker of a will received some increased power in determining the disposition of property, though he or she could not violate the stipulation on compulsory portions (Articles 1165, 1187). Compulsory portions amounted to one-half or one-third of the full successional portion, depending on the relationship of the heir to the deceased (Article 1223).

The spouse[2] was the first to inherit, and thus at the death of the first parent, the surviving spouse "inherited" the property, rather than just assuming the role of property manager, as had been the case in the Qing (Article 1138). The statutes also constructed a new order of inheritance: first, the spouse; second, lineal descendants by blood; third, parents; fourth, brothers and sisters; and fifth, grandparents (Article 1138). This was a dramatic change from the Qing, in which the order was, first, legal male heirs, then daughters, then close agnatic kin, and finally the state.

The new statutes also introduced the idea that a person could waive his or her inheritance rights (Article 1174). They did not include a statute accounting for division of property ordered and carried out by a living parent. Premortem division was later defined as a "gift" equal to an inheritance portion (Riasanovsky 1976:302; Article 1173).

It is no exaggeration to say that the Republicans were introducing an entirely new concept of family and inheritance property rights that implied less familial and greater individual control over property, and greater freedom of the individual to alienate property. These legal changes were designed to play a revolutionary role in Chinese women's inheritance rights as well. The designation of the spouse as the first heir meant that a widow now legally inherited her deceased husband's property. She thus gained greater control over the property, including the power to apportion it according to a will. Including in inheritance all lineal descendants by blood meant that a daughter now had inheritance rights beyond a dowry and equal to a son. The potential of these changes to create legal chaos in family property relations was well recognized, and thus this transformation was specifically made nonretroactive (Article 1).

But these new rights did not come without problems buried in the fine print. The new power given to the maker of a will meant that wives or daughters could legally be denied one-half of a full inheritance portion. The power to waive inheritance rights further opened the door to the coercion of daughters to give up in writing their new inheritance rights.[3] In sum, the Republican government established a new legal inheritance regime that, had it been properly implemented, would have dramatically changed family property relations in China and vastly improved the position of women. But, despite considerable differences in time, location, and law, the pattern of household division in North China during the Republican period was essentially the same as it had been in Taiwan during the Qing.

The sources for this chapter differ in nature and scope from those of chapters 4 and 5. While for Qing Taiwan the extant sources are primarily household division documents, for the North China Plain, I have used the *Chūgoku nōson kankō chōsa* (Investigations of Customary Practices in Rural China), the six-volume series of village investigations undertaken by the Japanese South Manchurian Railway Company (Mantetsu) in the early 1940s. The investigators surveyed a total of thirteen villages, all located on the North China Plain of Hebei and northern Shandong provinces. The five villages for which the information is most complete are Shajing, Houjiaying, and Sibeichai in Hebei and Lengshuigou and Houxiazhai in Shandong; they are the villages on which my analysis is based. In these interviews the voices of the peasants confirm the essential similarities of North and South, and they often provide a detailed and nuanced understanding of the inheritance process.

The Rights of Sons

As was the case in Qing Taiwan, the core of the inheritance regime on the North China Plain was equal division of property among all sons of the same father. The Yang family division of 1933 in Shajing is just one of many possible examples. The Yang parents were both dead, and the property, including housing, land, tools, and draft animals, was divided equally among the three brothers, Zheng, Yuan, and Hong. The eldest received 31.25 *mu* of land, eight rooms of housing, and the rights to a profitable shop. The second received 33.5 *mu* of land, five rooms of housing, all the draft animals, and the related accessories. The youngest brother received 36.5 *mu* of land and five rooms of housing (KC 1:292).

And as in Qing Taiwan, age was not a factor in equal division. A young son was entitled to a share equal to that of his older siblings. Two talks with Yang Ze of Shajing went as follows:

Q: At household division time, must all the brothers divide?
A: Yes.
Q: What happens if one brother is a young five-*sui*-old?
A: They must first all divide, and then he lives together with one of the others.
Q: So a five-*sui* brother can divide?
A: Yes. (KC 1:276B)

And again:

Q: In household division doesn't the eldest son get more?
A: It's the same. (KC 1:251B)

No distinction was made between hard-working and lazy sons, and no extra property was awarded to a son who had brought in family property (Shiga 1978:113–114).

Sons born to women other than the first wife were not a major concern, because instances of a man taking a second wife or a concubine were rare. Even peasant terminology for these women differed from standard Qing or Republican legal usage. One group of Shajing interviewees composed of Li Ruyuan, Zhang Yongren, and Yang Run did not recognize the Qing legal term for concubine *(qie)* and used instead the term *erfuren*. For women brought into the household when the first wife had no children, they used the term *erfang*. They further stated that such women were in fact wives, *qi*. Another category of women who lived with a man yet did not enjoy the status of wife or concubine was *kaoren* (KC 1:227C, 229A–B).

But while the villagers' terminology may have differed from Qing or Republican legal usage, the rights of the sons of these women were identical: all inherited equally. The following response of the three interviewees is typical:

Q: When the husband dies and the property is divided, isn't there a difference between the son of the first wife and the son of the second wife?
A: There is no distinction. It is all the same. (KC 1:227C)

And, according to Yang Ze:

Q: After the arrival of the concubine, does it sometimes happen that the original wife has children?

A: Yes.
Q: Who is the inheritor then?
A: The son of the concubine and the son of the wife are the same. (KC 1:250C)

As in Taiwan, adopted sons were of two types, *yangzi*[4] and *guoji*. While some interviewees were unaware of any distinction or used different terms (KC 3:146A–B), the rough consensus was that a *yangzi* was young, came from outside the lineage, and may have been a foundling, and his adoption was not formalized by a written contract. A boy adopted in the *guoji* manner could be adopted at any age and came from within the lineage, and his adoption was formalized with a contract (KC 1:248C, 1:315B). Though the processes by which the boys were adopted may have differed, their customary rights to inherit property did not. Unlike in Qing Taiwan, where adopted sons' rights were often negotiable, adopted sons in North China had clear and simple inheritance rights. Since adoption usually occurred only if there was no male heir by blood, a single adopted son inherited all family property. The adopted son's rights were only in question if his adoptive parents later gave birth to a son. In these rare cases, both types of adopted sons inherited equally with the blood son or sons. As Zhao Tingkui of Shajing says of adopted sons: "As regards property, they are the same. They divide the household equally" (KC 1:248C).

As in Qing Taiwan, sons suffering from physical disabilities were entitled not only to their equal share, but perhaps to a bit more. Zhang Jiwu, also of Shajing, states:

Q: If a family has a crippled person, is some special property left over and given to that son?
A: Prior to household division, he is taken care of in the house, and at household division a little extra is given to him. (KC 1:255A)

Even brothers who had been expelled from the household could not be denied their inheritance rights. According to Zhao Tingkui:

A: If a brother is expelled from the house, no document is drawn up. This is not household division, and the property is not divided. If in the future he reforms, he can return home. . . .
Q: If the expelled brother has not returned, and the remaining brothers divide the household, what happens to him?
A: The expelled brother will have his equal share retained for him. (KC 1:241C)

Sons who were unmarried at the time of household division were entitled to extra property to cover their future marriage expenses. This emerges clearly in an interview with Zhang Jiwu:

Q: The brothers' portions are the same?
A: Generally the same. But not necessarily, if one brother is married and one isn't. In that case the married one gets a little less, and the unmarried one gets a little more.
Q: Why?
A: To pay marriage expenses.
Q: And if they are all single?
A: The same. (KC 1:252A)

In 1936, when Du Chun divided his household among his four sons, the youngest boy, Guangxin, had not yet been married. As a result, the division document read:

The maker of this household division document is Du Chun. He has four sons, and three are already married. Only the fourth son is not married. Now, because I am old, my strength is declining, and I find it hard to manage family affairs. Therefore I have invited lineage relatives and village friends to take all my land, gardens, housing, and property and, after first removing my *yanglao*[5] portion and my fourth son's marriage expenses, divide the rest equally. (KC 1:291)

Liu Zhen's experience stands as another illustration.

Q: When did you divide your household?
A: Two years ago.
Q: And how was the property divided?
A: There were twenty-four *mu* to divide between three brothers. Elder brother got 3.5 rooms and six or seven *fen* of land. I was the second and got six *mu*. The third was younger brother, who got thirteen *mu*. Mom's 3.5 *mu* of *yanglaodi* went with younger brother and became his, so he got a total of 16.5 *mu*.
Q: Whose share was the best?
A: Younger brother's. But that was because he had no wife, and so marriage expenses had to be included. (KC 2:479C)

In sum, as was the case in Qing Taiwan, at the point of household division, all sons of the same father were entitled to equal shares of the family property plus additional property for marriage expenses if they were single.[6]

The Rights of Surviving Parents

In another parallel with Qing Taiwan, parents who were alive at the point of household division were entitled to support while they lived and funeral expenses when they died. These expenses and responsibilities could be handled in a variety of ways. In one common pattern, the parents extracted for themselves a portion of land called *yanglaodi*. The parents retained control of this land and used it to support themselves. They could work it themselves, or if they were too old, they could rent it out and live off the income. Liu Tanlin's experience stands as a good example.

Q: You divided your household after the harvest?
A: Yes.
Q: And so this year your parents lived with your younger brother. So who tilled the eight *mu* [of *yanglaodi*]?
A: Father himself hired somebody to work the eight *mu*, and it was not connected to younger brother. (KC 2:261C)

In a Houjiaying division in which three grandsons divided their household, not one but two shares of *yanglaodi* were first extracted. The brothers' mother and grandfather were both living, so the grandfather retained thirty-five *mu* for himself, while the mother retained thirty-two *mu* plus three *mu* extra to pay for her two daughters' dowries (KC 5:93).

The setting aside of *yanglaodi* was not the only method of supporting aging parents. The parents might have the sons provide support in the form of money, grain, or labor, which was usually referred to as *yang(lao)shan* or *yang(lao)fei*. One division document from Houjiaying reads: "As to my *yangshan*, eldest son Yuanzhen each year will pay one hundred *diao* of eastern money. Second son Yuanrui will pay five *dou* of grain. Fourth son Yuanlian will pay five *dou* of grain. I am now living with third son Yuanjun, but if in the future we do not live together, Yuanjun will also pay a share" (KC 5:92). Thus each son was paying a share of support, though Yuanjun was apparently paying in labor.

A final method of support for aged parents was to have the parents live in turn with each brother and his family. The parents moved from house to house for fixed periods of time, such as three days, a week, or a month (KC 1:241). In families that lacked sufficient land to provide a formal *yanglaodi,* this was the most common pattern (KC 1:240C). Thus, at the point of household division, parents were provided with support in either property, payment, or labor, just as was the case in Qing Taiwan.

Parents were also entitled to funeral expenses, and these could be paid in several ways. The brothers might agree to pay in cash when the time came. One Houjiaying division document states that the three brothers will in future pay equally for the funeral expenses of their parents (KC 5:97). If a *yanglaodi* portion was given to the parents at division, this land could be used to pay for funerals. The first choice was to use the income from the land; second best was to pawn the land and use the cash thus generated; the third and least desirable option was to sell part or all of the land to raise sufficient money. Once the funerals of both parents were complete,[7] any remaining land or money from its sale was divided equally among the sons (KC 3:79B, 157; 4:71A; 5:74B). Any household items the old couple had owned were also divided (KC 4:97B).

Hou Shupan of Houjiaying remembers the dispensation of his parents' *yanglaodi* this way. After household division, his mother and father chose to live with their third son. They kept 19 *mu* of *yanglaodi,* and the third brother worked it and used the income to support his parents. When his widowed mother died, they sold 4.5 *mu* to cover her funeral expenses and then divided the remainder among the four brothers (KC 5:69A).

The Rights of Women

And just as the rights of sons and parents paralleled those of Qing Taiwan, so too did those of women. The interviewees were unanimous in the opinion that daughters did not receive a share of property at household division. A talk with Zhao Tingkui, Yang Ze, and Zhang Yongren was typical:

Q: As to daughters who have not married out, are they treated
    equally?
A: Daughters do not receive land or property. (KC 1:232B)

Another conversation went like this:
Q: How is land divided among the brothers?
A: Equally. . . .

Q: Don't daughters receive a share at household division time?
A: No. (KC 1:8C)

Though the denial of a share to daughters was by now illegal under Republican law, the practice continued. An interview with a local court official makes this point.

Q: Do women have inheritance rights?
A: [They have] equal [rights].
Q: If there are two brothers and one sister, then it should be divided into three?
A: Yes.
Q: But in fact a little dowry money is given to her, and the three-way division is not done?
A: Yes, that is the custom. (KC 1:309)

Thus, despite a change in the political and legal-property systems occasioned by the Republican revolution, daughters' customary inheritance rights had not changed.

But daughters were still entitled to dowries, and if a daughter was single at the point of household division, this responsibility had to be fulfilled. One pattern was for the parents to take a slightly larger *yanglaodi* portion and then pay the dowry when the time came for the daughter to marry (KC 1:255A). Another solution was to set aside some land specifically for the dowry. Before her marriage, this land was generally sold or pawned to obtain cash to cover the expense (KC 1:20A). If the parents were dead, the brothers jointly inherited the dowry responsibility. In the case of Yang Ze, he and his brothers jointly sold twenty *mu* of land to pay for their two sisters' dowries. Each sister received the equivalent of ten *mu*, or three hundred yuan (KC 1:256A–B). Another possibility was for one brother to take full responsibility for his sister's dowry, in which case he received extra land to pay for her living expenses and future dowry (KC 1:251A). Finally, the brothers could divide all family property but promise to provide dowry money equally when the time came for their sister to marry (KC 1:6B).

As wives of living husbands, women seldom emerged as formal actors in the household division process, since their husbands took all formal responsibility. As widows, however, women emerged and played the same roles they had in Qing Taiwan. A widowed mother in the senior generation was entitled to a *yanglao* portion to support herself and provide for her funeral expenses. One example took place in Lengshuigou in 1935, when grandmother Li divided her house between her two grandsons. The division document states that she kept for herself a total of six big *mu* of land as her *yanglaodi*. When she died, the land was to be sold to pay for her burial expenses and any extra divided equally between her grandsons (KC 4:99, 100).

The case of Li Shulin of Shajing illustrates another pattern followed when a widow received land. When the Lis divided their household, Shulin's father and blind mother each received five *mu* of *yanglaodi*. When father Li died, his five *mu* went to his widow, giving her a total of ten, and she was free to do with it as she pleased. She turned some of it over to Shulin, who worked it and gave the income to her. Other pieces she rented to people from outside the village (KC 2:007, 2:100C, 2:103B). The case of Ren Zhengang's mother-in-law, a Shajing resident, was similar. She lived with her daughter and Zhengang, and had received twenty to thirty *mu* as her *yanglaodi*. She rented twenty *mu* to Zhengang at a low rent, and the rental payment went to her (KC 2:007A). An interview with Yang Ze serves to emphasize the point.

Q: If two brothers divide, and they get no land, the mother will go to live with the elder brother. If she has some *yanglaodi*, then will that land be managed by the elder brother?

A: It's not necessarily decided that way. If she stays with the elder brother, he manages the land; if she goes with the younger brother, he manages it. (It's up to the mother.)

Q: So as to where she goes, it's up to her?

A: Yes.

Q: When the elder brother manages the land, can he pawn it out?

A: No he can't. (It's up to the mother.) (KC 2:251)

If a woman was the widow of a brother in the generation receiving the property, her inheritance rights were affected by whether or not she had a son. If she had no son, she inherited the property outright; if she had a son, it went to him, though she might act as manager if he was young. A conversation with Yang Ze explains:

Q: If a husband and wife have no children, and the husband dies, who gets the property?

A: The wife. (KC 1:240A)

The Li family division, which took place in Lengshuigou in 1940, stands as a good example. Of the original three Li brothers, only the eldest, Changxun, was still alive. The second, Changshi, had died leaving his widow, née Zhu. The third, Changnai, had died unmarried at about age ten *sui*. The Lis decided to divide the family property and debts into two shares, ignoring their option of adopting an heir for Changnai. One share went to Changxun and one share went to widow Li (KC 4:127–128). Another instance, also from Lengshuigou, is the Hou family division of 1936. In this case, two of the four Hou brothers were dead, and both of their widows, née Jia and Ye, received the shares in place of their deceased husbands (KC 5.1:95).

In sum, the basic inheritance regime in rural Republican North China was the same as it had been in Qing Taiwan: surviving parents received support, unmarried siblings received marriage expenses, and brothers received equal shares of the remaining property.

The Priorities in Household Division

The *Kankō chōsa* sources confirm the existence of household division priorities that could only be guessed at in the Taiwan context. In families with sufficient property to fund all responsibilities, priorities were not a major concern. But in families with fewer resources, priorities had to be set. It seems clear that, in tight circumstances, parental support was given the highest priority. If the amount of land was only sufficient to support the parents, the parents could keep it. An interview with Yang Run went like this:

> Q: If a family has two brothers, a sister, and the parents are alive, how much is taken out for *yanglaodi*?
> A: Enough is taken out for the parents to live on, and then the rest is divided equally among the brothers.
> Q: If there are only three *mu* of land, what then?
> A: Then the three *mu* of land will all go to the parents, and the brothers will not divide anything. (KC 1:295C)

This priority does not imply that parents in poor families always kept all the property for themselves. It was possible for them to divide even small amounts of land and housing among their sons and then rely on the boys for support. As to why some parents kept the property while others divided, an interview with Qiu Haisen of Dayang village just outside of Longyan, Fujian, is revealing:

Q: Why did you give it all to them?

A: I trusted them, so I gave it all to them. They all love me, so it's no problem. (Qiu Haisen interview, p. 2)

Thus the key element for parents in deciding how to organize their *yanglao* portion may have been the level of trust they felt for their sons. The more the parents trusted the sons to provide support, the more likely they were to forgo *yanglaodi* and divide the property. But the parents had first choice regarding how the land would be distributed, which reflected their top priority at household division time (Shiga 1978:136; KC 5:101).

As to the relative importance of the brothers' equal shares and the unmarried daughters' dowries, the record is less clear. The following conversation with Yang Run of Shajing is suggestive, however:

Q: First you take out the parents' *yanglaodi,* then you take out the sister's dowry, and then if there's anything left over, the brothers divide it, right?

A: No. First you take out the *yanglaodi,* and the rest is divided between the brothers and sisters. The sister must be given something, but she is not provided for first, and then the remainder divided by the brothers. After the *yanglaodi* is taken out, the rest, even if it's small, is divided by the brothers and sisters. The [amount of the] sister's share is not the same as the brothers'. (KC 1:295C)

While dowry did not have as high a priority as parental support, it was probably considered as important as the brothers' equal shares. In the poorest families the potential conflict between brothers' shares and sisters' dowries was not severe, because the truly impoverished paid little if anything for dowries (KC 1:267A). As to the tension between the brothers' equal shares and their marriage expenses, it is difficult to tell, but I suspect that marriage expenses had a slight priority.

The Division of Property: Housing

Let us now turn to the actual division of property. Looking first at living space, the division of housing was most frequently done, as in Qing Taiwan, by the number of rooms. The two most common types of rooms in North China were *zhengfang,* the main rooms on the courtyard that sat opposite the main gate and often faced south, and *xiangfang,* the rooms on the two sides of the court-yard, usually to the east and west (see Figure 7). In a 1925 division in Houjiaying, the two Hou brothers, Tingwen and Tingwu, divided their house as follows:

Tingwen received

1.5	rooms on the east side of the western courtyard
3	rooms on two stories of *zhengfang*
3	rooms of east *xiangfang*
2	rooms on the south side of the eastern courtyard
1	side room of the *zhengfang*
5	rooms on the southern courtyard
15.5	

Tingwu received

1.5	rooms on the west side of the western courtyard
3	rooms on two stories of *zhengfang*
3	rooms of west *xiangfang*
2	rooms on the north side of the eastern courtyard
5	rooms on the southern courtyard
14.5	

It appears the Hous had four courtyards, and each was divided exactly in half. Tingwen received 15.5 rooms, while Tingwu received 14.5. But even this level of equality was not sufficient, as Tingwen had received an extra room of *zhengfang.* Recognizing this, the family set aside 2,900 *diao* of money to pay for both the mate-rials and the construction costs for a new room of *zhengfang* for Tingwu. Thus the division of the houses was made as equal as possible (KC 5:76).

In 1911 in Houjiaying, Hou Lianfa divided his house among his three grandsons as follows:

Yuanzhang, the eldest, received
3 rooms of south *zhengfang*
2 rooms of northwest *xiangfang*

Yuanwen, the second, received
3 rooms of *zhengfang*
2 rooms of southwest *xiangfang*

Yuangong, the youngest, received
    3 rooms of *zhengfang*
    3 rooms of rear *xiangfang*

Thus two brothers received five rooms and one received six, a situation of almost perfect equality. But even this minimal level of inequality was offset by another section of the division document. At the time of division, both the boys' mother and grandfather were living. The grandfather kept a room of *zhengfang* that, when he died, would go to Yuanwen, the second brother. The boys' mother was also awarded a room of *zhengfang* that, when she died, would go to Yuanzhang, the first brother. Thus all three brothers would in time receive six rooms, making the division one of perfect equality (KC 5:93).

When dividing living space, the allocation of courtyards and threshing grounds inside and outside the buildings also had to be considered. According to Yang Ze, courtyards were ideally divided equally, the brothers receiving the courtyard space immediately in front of the rooms they received (KC 1:272B). Boundary lines were drawn, using as a reference the point where a wall stood on the land or the point where rain fell from the roof. Many division documents have lines that read like this one from Hou Lianfa's 1911 division: "The attached land[8] runs north to the base of the north side of the *xiangfang* wall, which is the boundary" (KC 5.1:93). Hou Yongchun's 1920 division document reads, "The attached land runs north to the water-drip line on the north of the *zhengfang*" (KC 5.1:92).

Land attached to the outside of the buildings, often used for threshing grounds, could be divided or retained for common use. The above 1911 division of Hou Lianfa was among his three grandsons. The house had a threshing ground attached, and each grandson's division document has a line that reads, "The threshing ground will be retained for common use" (KC 5.1:93).

Pigsties were also considered when dividing living space. If by chance the number of brothers equaled the number of pigsties, each brother received one (KC 1:291, 5.1:93). If there was only one pigsty, it was awarded to one brother, the others receiving some form of compensation (KC 1:292). Outhouses, given the critical role they played in producing fertilizer, may have been awarded in a similar manner, or new ones may have been built (KC 1:220A, 2:62A–B). If a family had a well on their property, it too had to be considered.

These tended to be retained for joint use after division (KC 1:290–291). New kitchens also had to be built for the newly independent families (KC 1:233C).

The vagaries of dividing housing and the surrounding spaces often created problems of access. Since many household divisions divided rooms facing the same courtyard, the new families had to be certain they could move freely in and out of their new legal residence. Most frequently a path was to be used jointly, and in these cases the division document might read similarly to that of Wu Kui of Houxiazhai: "The common path on the south side of the West Building, and the common path on the south side of the East Building are both one step wide, and passage to and fro cannot be obstructed" (KC 4:456). An interview with Yang Ze and Zhang Yongren explained:

Q: When a house is divided, and they still live around the same courtyard, do they continue to use the same path?
A: That must be clearly written in the household division document. Then they use it jointly, and it's called a "common path." (KC 2:498B)

Failure to write in the paths of access could lead to disputes.

The ideal patterns for dividing living space as a whole were of two related types: separate courtyards for each brother or division of a single courtyard among the brothers. If a family was fortunate to have, for example, two sons and two roughly equal courtyards complete with *zhengfang, xiangfang,* kitchen, pigsty, and outhouse, then the division of living space was simple. Each brother received one courtyard, and any minor differences in value could be made up with money or land. Most divisions, however, were not so easily resolved and included the more complex division of a courtyard. In the ideal pattern (see Figure 7), each courtyard faced south, the most auspicious direction according to the geomancy *(fengshui)* masters, and the family altar was in the middle room of the *zhengfang* (KC 1:233A).

In the *zhengfang,* room C contained the family altar, and it was the largest room of the house. Next in size were B and D, with A and E being the smallest. Generally there was no wall between A and B, so they were in fact one large room, or A'. E was often a storeroom, and H and I either were kitchens or were left empty. The order of preference for the rooms was, A (with B often included), followed by

Figure 7
A Typical North China Home
Zhengfang

| E | D | C | B | A |

G		Courtyard		F
I	Xiangfang		Xiangfang	H
K				J

Main Gate

Threshing Ground

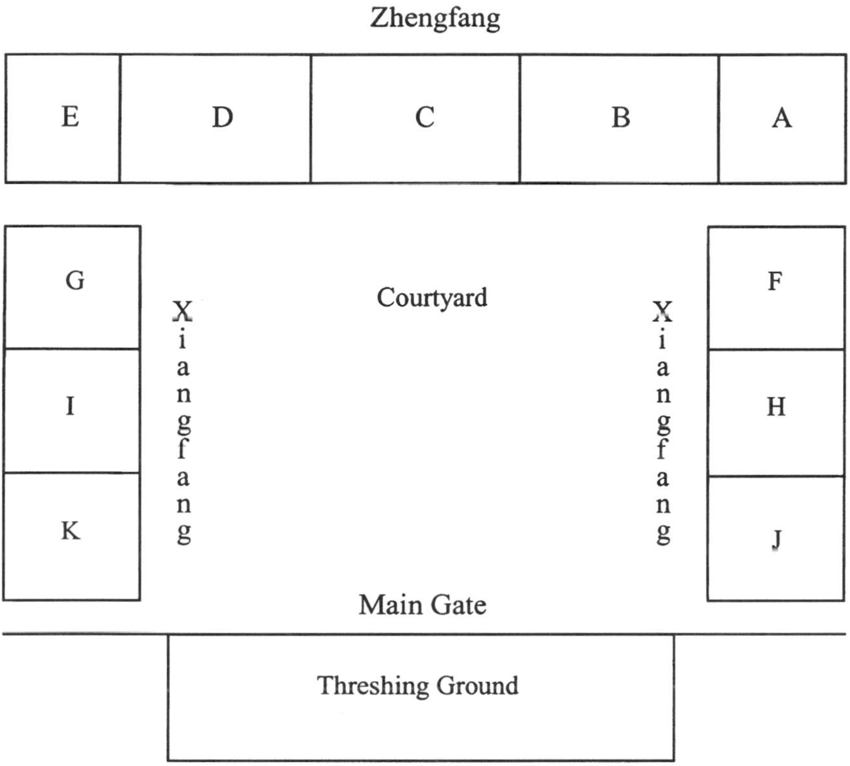

D, and then E, F, G, J, and K. If the brothers' mother or father was still alive at the point of household division, the senior generation received room A′, the eldest brother got D, the second brother F, and the third brother G. If the parents were dead, room A went to the eldest brother, room D to the second, room F to the third, and so on (KC 1:233–234). This preferential positioning of the parents and the eldest son matched the practice in Qing Taiwan.

Such were the models, and the Yang family of Shajing, who divided in 1928, were able to approximate very closely the ideal of providing each heir with one full courtyard. In this case the two Yang heirs, uncle Zhenlin and nephew Yuan (and his two brothers), each received a separate courtyard composed of five rooms of *zhengfang* and six rooms of *xiangfang*, three on each side. Each courtyard con-

tained a pigsty, and the external threshing ground was divided in half
(KC 1:291). But in the division in the next generation, partition was
not so easy. Yang Yuan's portion was divided into three shares among
the three heirs Yang Yuan, Yang Zheng, and Yang Ze. Yang Yuan was
awarded the five rooms of *zhengfang* and three rooms of *xiangfang*
in the original house. The remaining three rooms of *xiangfang* were
initially given to Yang Ze, but Yang Yuan bought them for fifty yuan,
thus retaining the entire courtyard. Because he received the best
housing, Yang Yuan's allocation of land was less than that of his two
brothers. Yang Zheng's original three rooms were located across a
path and were of considerably less value. As compensation he also
received some garden land, two carts, and a millstone. Yang Ze received another courtyard in a separate location. Thus, through bal-
ancing housing with other property, the three Yangs managed to
avoid dividing a courtyard (KC 1:256B–C).

In other cases, division was even more difficult, as the number of
brothers and the architecture of the house required more complex
solutions. Another Yang division, this one from 1919, did entail the
division of a courtyard. The house contained five rooms of *zhengfang* and four rooms of *xiangfang,* two on each side. In this case,
brother Shaozeng received the five rooms of *zhengfang,* while Puzeng
received all four rooms of *xiangfang.* The boundary was set at the
north wall of the *xiangfang,* the courtyard portion to the north staying with the *zhengfang,* that to the south staying with the *xiangfang.*
The threshing ground to the west was divided in half, and the pigsty
went to Shaozeng to use for thirty years (KC 1:292, 319).

The Division of Property: Draft Animals and Grain

Other critical assets for peasant families were the draft
animals essential to agriculture. A family that owned an ox, a mule, a
camel, or a horse faced a decision as to who should get the animal,
and the North China peasants devised a variety of ways to divide
these critical means of production. The most clear-cut manner was to
give to one brother individual ownership of the animal and all the
accoutrements, such as the pen, the harness, or the cart, while giving
the other brothers equal value in other property or money. In 1933
the three Yang brothers of Shajing gave the mule, the donkey, the
donkey pen, the reins and yoke, and two carts to their second sibling.

As compensation, the first brother received rights to the ownership of a shop, and the third brother received an additional 2.75 *mu* of land (KC 1:292). According to Yang Run, a cash equivalent was also possible:

Q: When there is one horse, what do you do?
A: If there is one horse and two people to divide it, and if the horse is worth 100 yuan, the person who gets the horse gives 50 yuan to the other. (KC 1:295B)

A variation on equalizing value was to pair the draft animal with debt and give both to one brother. In 1937 the four Xing brothers of Lujiazhuang divided their considerably debt-ridden household, and third brother Mingshan received the camel and cart, but these were specifically paired with a debt of 120 yuan (KC 4:363).

Instead of giving the draft animal to one brother, peasant families could try to maintain joint ownership of their animals in order to guarantee access to them at critical times such as planting and harvest. Thus in 1925, when the four Liu brothers of Sibeichai divided, the big cart and the mule were specifically set aside for joint use (KC 3:123). In another instance, the Houxiazhai division document drawn up during the Wang family division of 1936 read that brother Qingchang received "ox, one-half head" (KC 4:443). The Japanese investigators noted this oddity and asked:

Q: What is the meaning of "ox, one-half head" in the division document?
A: The brothers will use it together.
Q: Where will the ox live?
A: In its own place. The two of them will both feed it. (KC 4:443)

Such attempts to maintain joint ownership or access to draft animals were frequent during household division. Out of eight instances of division involving draft animals, four families tried to maintain some form of communal ownership. And while such instances were "common" according to one Houjiaying peasant (Uchida 1956:196), they were not always successful. Postdivision disputes could upset joint ownership, as the following conversation suggests:

Q: Who didn't divide the ox and kept it in common?
A: Hou Jinsheng and Hou Jinduo, when they divided [seven or eight years earlier].

Q: But when did they sell their jointly owned ox?
A: Two years ago.
Q: Why did they sell it?
A: Their relationship went bad, and neither of them fed it. . . .
Q: Now Jinsheng has an ox. When did he buy it?
A: He bought it this spring.
Q: Did Jinduo borrow Jinsheng's ox this year?
A: No. He borrowed Hou Yuanzhang's ox.
Q: Don't Jinsheng and Jinduo live around the same courtyard?
A: Yes.
Q: So their relationship is bad even now.
A: So it appears. (Uchida 1956:196)

Other instances of division of draft animals use strategies of both individual and joint ownership. When Wang Qingchang of Houxiazhai divided with his two brothers in 1936, the eldest and youngest jointly received the ox, so the second brother was given extra land:

Q: What did second brother get in place of the ox?
A: He was given about one-half extra *mu* of land.
Q: At the time you divided, what was the cost of an ox?
A: It was fifty or sixty yuan.
Q: And how much was one-half *mu* of land?
A: Thirty yuan. (Uchida 1956:195–196)

A similar strategy was used in Houjiaying in 1907, when four Hou brothers gave one-half mule to the eldest, Changhui; one-half mule, the cart, and the reins to the second, Chang'en; and nothing related to draft animals to Changde and Changyong. The latter two received equal value, however, as Changde's portion was a business of equivalent value to the mule, and Changyong assumed less of the family debt than either Changhui or Chang'en.

Since most acts of household division took place in the winter after the fall harvest, the division of the stored grain had to be considered, though this aspect of division was not entered into the division documents. Liu Tanlin was asked about his division following the harvest.

Q: What about the grain?
A: [I got] two *shi* of corn, one *shi* of gaoliang, and one *shi* of beans.
Q: Did your brother get the same?
A: Yes. (KC 2:261C)

The Division of Property: Land

But as in Qing Taiwan, when dividing the various forms of property, land was the most important for North China peasant families. Land was recorded in the division documents in terms of number of *mu* or some local equivalent, and, just as in Qing Taiwan, equal division was the rule. In 1933 the three Yang brothers divided their house, and the eldest received 31.25 *mu,* the second received 33.5 *mu,* and the youngest received 36.25 *mu* (KC 1:292). In a 1925 division in Houjiaying, Hou Tingwen received 43 *mu* and Tingwu received 46.5 *mu* (KC 5:76). In that same village in 1940, three Hou brothers divided the land as follows: Lianbi, 11.5 *mu;* Lianyu, 11.5 *mu;* Liankun, 12 *mu* (KC 5:78). In 1911 Hou Lianfa gave his first grandson 18 *mu*, his second grandson 19 *mu*, and his third grandson 18 *mu* (KC 5:93). In 1936 four members of a Hou family divided their land as follows: the first brother's widow received 32.5 *mu*, the second brother received 31.5 *mu,* the third brother received 31.5 *mu,* and the fourth brother's widow received 30 *mu* (KC 5:95). In 1936 in Houjiaying, the two Hou brothers, Yongjian and Yongqin, divided their land into two shares of 42 and 43.5 *mu,* respectively (KC 5.1:73).

The division of land on the North China Plain was considerably simpler than in Qing Taiwan. The peasants divided the land they owned equally among the sons, and the problem was solved. Multitiered ownership of land and permanent tenure rights never emerge in the household division documents, which testifies to the relative unimportance of these phenomena in the North.

The interview sources reveal, however, that the land systems in the North and the South were not fundamentally different. First, according to Yang Run, northern tenants could, at least in theory, divide rented land.

Q: If there are four *mu* of rented land, and two brothers divide the household, can the rented land also be divided?
A: Yes it can.
Q: Is it required to talk to the landlord?
A: No it's not. (KC 1:296B)

Second, permanent tenure and dual ownership had existed in the Qing era on land that was legally "owned" by the Qing state, specifically the Imperial Household Department and the Banner families of the Qing elite. Yang Ze owned land that had once belonged to the Imperial Household Department. A conversation with him on this theme went like this:

> Q: How long were the rental agreements on this land?
> A: Forever.
> Q: Was there any document giving this permanent right?
> A: No there wasn't, but the land was rented permanently.
> Q: Was the rent changed each year?
> A: It was set, and it definitely never changed.
> Q: From when?
> A: Long ago. (KC 2:129–130)

According to Du Xiang, such land was divisible.

> Q: If the owner [the peasant with permanent tenure] died, what procedure took place?
> A: In that case the sons and grandsons tilled the land.
> Q: If the owner died, was it necessary to report to the rent collector?
> A: No. (KC 2:132–135)

The tenants who worked this Qing land could sell or rent the land, in the latter case creating a classic two-tiered ownership pattern. The rental payment pattern is illustrated in Figure 8.

Figure 8
The Qing Land System on the North China Plain

Qing state

↑

zhuangtou (tax collector) pays Qing state

↑

Tenant 1 (with permanent tenure) pays
laozu "old rent" to *zhuangtou*

↑

Tenant 2 pays *xianzu* "current rent" to Tenant 1

Source: KC 2:110A.

In terms of the land system, pawned land often complicated the calculation of land value during household division, just as it had in

Qing Taiwan. As mentioned in Chapter 5, when the first party pawned a piece of land to the second party, usually for half of the land's market value, each party had certain rights. The first party had the right either to repay the money and reclaim the land, or to receive the remaining half of the value of the land and turn over complete ownership to the second. The second party had the right to use the land, usually for a fixed minimum number of years, and then to wait until party one exercised either of his or her options. Land held in pawn or pawned out thus required special consideration during household division.

In 1907 four Hou brothers of Houjiaying divided their 56.5 *mu* of land. Two plots, one of 9.5 *mu* and the other of 3.5 *mu*, were held in pawn. To spread the risk of having the land redeemed from them or having to pay the remaining value of the land, the brothers divided the larger plot into two pieces, one of 3.5 and the other of 6 *mu*. They then gave the former piece to the eldest, the latter to the second, and the other 3.5 *mu* plot to brother number four (KC 5.1:88).

Illustrating the other side of the pawn transaction are two division documents. In 1928 the wealthy Yang family of Shajing divided their 350 *mu* of land between two sons. Three plots totaling 14.8 *mu* had been pawned out, and the family was certain of being able to reclaim them the following fall. They decided that the two brothers would each pay half the 285 yuan to redeem the land and that the land itself would go the their father, Yang Fen, as part of his 30.8 *mu* of *yanglaodi* (KC 1:291).

In 1936, when the Hou family of Houjiaying divided their 158 *mu* between four branches, the family was less confident, or perhaps less desirous, of redeeming two *mu* of land they had pawned out for forty yuan. They decided that, when the time was right, they would ask for the remaining value of the land and divide the money equally among the four branches (KC 5.1:95).

Thus, from the perspective of the interaction of the inheritance and land systems, North and South China were essentially the same. While the potential for permanent tenure and multitiered ownership was more clearly elaborated in the South, these were fully understood in the North, and they had existed to a limited extent at an earlier time. The land pawn transaction was the same and required the same consideration during household division.

The Division of Debt

Finally, as in Qing Taiwan, families had to divide current debts. The division documents demonstrate that, if the family had debts, the brothers in principle inherited these obligations in equal shares. The family could first pay the debt from family money or property and then divide the house, thus equally reducing each brother's portion before division. In 1936 in Houjiaying, two brothers and their two widowed sisters-in-law divided their considerable holdings, and the document states that a total of 31.2 *mu* was first extracted from the family holdings and disposed of to repay various debts (KC 5:95).

A second pattern for handling debt was simply to divide the amount of debt among the brothers. An interview with Yang Run of Shajing demonstrates this possibility:

Q: If there are two parents, two brothers, and a sister, and there is a debt of 600 yuan, how is the debt divided during household division?
A: The brothers take responsibility for 300 yuan each. The sister has nothing to do with it.(KC 1:297)

In a 1920 division in Houjiaying, Hou Yongchun divided his house among his four sons. The family had quite a bit of debt, and he divided it this way: Yuanzhen, the eldest son, received 650 *xiaoyang* yuan and 760 *diao;* Yuanrui, the second son, received 400 *diao;* Yuanjun, the third son, received 150 *diao;* and Yuanlian, the fourth son, received 650 *diao.* Thus each brother inherited part of the family debt, and though in this case the amount varied, this variation was balanced by other aspects of the division. Yuanzhen, for instance, received an increased portion of debt, but he also received a family business, whose profits were specifically denied to the other brothers. Yuanjun received less debt, but he was living with the parents and did not receive a share of the house. He may also have been providing a larger share of parental support (KC 5:92).

Two Summary Examples

Taking together the elements of land, living space, household property, and debt, household division in rural North China had the same characteristics as household division in Qing Taiwan. A typical example, presented in summary, is a 1933 division among three brothers in Shajing. The household division document reads as follows:

> The creators of this document—Yang Zheng, Yang Yuan, and Yang Hong—because household affairs are very difficult and hard to manage, desire each to establish his own home and live and cook separately. Therefore they invite lineage members and relatives and take all the property, such as the land, houses, things, and so forth, and divide them into three equal shares, and each will receive one share. The property is listed below.

>> The eldest son's portion is five rooms of the northern tiled house, three rooms of the eastern tiled house, one building, and the courtyard 4 *zhang* 9 *chi*[9] wide inside the line where the water drops off the roof, four *mu* of *jingjiao*[10] land, 3 *mu* of *chadaozui* land, 2.5 *mu* of *xiaozuo* land, 7.5 *mu* of *datouyu* land, 6.25 *mu* of *changfuzi* land, and 8 *mu* of *xiaohe* land.

> The second son's portion is three rooms of brick building, two rooms of shed, a grindstone, a flat cart, a mule, a cart, reins and yoke, one piece of the eastern garden, 10 east-side *mu* of *beifaxin* land, 7 northern *mu* of *fenhou* land, 5 *mu* of *hetouzi* land, 3 *mu* of *caochang* land, 3 *mu* of *fenqianshuibian* land, 2.5 *mu* of *cipanzi* land, 3 *mu* of *yuantouzi* land, one donkey, one feeder, one pigsty, one pig feeder. The land on the east side that held the old home is in this portion. On the outside of the old home going north is a public walkway 1 *zhang* 4 *chi* wide that is for both families.

>> The third son's portion is two rooms of brick building, four rooms of tiled building ... 10 *mu* of *daxiezi* land, 10 western *mu* of *beifaxin* land, 7 southern *mu* of *fenhou* land, 6.25 eastern *mu* of *changfu* land, 3 southern *mu* of *fenqian* land, one big pigsty that may be torn down on its east, south, and west sides and built upon. In addition, this son may retain 10 *mu* of pawned out *zhangxiezi* land. ... If at a later date there are regrets or disputes, this will be the proof, along with the guarantors and lineage members.

> In addition, there is in Shunyi county a shop building owned jointly with the Ru family. This goes to eldest son, who pays fifty yuan [to second and third son], and later the business's profits and losses have no connection to second and third son.

This division may be roughly schematized as shown below:

> *Eldest brother*
> > 5 rooms in north building
> > 3 rooms in east building
> > 1 "building"
> > 31.25 *mu* of land in six plots
> > one-half ownership in a shop (the other half is owned by another family)
>
> *Second brother*
> > 3 rooms in east courtyard
> > 2 rooms in shed
> > 1 grindstone
> > 1 flat cart
> > 1 mule
> > 1 cart
> > 1 set of reins and yoke
> > 1 piece of garden
> > 33.5 *mu* of land in seven plots
> > 1 donkey
> > 1 donkey feeder
> > 1 pigsty and feeder
> > 1 piece of land under the old house
>
> *Third brother*
> > 2 rooms of mud house
> > 3 rooms of western house
> > 36.25 *mu* in five plots
> > 10 *mu*—the right to redeem this 10 *mu* of pawned land
> > (KC 1:292)

Each brother received rooms and land based on the rule of equal division. The specific amounts are, however, adjusted slightly owing to differing values. The eldest brother gets three more rooms in better buildings. He also gets an extra building of some kind and a shop, which is a profitable business. The second brother gets less and poorer quality housing, but this is offset by a little more land and all the agricultural implements and the draft animals. The third brother gets neither a business nor animals but gets more land and the rights to reclaim a large piece of pawned land.

A second example, this one from Shajing in 1919, demonstrates how property and family responsibilities could be divided.

> The creators of this document are Yang Puzeng and Yang Shao-zeng. The two brothers have discussed the matter and will publicly divide the family property, land, and house. The two brothers will both work the mother's five *mu* of *yanglaodi*. The land is named *langwo*. The two brothers will each work 2.5 *mu* and pay thirty *diao* of rent [to their mother]. The older brother will work the north; the younger brother, the south. Shaozeng's share includes five rooms of *shangfang*.[11] Puzeng's share includes four rooms of east and west *xiangfang*. The northern wall of the *xiangfang* is the boundary, with the south going to Puzeng, the north to Shaozeng. Shaozeng may use the pigsty for thirty years. One piece of west yard will be divided by the line formed by the gutter of the rear side of the *shangfang*. The southern part will go to Puzeng, the northern part to Shaozeng. In the southeast of the village, there is a piece of land called "Three Mu," which is seven *mu* in size. Each brother will receive 3.5 *mu*: the elder brother, the east; the younger, the west. Our *zhangjiafen* land of six *mu* will be divided into three *mu* for each brother: the elder brother gets the south; the younger, the north. The two *mu* of *dujiafen* land will go to Shaozeng to work as a tenant. Farm and household goods will be used jointly. The path by the *shangfang* will be used by both brothers. (KC 1:292, 319)

This division might be schematized as follows:

> *Puzeng*
> Property received:
>   4 rooms of *xiangfang*
>   one-half east yard
>   3.5 *mu* of land
>   3 *mu* of land
> Obligations received:
>   work 2.5 *mu* of *yanglaodi*
>   pay mother 30 *diao*
>
> *Shaozeng*
> Property received:
>   5 rooms of *shangfang*
>   1 pigsty

    one-half east yard
    3.5 *mu*
    3 *mu*
    2 *mu* of rented land
    Obligations received:
        work 2.5 *mu* of *yanglaodi*
        pay mother 30 *diao*

    Mother
        5 *mu* of *yanglaodi*
        60 *diao* of income

Thus the two brothers divided the land and garden precisely in half. They each provided exactly half of the support of their mother, including both *yanglaodi* and *yanglaoshan*. The house was divided almost equally, four rooms to five. Shaozeng received some extra value in the extra room, the pigsty, and the rented land, but this can be explained. Since Shaozeng was living in the *shangfang*, it is probable that their mother lived with him. Thus the extra room was the mother's, and the extra pigsty and rented land were to offset the increased labor that Shaozeng was providing to care for his mother.

Thus household division on the North China Plain embodied three essential principles: support for aged parents, marriage expenses for unmarried siblings, and equal division of family property among all sons of the same father. Despite the differences in time, location, and economic environment, the household division process was the same in Republican rural North China as it had been in Qing Taiwan: all families adhered to the three basic principles.

The evidence in this chapter also allows a view of the priorities of family members at the point of household division. If property was minimal, the first priority was the right of the parents to their *yanglao* support. The relationship of marriage expenses, dowries, and equal shares was less clear, but most likely marriage expenses for sons and dowries for daughters had a slight priority over the equal shares for the sons. Finally, it is clear that the revolutionary Republican laws promulgated in 1931 had no effect in rural North China on the inheritance regime as a whole or on improving women's property rights in particular.

Chapter 8

Region and Class: Exceptions, Strategies, and Orientations

As we have seen, the basics of household division were the same in Qing Taiwan and Republican North China. Household division documents and legal cases from other areas of China demonstrate that the pattern was standard throughout Han China. But even within this well-structured system, families could and did employ differing strategies of property dispensation for a variety of purposes. One strategy was to make use of accepted violations of the equal division rules, including set-asides known as the eldest grandson portion, the eldest son portion, and special gifts. Other strategies used acceptable property set-asides and trusts. When opting for a set-aside or trust at household division time, families dedicated specific property to some purpose other than equal division among the sons.

The major set-asides were the eldest grandson portion, the eldest son portion, and *yanglao* support, which benefited individuals. The major trusts were sacrificial property, joint ceremonial rooms, common property, educational property, and charitable estates, which went for more communal purposes. When families of a particular region or social class employed these strategies over several generations, significant variations could emerge in household division and property relationships as a whole. These inheritance strategies, both singly and in combination, I call "orientations," and to illustrate them I first analyze three exceptions to the general rules—the eldest grandson portion, the eldest son portion, and special gifts—and then several orientations typical of a certain region or class.

155

Three Exceptions

The Eldest Grandson Portion and the Eldest Son Portion

The eldest grandson, or more precisely the first son of the first son, was often though not always granted a special set-aside of property that varied considerably in both type and amount. Of 177 household division documents, sixty-two make a provision for the eldest grandson, suggesting that in 35 percent of Chinese household divisions, the eldest grandson so benefited. The practice seems to have been much more prominent in the South, with no cases occurring on the North China Plain (see Table 10).

Such a set-aside could be of any type of property. In 1773 the Lin family awarded .4 *jia* of land to their eldest grandson (TS 1910, 52:1626). In 1778 the Zhuang family offered their eldest grandson two water buffalo and a plot of land, which he refused, opting to take 76 yuan instead (TS 1910, 12:1543). The wealthy Han family gave 3,484.6 *liang* of silver to their eldest grandson in 1793 (TS 1910, 75:1667). In 1871 the Zhuang family awarded their eldest grandson 14.4 *shi* of *xiaozu* income, from which he had to pay 3.4 *shi* of *dazu,* netting himself 11 *shi* annually (TS 1910, 67:1652). In the Lin family division of 1886, the eldest grandson, Ying, received the annual interest of 2.76 *shi* of grain on a loan of 23 yuan. If the loan was repaid, the returned principal would be his as well (TS 1910, 15:1551). Those instances of division that allow for statistical comparison are presented in Table 11. The figures suggest that the amount of the eldest grandson's portion was negotiable and that it could range from a small, symbolic amount up to 85 percent of a brother's full share.

The eldest grandson portion was formally intended to go into the actual control of the eldest grandson, and this would certainly occur if the first son had already died. In one instance, widow Zhang divided the family property among her four sons in 1843. Her first son had died, and the first grandson, Jianpei, received his father's share along with the extra eldest grandson land. Jianpei signed the document as the "grandson" (TS 1910, 48:1619). A similar situation occurred in the Wu family division of 1893. The first brother had died, and his son Shiqing received both his father's share and an extra 1.6936 *jia* of land as the eldest grandson. He signed the document in two places, as son and as grandson (TS 1910, 45:1612). In the

Table 10

The Use of Trusts and Set-Asides in Six Provinces

Province	Total Documents	Yanglao Set-Aside	Sacrificial Trusts	Common Trusts	Eldest Grandson Portion	Eldest Son Portion	Educational Trusts
Anhui	35	13 (37%)	13 (37%)	19 (54%)	9 (26%)	0	6
Fujian	21	10 (48%)	13 (62%)	8 (38%)	5 (24%)	2 (10%)	4
Hebei	24	11 (46%)	0	0	0	0	0
Shandong	9	2 (22%)	0	0	0	0	0
Taiwan	75	39 (52%)	40 (53%)	26 (35%)	43 (57%)	0	6
Zhejiang	13	4 (31%)	5 (38%)	3 (23%)	5 (38%)	4 (31%)	2
Totals	177	79 (45%)	71 (40%)	56 (32%)	62 (35%)	6 (3%)	18 (10%)

Sources: KC, TWGS, TS, JJS, ZZM, ZPM.

Table 11

The Eldest Grandson's Portion as a Percentage of a Brother's Share

Year	Brother's Share	Eldest Grandson's Portion	Percentage
1725	2,808 liang	100 liang	4
1752	24 mu	1.44 mu	6
1773	0.55 jia	0.4 jia	73
1793	7,003 liang	3,484.6 liang	50
1816	5.4 jia	4.6 jia	85
1831	6.03 mu	1.1 mu	18
1837	1.06 jia	0.4 jia	38
1863	6.5 shi	2 shi	31
1865	55.8 gu	10 gu	18
1884	3,500 yuan	260 yuan	7
1886	55 shi	4 shi	7
1893	65 shi	26 shi	40
1897	900 yuan of land	120 yuan of land	13
1922	2.67 mu	0.4 mu	15

Sources: JJS, TS, ZPM, ZZM.

slightly more complex 1770 case of young grandson Xiao Chuan-sheng, the first brother (Chuansheng's father) had died, so Chuan-sheng received both his father's portion and the eldest grandson land. But, since he was young, he was going to reside with his uncle, second brother Yuncheng, and the document specifically states: "Eldest grandson's share of the property, as witnessed by many relatives, will temporarily go to Yuncheng to manage, and it must not be embez-zled. After Chuansheng is grown and married, the property from the division will be returned to him." Chuansheng also signed the division document, probably to strengthen his claim in any future dispute (TS 1910, 63:1645–1647).

But an eldest grandson was not limited to receiving his special portion only if his father was dead. In the Ye family division of 1897, for instance, the eldest grandson, Chengzhi, was specifically awarded land valued at 120 yuan, even though his father, Qizhen, was still living (TS 1910, 39:1593). In an 1887 Wu family division, the eldest grandson, Tanshi, was specifically awarded some rice land and housing "to be his forever," although his father was still alive (TWGS 1, 9:894).

If the first son was alive, possession of the eldest grandson property was negotiable, however, and actual control could go to the first son. Thus, in the 1819 Huang family division that occurred among the brothers Zhiyan, Zhinong, and two nephews, the document states: "The piece of dry land at Kuimuzizhuang that was bought from the Shi family will go to [Zhi]yan as the eldest grandson property to show our respect for the eldest" (TS 1910, 23:1567). In the Chen family division of 1879, the eldest brother, Guanfang, received both his share as a brother and an extra piece of rice land as the eldest grandson portion. He is called both the first son and the first grandson in different parts of the document (TS 1910, 24:1569).

Adoption could create a new category of grandson, who was similar to an eldest grandson and who might be entitled to a bit of extra property. If a family adopted their first son in the *baoyang* form, he strictly speaking had no blood relationship to the family, though his first son would be the eldest grandson. If at a later date his adoptive parents managed to produce a natural son, who then produced a grandson, this boy was then considered the *disun,* or "blood grandson," and might be entitled to some extra property. Thus, in the 1892 Li family division, two sons, Zengyi and Xu'er, had been adopted in the *baoyang* manner before the parents managed to produce a natural son, Senpao. In this situation, Zengyi's first son, Yanshu, was the "eldest grandson," and Senpao's first son, Housheng, was the "blood grandson." At division, Yanshu received three hundred yuan as the eldest grandson, and Housheng received extra land as the blood grandson (TS 1910, 13:1545).

Finally, the eldest grandson portion was sometimes specifically given to cover marriage expenses. Thus, in an 1857 Taiwan division, the eldest grandson, Gengxin, was awarded 24 big yuan to cover his marriage expenses, though his father would manage the money until the wedding (TWGS 2, 8:886). In the Li family division of 1886, eldest grandson Zhouqi received 100 yuan to pay for his marriage expenses (TS 1910, 6:1528). In the Xiao family division of 1770, the eldest grandson received a share of the property to fund his marriage when he came of age (TS 1910, 63:1645).

In some cases, the eldest son, rather than the eldest grandson, was the recipient of some extra property, though this practice seems to have been less frequent than the awarding of the eldest grandson portion. As presented in Table 10, only in six cases out of 177 divisions did the eldest son so benefit, and the practice seems to have been most common in Zhejiang. Francis Hsu reports that the eldest son received extra property at household division time in his West Town in Yunnan province (Francis Hsu 1967:114). As with the eldest grandson portion, the eldest son's extra property could vary in both type and amount, though it never was greater than a single son's share.

The practice of setting aside extra property for the eldest son or grandson was, in the strict legal sense, a violation of the law. There was no room in Song dynasty law for an extra portion for the eldest son, and there is no mention of the practice in the Southern Song collection of legal cases, the *Qingmingji* (Burns 1973:viii, 139). The Ming and Qing codes make no provision for such extra shares either. Yet in Qing customary practice, the awarding of such extra shares seems to have been perfectly acceptable, especially in South China. Oftentimes, the eldest grandson's portion was written up next to the stipulation for parental *yangshan* support, perhaps suggesting just how acceptable the practice was (TWGS 2, 8:886).

Given the widespread nature of the practice, scholars have offered varying explanations for its existence. Some have suggested that the practice is the residual effect of the *zongfa* system of Zhou dynasty China, in which primogeniture was the rule.[1] Others have suggested that the extra portion was given to cover the individual responsibility incurred by the eldest son to maintain the ancestral shrine or the ancestral cult (Freedman 1958:22–23; 1966:7n). One household division document does indeed state that the eldest grandson, Chuan-sheng, was given a piece of vegetable garden specifically to fund his sacrificial duties (TS 1910, 63:1645). Still others have postulated that the extra property might be for support of aged parents or because the eldest had more children (quoted in Freedman 1966:53). Another scholar has argued that in poor families the eldest grandson "usually gets at most 'enough to pay for a wife,' " suggesting that the property was designed to facilitate the marriage of the senior grandson and the extension of the family into the next generation (Arthur Wolf 1970: 196). But only six of sixty-two eldest grandson portions are specifically tied to marriage in the household division documents.

In the end, the evidence suggests that, except in those few cases in which the eldest grandson portion was specifically tied to sacrifices or marriage, the eldest grandson could in fact do as he pleased with the property, as Maurice Freedman has elsewhere argued (1966:50–51). Assuming that the eldest grandson had freedom to do as he pleased with the property, the question remains: why did he so benefit? My argument below is that the eldest grandson portion is part of a series of inheritance practices that form the lineage orientation common throughout South China.

Though the eldest grandson portion was frequently awarded in South China, it was not a universal practice, the amount was entirely negotiable, and it was never used as a subterfuge to create a de facto system of primogeniture that kept family property intact. In all cases of household division that used the eldest grandson strategy, the brothers received their portions, which were always larger and in most cases much larger than the eldest grandson's portion.

Special Gifts

Another type of true exception to the equal division rule was the awarding of special gifts to family members for unique reasons. In an 1810 Zhejiang division, second brother Yuankai received a gift of 5.06 *mu* for his "industrious labors." For purposes of contrast, each brother's portion totaled 105 *mu* (ZPM 1). In a 1924 division in Zhejiang, the three Wang brothers divided their property, and second and third brothers, Shizhou and Shibing, received small amounts of extra gift land for their undefined "special input" into the family estate (ZPM 3:8612).

In an 1838 division from Taiwan, four brothers had been orphaned when the eldest, Chengchang, was only eighteen *sui*. Because of his special efforts in raising his younger brothers and in building the family estate from literally nothing, Chengchang was awarded a special gift of some housing, a piece of land, and a total of 690 yuan in cash. Again for purposes of contrast, each brother's share equaled about four pieces of land and eight rooms of housing, suggesting that the gift was a small percentage of the total (TWGS 1, 9:830).

In an 1864 Fujian division, the eldest brother of the very wealthy

Chen family was awarded a double share because his branch had "many more mouths to feed" (ZZZ:2). A 1945 Li family division in Fujian included two special gifts, each of three *shi* of grain, the first for a widow and her son, the second for a nephew (DW:2). In an 1836 division of the Huang family in Huizhou, a daughter had been married out but had, for reasons unexplained, returned to care for a nephew. She was awarded four pieces of land to support herself and to fund her funeral when the time came (JJS:385). Finally, in the 1825 Sheng family division, eldest brother Yi'an was awarded a special gift of fifty *ping* of grain because he had sustained an injury (JJS:175). In total, of 183 total household division documents for which there is sufficient information to make a judgment, only ten (about 5 percent) have provisions for a special gift. They could be awarded for a variety of reasons—injuries, extra mouths to feed, special contributions to the family estate—that were, strictly speaking, a violation of the equal division principles. The amounts could be minimal or as much as a full brother's share. But, as in the case of the eldest son and grandson portions, the practice was so infrequent that it cannot be seen as a strategy to create a system of unigeniture and thus avoid the inevitable application of the household division rules.

The North China Peasant Family Orientation

Taking advantage of acceptable violations of the rules was not the only or even the most frequent manner in which Chinese families strategized at inheritance time. Much more frequently, the families tried to take advantage of a complex of legal and acceptable practices—the use of set-asides and trusts—that fall into patterns I have called "orientations." The simplest of these was the North China peasantry's family orientation. In this pattern, virtually all property was divided among the sons, and only the *yanglaodi* set-aside was used to any significant extent. After the deaths and funerals of the parents, any extra *yanglaodi* was divided among the brothers, and nothing remained as jointly owned property. Thus, once the family divided and the parents passed away, the extended family relationships between the brothers were not buttressed by property, and the brothers' families were, as far as property was concerned, completely independent.

Of the thirty-three household division documents extant for North China (here meaning Hebei and Shandong provinces), thirteen employ some form of set-aside or trust, all of which are for *yanglaodi* (see Table 10). These figures suggest that the use of sacrificial, common, or educational trusts was very infrequent. Furthermore, the disposition of the *yanglaodi* after the parents' deaths confirms that the maintenance of jointly held property was not a priority for North China peasants.

In one common pattern, all of the *yanglaodi* was simply used up to pay for the parents' funeral expenses, unless one of the brothers could pay for the funeral. A conversation with Li Yunjie of Shajing explains:

Q: If the parents die, is the *yanglaodi* divided among the brothers?
A: Well, for example, if there is fifteen *mu* of land, it will all be sold for funeral expenses. If a son has money equal to the fifteen *mu* and he uses it, the land is his. (KC 1:79C)

And, according to Shajing resident Li Shulin, who worked four *mu* of his mother's *yanglaodi*:

Q: [What happens] when your mother dies?
A: The *yanglaodi* will be sold for the funeral.
Q: And when your mother dies, if you use your own money for the funeral, can the land become yours?
A: Yes. (KC 2:100C)

Another common pattern was first to pay funeral expenses and then to divide any remaining land equally among the brothers. A group interview with five Shajing residents went as follows:

Q: Can the *yanglaodi* be sold while the parents are alive?
A: No, only after they die.
Q: Must it be sold after they die?
A: If the family has enough property to pay for the funeral, there is no need to sell it.
Q: If it isn't sold, who owns it?
A: Each of the divided families gets an equal share. (KC 2:90B)

An interview with Yang Run noted the same pattern:

Q: If the parents die and the *yanglaodi* remains, and if you sell some to pay funeral expenses and there is still some left over, what happens?

A: If there are three brothers who divided, the three divide it.

Q: In a case like that, if the three pay for the funeral together, is the *yanglaodi* then divided among each of the three?

A: Yes, it is. (KC 1:302C)

Some household division documents in North China contain a clause similar to this one from Lengshuigou, which mandates equal division of the *yanglaodi* after the deaths of the parents. In this case widow Li, née Lu, drew up a household division document to divide the family property between her two sons, Yongzhang and Yongxiang. After listing her two plots of *yanglaodi,* which totaled six big *mu*, the document reads: "After I die, with the exception of that which is taken out to pay for my burial apparel and funeral, the rest [of the property], no matter how much or how little, will revert to both Yongzhang and Yongxiang for them to divide equally" (KC 4:100). Thus, in most if not all cases on the North China Plain, the final dispensation of any remaining *yanglaodi* saw all land go into the hands of the sons individually, and none was retained for joint ownership.

The family orientation of household division is further characterized by the way families divided the ceremonial center of the household that held the family altar and tablets, usually the central room of *zhengfang* (room C in Figure 7). Though this was the ceremonial center of the family, when household division occurred, the room was simply awarded to one of the brothers. The other brothers established family altars and ceremonial centers in their own new living quarters. Most daily sacrificial ceremonies were then conducted in these new ceremonial rooms, as an interview with Yang Ze describes:

Q: After division, isn't there a special name for the house of the eldest brother?

A: No.

Q: Where are the sacrifices to the ancestors done?

A: In their own houses.

Q: Don't you go to the eldest's house for sacrifices?

A: No. (KC 1:256C)

Another talk with Zhao Tingkui, Yang Ze, and Zhang Yongren revealed much the same pattern.

Q: In this village, how many families live in one courtyard?

A: Usually two, at most three.

Q: In these cases, do the [brothers who have] divided build family altars?

A: Of course. It [the altar] is placed at the very center [of each household]. (KC 1:233C)

These findings do not deny the existence of jointly held sacrifices, such as Qingmingjie,[2] but rather emphasize that after division each new family established its own ceremonial room, or more likely a corner of a room, and there was no jointly owned ceremonial room that housed the family altar and tablets. Thus the ceremonial center of the house was divided, and no ceremonial property remained to strengthen the agnatic family ties.

The family orientation of household division practiced by peasants on the North China Plain is thus characterized by the total and final nature of the division. Neither land nor ceremonial space was set aside for joint ownership, and the only frequently used set-aside, *yanglaodi*, ultimately devolved into the hands of the individual brothers. Thus, when the parents' life cycles were complete, their property had devolved in its entirety to the individual sons and their families. No property was left to joint ownership for the purposes of strengthening agnatic ties or pursuing specific economic goals.

The Taiwan Lineage Orientation

The Taiwan lineage orientation of household division stands in marked contrast to the family orientation, because Taiwan families employed a wide variety of set-asides and trusts, both in housing and in land. While the set-asides of *yanglaodi* and the eldest grandson portion went to individuals, the trusts were jointly owned by the brothers and were designed to buttress, both symbolically and economically, the now more distant relationships between the brothers and to minimize the divisive effects of household division.

A prominent element of the lineage orientation, one of both symbolic and economic importance, was the set-aside of the eldest grandson portion discussed above. In the Taiwan lineage orientation, the eldest grandson portion was awarded approximately 52 percent of the time, and the amount could vary considerably. The purpose of this special set-aside was to celebrate the firstborn male guarantor of the family's and possibly the lineage's extension into the next generation. While in nuclear family terms the first grandson was critical only to the eldest brother, in lineage terms he was of critical importance for simultaneously extending into a new generation the father's line, the father's line within the lineage, and possibly the lineage as a whole. The awarding of property to the eldest grandson also emphasized the importance of the main branch of the lineage as it grew. To the extent that the property was to aid in the eldest grandson's marriage, it was designed to help extend the lineage even one generation further.

A second prominent element of the lineage orientation, one of primarily symbolic and ceremonial value, was the frequent creation of a ceremonial trust from the main room of the house, which contained the family altar and was used for joint sacrifices. Thus, in one 1868 division between four brothers, the rooms were carefully divided. A short sentence reads, "The main hall *(ting)* will be joint *(gong)*" (TS 1910, 8:1534). The 1825 Yang family division document contains a similar clause that reads, "The back and front halls will be retained for common use" (TS 1910, 17:1560). The Jian family division document of 1868 states, "The main hall will be retained as a joint hall, and this must not be confused" (TS 1910, 41: 1604). The prologue to an 1879 Chen family division document is more explicit in that it clarifies the use of the joint hall.

> Therefore we invite our relatives to participate in a discussion. We take all the land we inherited from grandfather, the land that was bought and pawned . . . , the family savings, the household items, the housing, and so forth, and we agree to take out one room of the main hall and leave it as a jointly owned ancestral hall–room, and the rest will be measured and valued, and will be divided by the three branches into three equal shares. (TS 1910, 24:1570)

The document drawn up for the Zhang family division of 1856 goes a step further by mandating joint repairs: "Let it be clearly stated: from the total land and housing we take out one room of the main hall, where we will jointly sacrifice to the ancestors and the gods. . . . If the walls of the main hall suffer damage, they will be jointly repaired" (TS 1910, 55:1632).

Beyond the eldest grandson set-aside and the ceremonial housing trust, Taiwanese families also employed other trusts in the lineage household division strategy. A frequently used trust, occurring in forty (53 percent) of the household division documents, was the sacrificial trust. This comprised land or income entrusted specifically to fund sacrifices to parents or other ancestors. One pattern for sacrificial trusts was to earmark the land for joint ownership and specify how the income was to be spent.

Thus in 1782 widow Lu set aside one "big piece" of land to fund specifically the present sacrifices to her deceased husband and later sacrifices to herself (TS 1910, 16:1555). In 1886 the Lin family set apart a house and a small piece of unirrigated dry land for joint ownership. The land was rented out for ten yuan. Three yuan would go to the eldest brother, Chengshou, to conduct sacrifices to a granduncle, three yuan would go to second brother, Fansheng, to conduct sacrifices to another granduncle, and the remaining four yuan would be used for upkeep of the family graves. The Lins also decided to award five *shi* of grain income to their fourth brother, Qingxiang, for which Qingxiang would sacrifice specifically to his father's deceased first wife, née Wang (TS 1910, 15:1551–1552).

Another common pattern was to rotate management of the sacrificial property. In 1836 the two brothers Bilan and Bitao allocated two plots of land for sacrifices. The first was rented out for nine yuan per year, and the income was to pay for sacrifices to their grandmother; the second, which brought in sixteen yuan per year, was to pay for sacrifices to an uncle and aunt. Both relevant clauses contain the phrase "We two brothers will rotate management" (TS 1910, 43:1608).

In 1819 the four Huang brothers divided their household, and they wanted to reserve one piece of land for sacrificial purposes. Their document reads:

> Therefore we have decided to invite the lineage head and to take all the property we have acquired over the years, and to first take out the piece of unirrigated land we bought from Wang Bianguan and establish it as jointly owned property. The four branches and their descendants will use it in rotation to pay for incense and sacrifices to the ancestors. (TS 1910, 23:1567)

In 1835, when four Lin brothers divided their household, they owned, in addition to other properties, a house and a piece of land that they wished to maintain jointly for sacrificial purposes. Their document reads:

Now, because we brothers are dividing, we want to retain this property in common. The main hall will be used for sacrifices and to hold the brothers' tablets [when they die]. The dry land for which we receive eight *shi* of *xiaozu,* but from which we must pay 5.631 *shi,* so we retain 2.369 *shi,* will be used to fulfill sacrificial responsibilities. The four brothers will manage the land in turn, and they must not argue, selfishly fatten themselves, or disrupt family harmony. (TS 1910, 22:1566)

At times the sacrificial lands were sufficiently large and their management sufficiently complex that they required a separate contract. Thus in 1893 the three Cai brothers drew up a division document whose primary purpose was to regularize the management of their jointly owned sacrificial lands. These totaled at least forty-three plots measuring about seven *jia* in area, some held in pawn and some owned outright. The prologue to the document reads:

We know we are brothers, but that there comes a day of division. We three brothers inherited joint-rotated property from our grandfather, and we three brothers will rotate it, with each brother managing the property for one year, and the profits from the irrigated and unirrigated land will be used to pay the various expenses for the annual sacrifices to the ancestors. (TS 1910, 20:1562)

Only three of the documents allow for a statistical determination of the amount of sacrificial trust property as a percentage of the family's total property. In 1770 Xiao Guanghe and his second wife, née Zeng, divided their household among their four sons. Each son received housing and an income of 19.44 *shi.* Forty *shi,* approximately 33 percent of the total family income, was reserved for sacrificial purposes (TS 1910, 63:1645). In 1773 the four brothers of the Lin family divided their 8.1 *jia* of land and allocated for sacrificial purposes 1.2 *jia,* or 15 percent of the total (TS 1910, 52:1626). In 1793, when the wealthy Han family divided their property valued at 64,280 taels of silver, 7,837 taels, or 12 percent, was marked for sacrificial purposes, more than the average 7,000 tael portion that was awarded to each brother (TS 1910, 75:1667).

Thus at least half of Taiwanese families in my sample allocated some property to be owned jointly by the brothers with the income dedicated to sacrificial purposes. This land could total up to as much as one-third of the family property, and management was either given to an individual or rotated on an annual basis among the brothers. And, while the total income from the trust was supposed to be spent on sacrifices, some portion probably went as income to the family handling the management in a given year. The rotation of management was most likely designed to equalize the distribution of this income.

In the Taiwan lineage orientation, another common set-aside was *yanglaodi,* which emerges in thirty-nine (52 percent) of the documents. And while the legal ownership and use of the *yanglao* property was the same as in the North China family orientation, the final dispensation of the property differed. In most cases, after the parents died and the funeral expenses were paid, any remaining property was kept as jointly owned by the brothers, who used the income for sacrificial purposes. The division orchestrated by widow Li in 1895 contains the following clause: "From the sixty *shi* of rent (income) that we bought in Nangang from Chen Chengqi, take out ten *shi* for my *yangshan*. One hundred years from now,[3] take this ten *shi* and give it to the two brothers in rotation to use for sacrifices to their mother and father" (TS 1910, 9:1535). When widow Wang divided her property among her sons, she inserted the following clause into the division document: "As for the piece of land we bought from Chen Guangping, I will keep it as my *yangshan,* and after I die, give it to the four brothers Yubi, Yuqing, Yushen, and Yubin as joint property to be rotated and used to provide for sacrifices. If heaven should allow me to live a long life, then the grain from the harvest or the savings from it all will go to the four brothers" (TS 1910, 10: 1537). The 1838 division directed by widow and stepmother Zheng was explicit to the point of discussing an adopted brother:

And as to the . . . piece of unirrigated land, as long as I am alive, it will be for my *yangshan* expenses, and when I die, it will be for my funeral expenses. If it is insufficient, the five brothers will pay equally; if there is a surplus, it will be rotated by the five brothers forever to pay for sacrifices. The brother who has been adopted out has no part in this, and no one may disagree. (TS 1910, 11: 1542)

In 1868 when widow Jian, née Huang, divided the household property among her three sons, she kept two *jia* of land and a shop as her *yanglaodi.* The final disposition was to be as follows: "Mother's *yangshan* land and shop, in the days when mother is more than one hundred years old, after taking some out to pay for the funeral, all that remains will be kept jointly and rotated by the three branches" (TS 1910, 41:1604).

Not all families kept the *yanglaodi* under joint ownership following the deaths of the parents, however. Some, such as the Wu family who divided in 1893, opted to leave the final decision on the *yanglaodi* for a later time:

> The piece of land that we bought from Han Ganyu will be stepmother's *yangshan*. . . . Each year we pay 7.7 *shi* of *dazu* and receive forty *shi* of *xiaozu*. It will be for mother's living expenses and may not be selfishly sold by either branch. One hundred years from now, it may be made joint [property] or may be divided equally. (TS 1910, 45:1613)

A few others divided it up after the parents' deaths.

> We received the property and debts that had been taken by father as his *yanglao* support. We originally desired to rotate it among the three branches, but after a time the children and grandchildren became too numerous, and we feared there might be disputes. So we are now inviting relatives to take the *yanglao* property and debts noted in the household division document and, after first extracting enough for father's funeral expenses, to divide the rest into three equal shares, burn incense to announce this to the ancestors, and draw lots to settle the question. (TS 1910, 44:1609)

Of thirty-nine Qing Taiwan household division documents that contain a trust for *yanglao* support of aged parents, seventeen specify how the property is to be used after the parents die. Of these, thirteen mandate continued joint ownership, while four mandate equal division. So by a ratio of roughly three to one, lineage-oriented household divisions tended to keep *yanglaodi* as joint property sacrificial trusts after the deaths of the parents.

In addition to sacrificial trusts and *yanglaodi* set-asides, many families also chose to use a third type of property trust, referred to simply as joint *(gong)* property. In this type, which I have labeled the common trust, the proceeds from the property went equally to the brothers' families simply as income and were not tied to any sacrificial, parental, or other responsibility. Some of these common trusts were of valued property such as irrigated land.

In 1838 a four-way division left two plots of land as joint property to be used to pay joint expenses, and "after taking out expenses, each year's rental income and interest will be divided into four equal shares. Four record books will be drawn up, and each transaction will be written in clear detail" (TWGS 1, 9:830). In the Chen family division of 1854, the two heirs had three sources of rental income—two plots of irrigated land and one set of water rights—that they opted to maintain jointly. The rental income was to be divided in half each year (Okamatsu 1971:84–85). In one four-way division in 1868, the two brothers and two nephews agreed to allocate one piece of irrigated land, two bamboo groves, a fish pond, and a vegetable garden as joint property (TS 1910, 8:1532). In the Yang family division of 1897, the two brothers stipulated that at least eleven plots of land were to be jointly owned. The income "of the common irrigated and unirrigated land will be stored up to pay for fourth sister's wedding, and after that is cleared up, it will be rotated between [brothers] one and two" (TS 1910, 62:1644).

In other common property trusts, the property was of lesser market value. In 1773, when the Lin family divided, they had two plots of land that had been flooded, the first being 1.4 *jia* in size. The brothers opted to leave both plots as joint property to be jointly cultivated (TS 1910, 52:1626). And in the 1782 Su family division, one piece of mountain land was reserved so that "hereafter the three branches can forever jointly use it to graze water buffalo" (TS 1910, 16:1557). In the Zhang family division of 1843, the family earmarked two tracts of uncultivated hill land. If at some future date a family member wished to plant orchard crops, he was required to inform the other branches of the family; if he wished to plant grain crops, he could do so and reap the harvest individually (TS 1910, 48:1620). In 1880 two Lin brothers opted to leave their betelnut grove as jointly owned property (TS 1910, 51:1624). And in a three-way division in 1883, two brothers and a nephew agreed to retain one bamboo grove, three unspecified trees, a longan tree, and a hillside shack as common property (TS 1910, 50:1623).

In sum, the establishment of jointly owned trusts solely for purposes of use or income was a frequent occurrence in Taiwan's lineage-oriented household division. Of the seventy-five documents, twenty-six (35 percent) contain this type of trust.

At the point of household division, the tradition of employing trusts and set-asides presented yet another problem for families. The members had to decide how to manage or divide trusts that had been established in previous generations and were therefore already jointly owned. The 1886 Li family division illustrates one manner of handling old trusts. It also demonstrates how rapidly these property rights could become complex and attenuated. Father Li was dead, and he had six sons, four by his wife and two by his concubine. In previous generations, two plots of land had been entrusted for sacrifices to specific ancestors. Management, including payment of taxes, was rotated each year. Father Li's was thus one of at least two branches involved in the rotation, but father Li's branch was now dividing into six new branches. It was decided that, in relationship to this sacrificial trust, "when it is the year of our branch's turn, our six shares will do it in turn." Therefore, assuming father Li had had only one brother and that the trust was established when father Li and his brother divided, the situation would be as follows: father Li's eldest son, Long, would manage the sacrificial responsibilities in the first year; second son Feng in the third year; third son Jin in the fifth year; and so on. Each brother would be responsible every twelve years. But this is just the simplest possible pattern. If we assume that father Li had had more than one brother or that the trusts had been established in an earlier generation, we could expand the pattern geometrically and make each brother responsible every twenty-four or thirty-six years, perhaps only once or twice in a lifetime (TS 1910, 6:1524).

In the *yizhu* document drawn up in 1898, the Chen family had several joint properties inherited from previous generations, and they opted for a management pattern similar to the Lis' above. The trusts were covered with a clause that read: "No matter from which generation the joint property came, and no matter whether it has rent or not, it will be rotated by each branch, on the basis of seniority" (TS 1910, 47:1617).

As opposed to rotation, some families decided to fulfill trust-related responsibilities jointly. In a six-way division orchestrated by widow Wang in 1826, the family had to decide what to do with their rights to a sacrificial trust of unirrigated land established by the father and his brothers in the previous generation. This land rotated among the father and his brothers. Now that the father was dead and his six sons were dividing, they decided to fulfill this responsibility jointly when their turn came around (TS 1910, 10:1537). In a four-way division in 1861, the heirs had inherited one plot of sacrificial trust land dedicated to a specific uncle. They decided to maintain the plot under joint ownership and management (TS 1910, 14:1550). In the Lin family division of 1884, the family was responsible for two rotational sacrifices. They decided that, in the years that they were responsible, "all three branches must go together to the land to collect [the rent from the tenant] and pay [for the sacrifices], and if there is any surplus, it will be divided equally among the three branches" (TS 1910, 69:1657).

Thus Taiwanese families used a variety of set-aside and trust strategies, both symbolic and economic, to strengthen agnatic ties in the postdivision period. As several household documents state, such strategies were an attempt to inculcate the attitude that "although we divide the hearth, we should not divide the heart" (TS 1910, 63: 1645). And, while the evidence is strongest for Taiwan, the data in Table 10 suggest strongly that the lineage orientation was common in Fujian, Anhui, Zhejiang, and by implication throughout South China.

The Zhejiang Eldest Son Orientation

Household division practices in the hills of southwest Zhejiang seem to have incorporated elements of the strategies in Taiwan and Fujian.[4] On closer inspection, however, the thirteen extant division documents from this region suggest that Zhejiang fell roughly halfway between the Taiwan lineage orientation and the North China family orientation but had the almost unique practice of often providing some extra property for the eldest son. For these reasons I have labeled the inheritance pattern of Zhejiang the eldest son orientation.

Of the thirteen documents, four set aside *yanglao* property for aged parents and three set aside property to cover marriage expenses of unmarried brothers. Five set aside property for the eldest grandson and four set aside property for the eldest son, with three of these families setting aside some property for both. Sacrificial trusts are established in three cases; a common trust is mentioned twice. There are even two mentions of educational trusts (ZPM:1–15).

One educational trust is instructive. In a 1752 division among four sons, each received several plots of land totaling approximately nineteen *mu*. The division document further set aside eight varied plots of land, all of which were rented out and from which the family derived rents in grain. This income was, in effect, a special gift to be spent on the education of one son, Shixue. This income was in addition to his nineteen *mu,* and it was to support his study. If he did not take the *xiucai* examination, he would lose the income, and it would be divided equally among the four brothers. This trust differed from those of the Fujian gentry, which were designed as a permanent aid to an entire growing lineage. (See the discussion of the Fujian gentry below.) Here one family was attempting to get a particular brother into the gentry class, and if he failed, the income would be divided equally. In the final analysis, this strategy was more akin to the family orientation in North China (ZPM:8).

The use of set-asides and trusts suggests both similarities and differences when compared to the Taiwan lineage orientation. According to Table 10, sacrificial trusts are used in 53 percent of Taiwan divisions, as opposed to 38 percent in Zhejiang. Common trusts are mentioned 35 percent of the time in Taiwan and only 23 percent of the time in Zhejiang. The eldest grandson receives his portion in 57 percent of the Taiwan divisions and in 38 percent of those in Zhejiang. In the most striking contrast, the eldest son portion is never used in Taiwan but is used in 31 percent of the Zhejiang divisions. Thus the defining qualities of the lineage orientation—the use of the sacrificial trusts, the common trust, and the eldest grandson portion —are only half as evident in the mountains of southwest Zhejiang, suggesting that the lineage-building strategy was somewhat stronger than in North China but weaker than in Taiwan.

The Fujian Gentry and the Education Orientation

The province of Fujian lies across the Taiwan strait from the island of Taiwan, and most of the Han Chinese immigrants that settled Taiwan came from Fujian. Therefore, it is not surprising that the Taiwanese lineage orientation was practiced in Fujian; indeed it most likely had its roots there. Sixty-two percent of Fujian families used sacrificial trusts, 38 percent used common trusts, and 24 percent used the eldest grandson portion, percentages roughly the same as in Taiwan.

The evidence from Fujian is striking, however, not in its lineage orientation, but in that some of the division documents use a strategy of establishing trusts for the purposes of fostering education and examination success. These documents allow a glimpse into the educational strategy employed by one part of the Fujian elite for purposes of attaining and retaining the coveted gentry social status.

In 1809, for instance, the Ouyang family of Taining, Fujian, divided their household. Of the three original brothers, the second and third had died, but they were survived by their widows and children. Of the total family income of 666.1 *shi,* 12.3 was set aside for the marriage expenses of an unnamed grandson, 52.2 for sacrifices, eighty for *yanglao* support, and fifty for education. The various set-asides and trusts thus totaled 194.5 *shi,* or almost 30 percent of the family's income. Each new individual family received 157.2 *shi* and twenty-four rooms of housing.

But beyond the economic fundamentals of the division, the division document contains a brief family history and the details of how the educational trust was to be administered. Since the time grandfather Ouyang had emigrated from Quanzhou to Taining, the family had managed to buy enough land to pay taxes in the area and thus to qualify for admission to the Qing state's civil service examination system. They owned sufficient property to guarantee family members enough to eat, and the elder generation was becoming concerned that the younger members would not take education seriously. It was decided, therefore, that the fifty-*shi* education trust would go the family member or members who passed the first level, *xiucai,* in either the civil or the military examination system. This income was designed to support them in their quest to reach the next two levels of the system, the *juren* and the *jinshi.* If a family member passed one of these higher-level exams, he received the entire fifty *shi* for that year. If several passed in one year, they each received the fifty *shi* over the next few years in rotation. If the successful members became too numerous and the rotation became too extended, they simply would begin to divide the income among all eligible family scholars. If a family member purchased a degree, he was not eligible for the income. And if a successful scholar actually took office in the civil service, he too was no longer eligible, most likely because his income while in office was deemed more than sufficient (ZZM:3).

The Yang family established an even more elaborate system to encourage education and examination success.[5] One trust of forty-nine plots of land and five shops netted the family 18.6 *shi* and 26,000 *wen* in rents. This income was to be awarded to those who achieved success in the examinations: one year's income for a *xiucai,* two years' for a *juren,* and six years' for a *jinshi.* The family also had a library-academy, which had thirteen plots of land attached to it and generated 15.6 *shi* and 10,000 *wen* of income. The academy was to be owned jointly, and the eight brothers were to rotate management. Lastly, the family allocated 10,000 *wen* of annual income from a shop to fund travel to and from the examinations. Ten thousand *wen* went to those who attended the annual *xiucai* examination, 10,000 *wen* for a prefectural examination, and 40,000 *wen* for the triennial *juren* examination (ZZM:19).

Even as late as 1904, when the Qing examination system was well on its way to oblivion, another Fujian family with well over 52,000 *jin* of grain income allocated 2,000 *jin* for those who passed the *xiucai* examination and needed travel money for the *juren* examination (DW:1).

An eloquent explanation of the rationale for the educational trust is found in the Han family contract of 1797 from Tongan, Fujian. Father Han had just died, and of his *yanglao* set-aside of 40,000 *jin,* 29,500 had been spent on his funeral. The family decided to take the remaining 10,500 *jin* and establish the "Nimble Memory" *(jieji)* educational trust. The contract reads as follows:

> We feel that study can raise social status and that such honors can bring glory to our ancestors; however, even though in each generation we have sons who dedicate themselves to study, the honors seem ever more distant, and we have only [lower-level scholars such as] *xiucai,* salaried *xiucai,* and senior *xiucai.*[6] What is the reason for this? It is not because our sons do not aspire, so perhaps it is the lack of travel money that denies them the chance to go and compete; it is not that they do not dedicate themselves to study, so perhaps it is because the families are too poor, and their desires become empty hopes. Thus their efforts produce small results, and the honors are few, and our social status declines. . . . The educational trust is designed to encourage the grandchildren to succeed [in the examinations] in order to become officials above and bring honor to our homes below. . . .
>
> As to the education trust, father died before he could complete its establishment. Now that father has passed on, we brothers wish to continue his hopes and works. So we have taken his *yanglao* prop-

erty of more than 40,000 *jin,* and after paying his funerary expenses, there remains . . . 10,500 *jin.* We have decided to establish a trust, named "Nimble Memory," . . . to continue father's desires and to inspire future generations.

Each person who obtains the *shengyuan* degree, be it civil or military, shall receive one share to use for the various expenses of the *juren* examination; those who obtain the *juren* degree shall receive two shares to use for the expenses associated with the capital examination; those who obtain the *jinshi* degree shall receive three shares to use for the expenses associated with the palace examination. . . .

A civil and military *shengyuan* who tries the *juren* examination gets one share per year to pay expenses. He shall receive it from the year that he passes the examination until the year that he dies. Each year [the division of the income] depends on how many *shengyuan* there are: if there are many, then divide it into many equal shares; if there are few, then divide it into few equal shares. . . .

If a man passes the civil or military *juren* examination, then the trust will stop payment for one year, and the income will go to him alone to fund his expenses related to the Preliminary and Capital Examinations, after which payment to the *shengyuan* shall resume. The *juren* shall receive two shares a year until the year that he dies.

At the point a man passes the civil or military *jinshi* and he wishes to try the Palace Examination, the trust shall stop payment [to the *shengyuan* and *juren*] for two years, and the income shall go to said *jinshi* to pay for the expenses associated with the Hanlin Academy Examination and the Palace Examination, after which payment to the *shengyuan* and *juren* shall begin again. A *jinshi* shall receive three shares per year until the year that he dies. (TS 1910, 76:1670)

These education trusts have at least several elements in common. Perhaps most striking, nothing is allocated to fund the years of initial study necessary to achieve success at the first, *xiucai,* level. The individual families were apparently required to fund this study independently. The trusts were designed as incentives to, first, reward success at the *xiucai* level and, second, facilitate and reward success at higher levels. Once a man became a *xiucai,* he could then use the added income to help with the study, travel, and gifts necessary to climb what Ho Ping-ti has called the educational "ladder of success" (1962). At the *juren* level his income from the trust increased, and at the *jin-shi* level it increased once again. Thus the incentives enticed scholars to strive for the highest degrees and rewarded them for each added success. They could receive this income for their entire lives but could not pass it on to their children when they died. Thus the educational orientation was a strategy adopted by gentry families to maintain both gentry status and the implied dominance in local society.

The Huizhou Merchant Phased Division Orientation

The area of Huizhou in Anhui province stands out in the documents because of a practice that occurs infrequently in other areas but is common there. This is the practice of dividing family property in a phased manner over time, rather than all at once, and it emerges in fourteen of thirty-six documents (39 percent) from the Huizhou area. A simple example of phased division is the Wang family division of 1865. In that year the family divided their land but kept the housing in common. Three years later, in 1868, they divided the housing, but kept the temples that they owned under common ownership (JJS:227). In 1826, a wealthy Huizhou family divided their rice and dry land into six shares for six sons but kept their housing, ancestral halls, lineage lands, sacrificial lands, and two shops in the city under joint ownership (JJS:590).

In 1825 the Wu family divided their property. The Wus were a moneylending family, and the three-way division netted a nephew and two brothers loan contracts worth about 2,385.5 taels of silver each. Twenty-one contracts were kept in common, and the business itself was not divided (JJS:287).

In a 1794 division, surviving concubine née Sun orchestrated the division of her wealthy pawnshop-owning family. The family owned pawnshops in two areas but lived in Huizhou, so the actual division was done by their hired manager, Jin Douxian. The pawnshops themselves were not divided and would remain under Jin's management. Each of the three branches received an extended list of the items that had been pawned but never reclaimed: jade hairpins, gold rings, pearls of various sizes, pearl jewelry, pearl and silver hat pins, jewelry boxes, jade items (dogs, people, Buddhas, bowls), ivory chopsticks, silver inlaid tea and wine cups—the list goes on for well over a hundred pages. The family was in effect dividing the profits but not the business (JJS:282).

The most illustrative of the phased division strategy was the Chen family division that took place first in 1725. Father Chen had had a checkered history of alternating success and failure in iron and paper business ventures but had finally, after twenty years of effort, established a very successful cloth business located in Suzhou. Most of the family still lived in Huizhou, however. The Suzhou business was composed of five cloth shops that used the same name and a dye works that they owned in order to make sure that they produced only high-quality cloth. The business was worth 26,970.8 taels of silver, and as father Chen had nine sons by two wives, there were now nine branches in the Chen family. After subtracting for *yangshan* support, dowries, and marriage expenses, each branch received housing, land, and 2,807 taels. They did not receive the silver in cash, however, and took instead the profits based on their ownership share. Thus the business remained intact, and the branches lived off the profits. Their income was not limited to the Suzhou business, however, as they owned and rented out at least fifty-six plots of land in Huizhou, using the income for consumption and sacrificial purposes.

Further, each member of the family who dedicated himself to study would receive twenty-four taels annually, as long as he took an examination each year. One of the family scholars' crucial jobs was to represent the family in case of local lawsuits. Anyone who bought a degree would have his stipend terminated. Father Chen further mandated that most of the family continue to reside in Huizhou, in order to maintain a frugal and responsible lifestyle, and that the sons had to marry local girls, rather than Suzhou girls, because of the latter's proclivity for extravagant lifestyles.

By 1756 the family had grown in number, and the business had appreciated in value by about 18,000 taels. These new conditions demanded adjustments in ownership and management. Father Chen's surviving widow orchestrated a redivision that accomplished two things: it kept the business intact, and it turned over the management of the business to the eldest brother for five years. The 18,000 taels of increased value was deemed a loan to the eldest brother, for which he would pay 1.2 percent interest per month, to be divided between the nine branches. The branches now lived off this interest income, rather than the profits as before. If, at the end of the five-year term, another branch wished to take over management, such a change was possible but had to be agreeable to all (JJS:117).

By this point, the Suzhou business had been in existence for sixty years and had passed though two household divisions. While the family's land and housing had been divided, their most profitable possession—the Suzhou dye works and cloth shops—had survived intact. Thus by using the phased division strategy and keeping businesses intact, the Chens maintained their wealth and power over several if not many generations. In this way they could protect the increasing value of their estate from the inevitable disruption and downward mobility associated with repeated household division.

In sum, the Huizhou merchants' phased division orientation was characterized by the division of land, housing, and other assets over a period of time, rather than all at once. It also included a strong tendency to maintain over time their commercial, moneylending, or pawnshop capital, allowing their businesses to grow while adjusting to different types of management as the need arose and distributing only profits or interest to the branches of the family.

The Charitable Estate Orientation

From the time that Denis Twitchett wrote his seminal article on the Fan clan's charitable estate, interest in such estates has remained high, though extensive research into the topic has yet to be done (Twitchett 1959).[7] The connection between household division and charitable estates seems, at first glance, to be an obvious one. The land or property set aside for charitable purposes had to be extracted from the family estate, and this might well be done at household division time. But, unfortunately, there are almost no extant household division documents from the Lower Yangzi Delta, where such estates were most common. Thus it is impossible to test for the frequency of the use of charitable estates at household division time. Nevertheless, there are a large number of lineage genealogies from the Lower Yangzi, as well as other areas, and these can be used as a source for information on charitable estates. These records do suggest a connection to household division, and they reveal a wide variety of practices associated with such estates.

One striking example comes from Guizhou province during the Jiaqing period (1796–1820). In this case, father Zhou established a charitable estate that was in many ways similar to Fan Zhongyan's original model: the purpose was to feed every member of his family, regardless of need. Each person was allowed to take food grain, three *shi* for those sixteen *sui* and older, 1.5 *shi* for those younger. He argued that, in this way, those with ability could emerge, and those who lacked ability would have survival insurance. At the time of writing, the estate had been in place for fifty years. Some land was also set aside to fund education and the publication of the lineage genealogy (*Zhoushi fangpu* 1924:32).

Another example, this one from the salt fields of southern Sichuan, had a direct connection to household division. The Wang family divided into three branches in 1835, setting aside 150 *mu* of land and a little more than ten salt wells to fund sacrifices. In the years that followed, one salt well became so profitable that the income was sufficient to buy six hundred *mu* of land and twenty more salt wells. This property came to 46,890 taels in value, with 6,000 taels in annual income.

In 1877 the family asked the government to declare the property a legal charitable estate, and the government agreed. Governmental agreement to recognize a charitable estate legally was a difficult and time-consuming process, but once the family managed to clear all the bureaucratic hurdles, the estate became tax-exempt (Twitchett 1959). This tax-free income was used to build a school and hire a teacher, and to fund sacrifices, funerals, marriages, *yangshan* expenses, and orphan support. The money could also be used to help those outside of the three original branches to take examinations. Any extra was to help in time of natural disasters (*Ziliujing Zhenzhushan Wangshi baoshanci sixiu jiapu* 1911, juan 12:80–81).

Another charitable estate that had a direct relationship to house-hold division was established by the Wu lineage from the Suzhou area. In 1602 father Wu divided his land among his children but was able to extract six hundred *mu* to establish a charitable estate. The income from the first two hundred *mu* was to go to pay taxes and corvée labor responsibilities, fifty *mu* was to cover sacrifices, fifty to take care of the aged, fifty for marriage expenses, fifty for funerals, one hundred for education, and one hundred for natural disasters.

The two hundred *mu* to cover taxes was so large because the family was a *lizhang*, a position in the Ming dynasty taxation system that imposed onerous expenses for payment and delivery of taxes.

For the elderly, defined as those sixty *sui* and older, three *shi* of grain annually was given in order "to buy meat." At seventy, four *shi* was given to "buy clothing." If the support for the elderly was unnecessary, the grain could go toward lineage or educational responsibilities. A son's marriage was awarded four *shi;* a daughter's dowry received two; a funeral received four. The education money was to hire a teacher and to reward those who attained the *xiucai, juren,* or *jinshi* level. The money for natural disasters was justified because, on average, there were problems with the harvest three times in ten years (*Wushi zhipu,* juan 12:3).

In the Ma lineage of Kunshan, Jiangsu province, a charitable estate was established in the late Qing and continued into the Republican era. Five hundred *mu* was entrusted, and the Qing state gave its approval, thus removing the land from the tax rolls. The first priority for the income was to fund sacrifices to the ancestors; the second was for various charitable tasks; and the third was to fund the maintenance of the lineage's several ancestral halls. The charitable payments would go to the aged without means of support; to poor children from the time they were four *sui:* boys until they were seventeen *sui* and able to support themselves, girls until they were married out; to people with physical disabilities and without support; for disasters such as fire and theft; for sons' marriages and daughters' dowries, funded at equal levels; and for a deceased lineage member's funeral expenses (*Kunshan Mashi zupu,* juan 5:25).

Another Jiangsu charitable estate displayed the same variety of characteristics. In 1887 Lu Yingchang, following his father's *yizhu,* set aside just over one thousand *mu* of land for charity and made an announcement to the government, though it is not clear if the estate gained tax-exempt status. According to the rules, payment would go for maintenance of ancestral halls, sacrificial expenses, charity, and taxes. The charitable expenses would go to a variety of people. The aged who lacked family support, starting at fifty *sui,* would receive three *dou* of grain each month, increasing to four *dou* at seventy *sui,* six *dou* at eighty, and eight *dou* at one hundred. Orphans received one *dou* from birth to age ten *sui,* 1.5 *dou* from eleven to fifteen, 2.1 *dou* from sixteen to twenty, and nothing after that. Widows received three *dou* per month at any age. Daughters who stayed home to care for aged parents received the same as widows; daughters who married out into poor families could also receive the same as a widow.

Members with physical disabilities received substantial support, ranging from one to four *dou* per month based on age. The unemployed received some support as well: four *dou* per year for a single person, eight *dou* per year for a family. Every third year one set of winter clothing was supplied to all those receiving aid. A son's marriage expenses were covered at 12,000 coppers, a daughter's dowry at 8,000. A detailed scale of payments was made to those who wished to study and had success in the examinations (*Pingyuan zongpu* 1906, juan 20:14–24).

Not all charitable estates were based on land and rental income. In 1845, a member of the Guo lineage in Hunan left an *yizhu* instructing his son to establish a charitable estate. At the time he counted about one hundred qualified lineage members in need of aid. The son took one thousand taels of silver and lent them out at interest. The interest was used to aid those three to ten *sui* and those fifty *sui* and older. The young received one-half *sheng* of grain a day, while the elderly received one *sheng* per day. Money was also provided for winter clothing.

Another charitable estate, this one in Zhejiang, was established around 1889, when Zhou Changchi died heirless. He willed 520.3 *mu* of land to his ancestral hall, but the lineage leaders apparently decided to give 40 percent of it to an appointed heir to conduct sacrifices to Changchi. The remaining 60 percent was made into a charitable estate. The income was to go to orphans, widows, the elderly, and for funerals. Families in difficulties who had just had their first child could also get one thousand coppers each month, provided the mother did not return to work (*Nanxun Zhoushi jiapu* 1911, juan 5:2–7).

In summary, the strategy of establishing charitable estates, though practiced in many parts of China, was most common in the Lower Yangzi Delta provinces of Jiangsu and Zhejiang. The property was often willed by the use of an *yizhu* or extracted from the family estate at household division time. The income often went first to cover such expenses as taxes, sacrifices, and the maintenance of ancestral halls. Educational expenses were frequently covered, as were marriage and dowry expenses. The truly charitable aspect comprised support for the needy: orphans, widows, the handicapped, and the elderly.

The charitable estate orientation seems to have been designed, much like the lineage orientation of Taiwan, to buttress lineage strength. The sacrificial and ancestral hall expenses were designed to maintain the cultural capital of the lineage; the education expenses, to support success in the examination system and thereby bring honor and money into the lineage; the marriage and dowry expenses, to assure good marriage alliances for the lineage children; and the aid to the needy was a statement to the surrounding community that this lineage was rich enough to take care of its own poor.

A Summation

Thus, while the three rules of household division—support for parents, marriage expenses for unmarried siblings, and equal shares for all sons—acted as fundamental guidelines, the actual practice of household division did in fact allow for variations. Families could and did employ trusts and set-asides as strategies to pursue their interests, and when carried out over time, these variations became patterns or orientations typical of a region or a class.

The figures in Table 10 indicate that the lineage orientation, with its extensive use of trusts and set-asides, was strongest in Taiwan and Fujian but probably was common throughout South China. Fujian also shows a strong tendency toward the use of educational trusts by the wealthy. On the North China Plain, the family orientation, which shunned the use of trusts, was clearly dominant. The mountainous area in southwest Zhejiang seems to occupy a position halfway between the lineage and family orientations, with a striking emphasis on giving property to the first son. The Huizhou merchants practiced a phased division style, which allowed them to keep businesses intact over the generations. And a few families, particularly in the Lower Yangzi Delta, used charitable estates to buttress lineage strength, while simultaneously providing for a variety of purposes that ranged from simple support of widows and orphans to all-out cradle-to-grave support for all family members.

Chapter 9

Household Division and Society: Land, Orientations, and Social Mobility

T HE treatment of property during household division raises questions central to the functioning of China's economy and society. Because land was the most important means of production and because it was divided equally among the sons, it is first useful to ask, what were the effects of this inheritance regime on farming and land-ownership? Available evidence allows us to answer this question posed from three perspectives: Did China's peasants divide farms beyond the point necessary for survival of a single family? Did China's peasants fragment plots to the point of agricultural inefficiency? Did regional and class orientations significantly affect landholding patterns? A final related question we might ask is, how did the interaction of division, fragmentation, and regional or class orientation affect social mobility?[1]

Did Chinese Peasants Divide Land beyond Survival Level?

When household division occurred, there was an inevitable decline in farm size. As we have seen in Qing Taiwan and Republican North China, peasants divided both house and land into equal shares rather than giving all the property to one brother. By its very nature this system caused a diminution in the size of landholdings for each brother.

Philip Huang has shown that rich peasant and managerial landlord families could not avoid the downward mobility caused by household division. He writes of the Mantetsu villages:

> A family might in one generation move from family farming upward to managerial farming, but a single partition among two or more sons was apt to force each household back into family-farm status. That is why . . . few village "rich" were able to remain rich across several generations. Of the 19 households in the nine villages who could be clearly identified as rich in the 1890's, only three still had rich descendant households (a total of five) in the 1930's. (Philip Huang 1985:117)

This being the case for village rich, what happens if we focus lower on the economic scale? Was there a moment at which middle

Table 12
Land Division on the North China Plain

Date	Total *Mu*	Number of Brothers	Size of Each Brother's Share *(Mu)*
1908	17	2	9–8
1919	18	2	6.5–6.5*
	38	4	4–4–15–5
1940	39.5	3	11.5–11.5–12
1907	56.5	4	15–25.5–0–16
1873	72	3	27.5–32.5–12
1936	88.55	2	45–43.55
1925	89.5	2	43–46.5
1933	101	3	31.25–33.5–36.25
1911	125.5	3	18–19–18
1936	158.7	4	32.5–31.5–33.5–30
Total	804.25	32	Average share: 25

Source: KC.

* The sum of the brothers' share often does not equal the total number of *mu*, because land was first set aside for parental support and other responsibilities.

or poor peasants stopped dividing land because further division would decrease farm size to the point where it could no longer support a family? Table 12 summarizes the figures from the North China household division documents.

Regarding whether there was a line below which peasant families would not divide, Table 12 can be read in two ways, both leading to the same conclusion. First, consider the size of the farms, which ranged from as large as 158.7 *mu* to as small as seventeen *mu*. All were divided. Second, from the perspective of the brothers' shares, share size went down to as low as four or five *mu* in some cases and zero in one case. These data suggest strongly that on the North China Plain there was no minimal survival line at which peasants ceased dividing land.

Shifting to Qing Taiwan, the eight division documents represented in Table 13 contain figures precise enough to allow a calculation of the total amount of land the family owned and how it was divided. The evidence again suggests that families had no qualms about dividing beyond any hypothetical minimal level. Total farm size ranged

Table 13
Land Division in Qing Taiwan

Date	Total *Jia*	Number of Brothers	Size of Each Brother's Share (*Jia*)
1880	.55	2	.275–.275
1842	1.2	3	.3–.3–.3
1796	3.005	3	.5–.515–.515
1857	4.4	3	.33–.33–.33
1773	8.1	4	.55–.55–.55–.55
1868	14.9	3	4.45–1.9–1.9
1837	16.42	7	1.2–1.0–.95–.85–1.25–1.75–1.65
1816	28	3	4.6–5.4–9.6
Total	76.575	28	Average share: 2.73

Source: TS, TWGS.

from a mere .55 to twenty-eight *jia,* yet division was done equally. The brothers averaged only 2.73 *jia* per division. Finally, of twenty-eight heirs, only two received more than five *jia,* many receiving less than one *jia.* Again, there was no minimal farm size for family support beneath which families would not divide.

Did Chinese Peasants Fragment Plots?

Turning to the question of whether Chinese peasants divided individual plots of land to the point of agricultural inefficiency, the situation becomes more complex, because household division did not legally require plot fragmentation. Chinese peasant farms were seldom composed of one large contiguous plot of land. Most, if not all, were composed of several to many plots, scattered at various distances from the nucleated villages in which the families lived.

The Hou family of Houjiaying is a good example. The Hous owned a total of eighteen plots of land that totaled 85.5 *mu.* This scattered pattern of landownership meant that, at division time in 1936, they might have avoided fragmentation by dividing eighteen plots into two groups of nine. But the actual division of land between the two brothers, Yongqin and Yongjian, was done in the manner detailed in Table 14.

The division of the land is almost exactly equal numerically. The brothers divided the 85.5 *mu* into shares of 42 and 43.5 *mu.* But, beyond the division into roughly equal sums, they divided the land on a plot-by-plot basis. They began with a total of eighteen plots, and they chose to divide almost every plot into two equal pieces. As the chart shows, fourteen plots were clearly divided, two plots (numbers 2 and 7) were probably divided, while only two (numbers 14 and 18) were left intact. Thus eighteen plots became at least thirty-two and possibly thirty-four plots. While this pattern allowed for the equal division of the landed area, taking into account the special farming characteristics of each plot, it also caused plot fragmentation.

Such a pattern of plot division is evident in many other division documents. Of the thirteen North China household division documents that allow for a calculation, eleven families divided in the plot-splitting manner of the Hou family described above, while only two did not. The figures appear in Table 15. Table 15 suggests several conclusions. First, at household division time, roughly half of all plots,

Table 14
The Hou Family Division of Land in 1936

Yongjian		Yongqin	
Plot Number and Name	*Mu*	Plot Number and Name	*Mu*
1. jia xinan shangdi	3.5	1. jia xinandi	3.5
2. jia dongnan tudi	3	2. jia dongnan changlongdi	3 (?)
3. Lijia fendi	3	3. Lijia fendi	3
4. jia xiaofen shangdi	1.75	4. xiaofen shangdi	1.75
5. xiaogou dongdi	4	5. xiaogou dongdi	4
6. daoguangdi	4	6. daoguangdi	4
7. dairen tuodi	2.75	7. canren tuodi	2.75 (?)
8. gegoudi	1	8. gegoudi	1
9. xiao shulindi	3	9. xiao shulindi	3
10. caihuangdi	1.5	10. caihuangdi	1.5
11. Lanjia fenxidi	2	11. Lanjia fenxidi	2
12. Yejia fendi	2	12. Yejia fendi	2
13. youhuangdi	1	13. youhuangdi	1
14. Liujia fennanbei	1.5	14.	
15. Liujia fenbei	3.5	15. Liujia fenbeidi	3.5
16. shuikeng yaodao xidi	3	16. shuikeng yaodao dongdi	3
17. dahao shangyao-dao dongdi	1.5	17. dahao shangyao-dao dongdi	1.5
18.		18. shuikengdi	3
Totals	42.0		43.5

Source: KC 5.1:73.

Table 15
Fragmentation of Plots during Household Division

Date	Divided Plots			Undivided Plots		
	Plots	Total *Mu*	Average Size	Plots	Total *Mu*	Average Size
1873	1	40	40	1	2	2
1883	3	34	11.33	0		
1907	1	9.5	9.5	13	48	3.69
1908	3	17	5.67	0		
1911	8	60	7.5	18	58.5	3.25
1919	2	13	6.5	0		
1925	7	48.5	6.93	6	32.5	5.42
1928	11	225	20.45	5	20	4
1928	2	11.27	5.64	3	20	6.67
1933	4	52.5	13.1	10	48.5	4.85
1936	16	81	5.06	2	4.5	2.25
1936	10	85.5	8.55	11	42	3.82
1940	2	19	9.5	5	16	3.2
Total	70	696.27	9.95	74	292	3.95

Total plots: 144
Total *mu*: 988.27

Source: KC.

seventy of 144, were divided. Next, the probability of a plot's being divided varied with its size: the average divided plot was ten *mu* in size, while the average undivided plot was four *mu*. These figures suggest strongly that, while plots of any size could be divided, the peasants tended to divide large plots first and small plots later. This finding in turn suggests that, while peasants tried to avoid fragmenting plots to the point of inefficiency, plot splitting, as illustrated above by the division of plots even two *mu* in size by the Hou family, was indeed inevitable.

The precise point at which the division of a particular plot would render it inefficient was affected by a variety of variables, such as the family's size, structure, and consumption needs, the total amount of family land, the total number of plots composing the family's land, the size of each plot, the distance of the plots from the village, and the availability of sideline and wage labor opportunities. Thus, while there was a point at which a divided plot became too small or too distant to be worked efficiently, the determination is not possible given the available sources. It must suffice to say that such a point existed, yet the peasants divided beyond that point with regularity.

The relationship between China's inheritance regime, declining farm size, downward mobility, and peasant poverty has not gone unnoticed in the literature on China's peasant economy. In his classic study of Chinese agriculture in the early 1930s, John Lossing Buck argues specifically that Chinese farmers' low standard of living was directly related to farms and plots that were too small to be worked efficiently (1937a:267–288). While Buck did not see the inheritance regime as causing this state of affairs, Ramon Myers has argued that household division was indeed the cause of inefficiently small farms and plots. Myers demurs on the question of poverty, however, arguing that the inefficiencies so created could have been offset by "expanding farming knowledge and evolving new techniques" (1970: 159–166, 183). Finally, Philip Huang states that there was an "unequivocal correlation between poverty and the incidence of family division" (1985:304). Clearly, Buck and Huang are closer to the point: declining farm and plot size over time had a deleterious effect on the ability of a peasant family to work land efficiently. And though improved knowledge and techniques might have temporarily offset such declining efficiency, any permanent solution also had to resolve the problem of ever smaller farms and morcellated plots created by household division.

Household Division Orientations, Landownership Patterns, and Social Mobility

Given that household division had a deleterious effect on farm and plot size, the next logical question is, did the different household division orientations affect landownership patterns? The evidence suggests that orientations did indeed affect landownership and further that these orientations were designed to help offset the inevitable problems of declining farm size, smaller plots, downward mobility, and poverty associated with equal division.

The effects of orientations can be clearly seen in the relative amounts of jointly owned land in different parts of China. On the North China Plain there was little jointly owned land. What did exist was grave land on which families buried their dead, but in some places the grave land had arable land attached to it. The genesis of this land was often household division, as a talk with Du Xiang and Zhao Tingkui reveals.

> Q: Where did the lineage grave land come from?
> A: In the old days, at the point of household division, some land was set aside to start it. (KC 1:247B)

This land was managed by the lineage, and any sale or pawn had to be cleared by the entire lineage (KC 1:247B). In the case of the Li family, the family divided their grave land at household division time. One branch then pawned out their portion out of poverty, but the lineage members redeemed it. The land was then deemed to be jointly owned (KC 1:258C). Thus the North China peasants understood the concept of jointly owned land and applied it in a few instances. But the more common practice of dividing all land at household division time kept the total amount of jointly owned land down to minuscule proportions. Table 16 gives some sense of how much

Table 16
Jointly Owned Land in Four North China Villages

Village	Total Cultivated Land *(mu)*	Total Grave and Lineage Land *(mu)*	Percentage
Shajing	1,182	44.5	4
Houjiaying	2,979	0	0
Houxiazhai	2,530	15	0.6
Lengshuigou	4,200	6.4	0.2

Sources: Philip Huang 1985:74–75; KC 1:247A–B; 4:202B, 216B–C, 419A, 435C, 452C; 5:67C.

land was jointly owned on the North China Plain, the totals ranging from a low of zero to a high of 4 percent.

In Fujian province, by contrast, the percentage of jointly owned land was higher by far. The lineage orientation of Fujian mirrored that of Taiwan, where at household division time considerable amounts of land were set aside in trusts. Table 10 confirms the frequent use of set-asides and trusts in Fujian.

But land set-asides and trusts created at household division time did not always survive over the generations. Families could and often did divide trusts after a period of joint ownership. Thus we read of one division of inherited lineage land that was established as a trust in 1795 but divided in 1861: "As I am now becoming old and I wish to retire, I have asked the relatives and lineage head to discuss late grandfather's bequeathed property and irrigated and mountain lands, and to divide them according to the old household division contract, and each will control his own" (TS 1910, 14:1549).

While trust land could be divided into family property, it was also possible for trust managers to acquire land and add it to lineage trusts over time (Zhang Youyi 1984). Commonly owned trusts were seldom static over time. They were constantly being established, expanded, divided, and dismantled, but the evidence demonstrates that the amount of trust land remained high in South China.

To get a sense of the amount of trust land in existence at one time, it is necessary to view such lands in the context of all arable land in a given area. One such study was conducted in May 1930 by the young Mao Zedong in the area of Xunwu in southeast Jiangxi, close to the Fujian and Guangdong borders. Mao estimated that fully 40 percent of the land in the area was in trusts, with ancestral trusts making up 60 percent of that total, religious trusts 20 percent, administrative and educational trusts 10 percent, and public works trusts 10 percent. The genesis of the ancestral trusts was the combination of *yangshan* set-asides and sacrificial trusts described in Chapter 8 (Mao 1990:122–132).

An even more comprehensive picture can be derived from the post-1949 Chinese-government-sponsored village investigations leading up to land reform in Fujian. The investigators covered ten Fujian counties, and their data provide a good view of the situation in that province in about 1951. The numbers are presented in Table 17.

The effects of the lineage orientation are striking. The percentage

Table 17
Jointly Owned Land in Fujian Province

Location	Trust Land as a Percentage of All Land	Total Trust Land (mu)	Lineage Land		Education Trust Land		Other[a]	
			mu	%	mu	%	mu	%
Gutian county								
Qibao	76	4,545	3,986	88	365	6	295	6
Luohua	58	2,445	2,029	83	139	6	278	11
Guoqi	61	1,444	1,409	98	0	0	35	2
Jianyang county								
Yingqian	37	1,051	954	91	80	8	18	2
Jian'ou county								
Songshan	19	195	195	100	0	0	0	
Fuzhou suburbs	8–14[b]							
Jiayang		112	22	100	0	0	0	0
Hutang		55	52	93	0	0	4	7
Qikou		53	19	36	0	0	34	64
Kuiqi		75	60	80	0	0	15	20
Minhou county								
Changbing		379	373	98	6	2	0	0
Fuqing county								
Wuyu	9	120	106	88	11	9	3	3

Putian county							
Huaxi	22	385	232	60	126	33	27	7
Jinjiang county							
Hanban	32	517	517	100	0	0	0	0
Yongding county							
Zhongchuan	70	1,891	1,822	96	70	4	0	0
Xihu	60	324	223	69	0	0	102	31
Yong'an county							
Jishan		1,534	,3121	86	0	0	221	14
Total		15,127	13,400	89	696	5	1,030	7

Source: Huadong junzheng weiyuanhui 1952:109–110.

Note: Some figures, such as those for Minhou and Yong'an, are incomplete. Figures in the original table were calculated to tenths and hundredths of a *mu*. To save space and to simplify matters, I have rounded off to the nearest *mu*, though this means some totals will be incorrect by one mu or 1 percent.

[a] Includes temple and *huiguan* lands. *Huiguan* were halls established by guild, lineage, or locality groups to aid members who were traveling through, residing temporarily, or immigrating.

[b] These figures are for eight villages in the Fuzhou suburbs, but subtotals are not assigned to the individual villages.

of trust land varied in different parts of the province: in Qibao fully 76 percent of the land was jointly owned, while in the Fuzhou area the total dropped as low as 8 percent. For those areas where the calculation can be made, arable land totaled 27,052 *mu,* and jointly owned land totaled 13,214 *mu,* fully 49 percent of all arable land. The authors of the investigation speculated on the pattern: "It can be stated that in Northern and Western Fujian, they [the jointly owned lands] comprise over 50 percent of the land, while on coastal areas they comprise 20 to 30 percent" (Huadong junzheng weiyuanhui 1952:109). Thus, in the more rugged and remote areas, the percentage of jointly held land was higher, while in the more accessible coastal areas, the percentage dropped. This pattern suggests that the extra-agricultural and market opportunities available to coastal inhabitants made the use of jointly owned land less of an economic necessity.

The investigators further speculated on the origins of this vast amount of trust land.

> From what we have found, most people feel that the reason for the emergence of lineage land is that when officials, merchants, and landlords are alive, they set aside *yanglaodi.* After they die, their heirs maintain it as sacrificial land, and after one or two generations it becomes lineage land. . . . But not only do the landlord and rich peasant classes set aside lineage land, so too do some middle and poor peasants. . . .
>
> As to the portion of land taken out by landlords as lineage land, of course, some is to be used for sacrificial purposes after death, but most important is that they fear their sons and grandsons will lose all the property. They establish lineage land so that the land they own can be maintained a little more securely. Middle and poor peasants do so in part because of the influence of sacrificial ideology, but much more often because their land is so limited. If they divide the land among their heirs, it will not only be insufficient to support a livelihood, but will also result in the land becoming too morcellated and inefficient to cultivate. But using the lineage trust method to maintain [the land] allows the heirs to use the land in a more efficacious manner. (Huadong junzheng weiyuanhui 1952:111)

Thus, for both rich and poor, joint ownership of land in a lineage trust made sense, though for different purposes. For the rich it guaranteed sacrifices after death, protected wealth from the destructive effects of household division, and shielded property from the serious threat of a wastrel son. For the poor, the lineage trust kept the family land from shrinking beneath a minimal size necessary for efficient work. One pattern for poor people was for the brothers to work the land in rotation, with the nonworking brothers in a given year finding income from other sources. Thus, while the lineage trust strategy did not solve the problems of too little land among poor families, it could delay the threat of plot splitting and morcellation posed by household division. By opting for a common trust, the household could divide but avoid either selling off the land or dividing it to the point of inefficiency.

Thus most lineage and trust land had its origins in the lineage orientation of household division. The lineage orientation was an extremely popular household division strategy in Taiwan and Fujian, and as a consequence, jointly held property averaged about 50 percent for Fujian and reached as high as 76 percent of the available land in some areas.

The economic consequences of the Fujian gentry's education orientation were not quite as striking as those of the lineage orientation. As the examples in Chapter 8 suggest, only wealthy families established such trusts, and the size of the property so dedicated was generally a small portion of total family property. As a result, only 5 to 6 percent of Fujian's trust land was in educational trusts as of 1951. This proportion suggests that educational trust land, while crucial to gentry class longevity, never became a major economic phenomenon in Fujian as a whole and most likely constituted only 2 to 3 percent of all land.

If the focus is on land, the same general conclusions can be applied to the Huizhou merchants and the phased division orientation. Though the use of sacrificial trusts was lower than in Fujian, the use of common trusts was significantly higher (see Table 10). Thus the total amount of land owned in all trusts might have been high as well. But because the merchants' main means of production were shops and commercial ventures, the conclusions relating to social mobility differ. The evidence suggests strongly that these families had found a way to maintain key commercial property intact over generations and thus maintain their wealth and class status as well.

The evidence on the charitable estate orientation, though admittedly slim, suggests that little of the total amount of arable land was dedicated to such purposes. The evidence further suggests that the estates were not designed to stop the downward mobility occasioned by household division. In fact, the estates had as a first priority the strengthening of the lineage's cultural capital. Only second came a concern for the poor, and their function in this respect is best viewed as an attempt to ameliorate the inevitable poverty caused by repeated household divisions, not to prevent it from happening in the first place.

To sum up, there were both similarities and differences in household division as it was practiced in different places and by different social classes. All families, rich or poor, North or South, were bound by the basic rules: support for aged parents, marriage expenses for unmarried siblings, and equal shares for all sons. The effects of this inheritance regime on farm size and plot size meant that, in each generation, families with two or more sons faced the necessity of dividing the family property. As they did so, farm size diminished, and the amount of diminution increased with each additional son. In terms of the fragmentation of land in North China, about one-half of all plots that contained 70 percent of the family land were fragmented. Though larger plots were divided before smaller plots, fragmentation generally continued to the point of inefficiency. As a rule for North and South China, both farm size and plot size tended to decline over time, and downward mobility was inevitable.

But under the three rules of household division, the use of set-asides and trusts allowed families to pursue specific interests and goals. On the North China Plain, peasants seldom used trusts, leaving the vast majority of land in family hands. In Fujian and Taiwan, wealthier families used trusts to minimize the effects of division, to avoid the disaster of the wastrel son, and to buttress lineage solidarity. Some gentry families used educational trusts to attempt to delay downward mobility and maintain their position and status over generations. Poor peasant families could use trust strategies to delay farm and plot division. These strategies led to the vast amounts of jointly owned land in Fujian and most likely in other parts of South China as well. The phased division practices of the Huizhou merchants, particularly the insulation of commercial capital from the effects of household division, allowed them to maintain their wealth over generations. Finally, the wealthy lineages of the Lower Yangzi

Delta established charitable estates to strengthen lineage power and care for their poor. Thus, while the rules were the same, strategies based on geographic location and class position could and did differ, and these differences over time had important consequences for economic structures, social structures, social mobility, and the quality of life of each family and individual.

Chapter 10

Conclusions and Speculations

I N the centuries prior to the Qing, Chinese inheritance law was not entirely static. As the dynasties came and went, inheritance law underwent changes in key areas of adoption, women's property rights, and perhaps the power of the will. But more important, the principle of equal division of property among all sons was the consistent legal principle guiding inheritance. Through an analysis of pre-Qing household division documents and legal cases, we can see that the basic principles of Chinese household division practices were three: living parents received support, unmarried siblings received marriage expenses or dowries, and all sons inherited equally.

For the Qing dynasty and the Republican period, this pattern remained intact. In the chapters of this book it has been possible to analyze the patterns regarding why, when, and how household division occurred. Household division happened because of the tensions inherent in the relationship between an expanding family and the property it possessed, and not because of community or legal pressures, or even necessarily the deaths of both parents. The tensions often centered on the per capita nature of daily consumption and the *per stirpes* nature of household division. These tensions were most often expressed as disputes between brothers, between sisters-in-law, and between parents and children. Although theoretically household division could take place at any point after the birth of two sons, it tended to occur after the marriage of the sons, yet before the deaths of both parents. This early timing of household division tended to keep family size small. When household division occurred, the process was composed of five stages that took from two days to two weeks. The process was firmly rooted in custom that legalized the proceedings and was family and community based with no state registration of the land and housing transactions involved in division.

In rare instances, however, household division disputes could become so severe that the family went to court to seek a resolution. And though Qing courts were used infrequently relative to the number of household divisions, China's historically large population naturally generated many such court cases. The Qing legal cases suggest that when adjudicating household division disputes, the magistrate used a civil law approach and used the Qing Code as a guide.

In an extended case study of household division in Qing Taiwan, earlier chapters of this book have described the rights of all individuals in the family at the point of household division. The case study has demonstrated that parents received support, unmarried siblings received marriage expenses, and all sons received equal shares of property. It has also described the common ways in which families divided property such as housing, land, rental income, pawned land, taxes, documents, and debts. The example from North China suggests the durability of the tradition, even in the face of the Republican revolution and its revolutionary legal changes regarding inheritance. It demonstrates that the household division process was fundamentally the same as it had been in Qing Taiwan. The two examples of Qing Taiwan and Republican North China suggest further that the priorities in household division went first to parents and then to any unmarried siblings' marriage costs and the brothers' equal shares.

Exceptions to the rules and strategic orientations within the rules also existed. The exceptions, such as special gifts and eldest son or grandson portions, were common in some parts of China, but they were not de facto attempts to avoid the rules of equal division. The orientations that varied by region and class were more significant, and families of certain regions and social classes could and did make use of property set-asides and trusts to pursue particular interests. Among North China peasants the predominant family orientation saw all property divided equally among the sons with little use of set-asides or trusts. In Taiwan and Fujian the lineage orientation predominated and was typified by the use of common ancestral halls, the eldest grandson portion, and the lineage trust. It is clear that

South China's lineage society owes its structure to inheritance strategies. Among wealthy Fujian families, there was a distinct tendency to use educational trusts to foster examination success. In Huizhou, the merchant families used a phased division orientation, combined with the protection of commercial capital, to maintain their social status over generations. And the great lineages of the Yangzi Delta often used charitable estates to strengthen lineage solidarity and care for their poor.

Finally, this book has argued that household division and its orientations had an impact on farm size, plot size, landholding patterns, and class structure. Household division meant inevitable declines in both farm and plot size as well as downward social mobility and poverty. Differences in orientations, such as the lineage orientation in South China, produced vast differences in landholding patterns, such as the 70 percent of lineage-owned land in some areas of Fujian. The orientations, both individually and in combination, could try to delay division and its attendant consequences or provide a safety net for those impoverished by division. The ability to avoid impoverishment was directly related to the family's wealth. The more wealthy had more options, but relatively few were completely immune from the downward mobility occasioned by equal division.

Household Division and Qing Social Structure

Given this analysis of household division, it might prove useful to speculate on its effects on Qing social structure and social mobility as a whole. One traditional view sees China as a relatively egalitarian society. Thomas Malthus emphasized the relationship between equal-male division and egalitarianism in his early treatise (Malthus [1914] 1982). Research from Stevan Harrell (1985), Lavely and Wong (1992), and others could be construed to support this view, particularly if the focus of analysis is on a class range from small landlord to poor peasant and includes the propensity for landlords and rich peasants to have more male children. Thus household division meant downward mobility for all, including and perhaps especially for the rich. The often-heard Chinese phrase *fu buguo san dai* (wealth never survives more than three generations) makes a concise summary. A focus on this leveling tendency is often combined with a view that Qing China had a market economy with a mix of economic opportunities for individuals. Add to this the argument of Ho Ping-ti (1962) that the Qing civil service examination system was open to almost all male members of society, and there emerges a view of Qing China as a society of relatively egalitarian wealth and equal opportunity to rise.

Needless to say, this view has not gone unchallenged. Chang Chung-li (1955), Ch'u T'ung-tsu (1961), and Joseph Esherick and Mary Rankin (1990) are just four of the noted scholars who have argued strenuously that Qing China was a seriously stratified society both economically and legally. While this study recognizes the leveling tendency emphasized by the egalitarian view, it strongly supports the latter view of stratification. The orientations used by the very wealthy were strategies available to delay and in a few cases completely offset the effects of division. The education-oriented gentry, the great lineages of South China, and the Huizhou merchants were able to use one or, more likely, a combination of strategies by which wealth could be maintained for more than three generations and perhaps for a century or more. The Wu family of Fujian, with their imperially sanctioned medicinal wafer, was a perfect example. A view that is limited to peasants or those of middling wealth alone probably does give the impression of leveling. But the truly rich had more options available to maintain their wealth and status over time, and they could be quite effective in doing so.

Qing Women's Property Rights

Another key issue in Chinese social-economic history is the property rights of women. Can we fairly say that women inherited, possessed, and managed property in traditional China? Following Jack Goody (1990), I propose to do this through a discussion of dowry, the conjugal fund, the daughter-in-law's continuing connection to her natal family, and widows' property.

As to dowry, the evidence demonstrates that funding for dowries was included in inheritance documents and suggests that dowry was held at roughly the same level of concern as brothers' marriage expenses and equal shares. In this sense, property did indeed devolve to daughters. But this fact should not imply that property devolved equally or that daughters' property rights were as strong as sons'. The amount of a daughter's direct dowry from her natal family was not guaranteed by law, and the few figures available in the sources do not allow for a determination of the amounts customarily provided. We do not know how much the daughter received relative to her brothers in different social classes and in different regions. Also an unmarried daughter did not sign the household division document and therefore had less power to affect the proceedings and defend her interests.

The evidence on women's individual, usually dowry-derived, property suggests that the property was hers, and she placed it into her and her husband's conjugal fund if and when she chose to do so. The dowry property of an incoming daughter-in-law did not go to the family head, usually her father-in-law, and it remained within her own conjugal unit. She could keep it for herself as individual property, or she could give it to her husband, in which case it became truly conjugal property and the basis of her future independent nuclear family. Thus women did control and guide individual property, though again the amount and its significance should not be exaggerated. While such property may have been extensive for the rich, the dearth of individual property in the Mantetsu villages suggests it was minimal for the masses of middle and poor peasants.

That married daughters received continued support from their natal families is confirmed by the evidence in two ways. First, the mother's brother was frequently called in to ensure fairness in the division, and he often signed the document as a witness. Also, the evidence from Fujian on the ceremonial offering of gifts by the families of the daughters-in-law confirms the existence of a continuing tie. The nature of the gifts, basically kitchen and household articles, could be seen as increasing that portion of the family property that was under her control.

But it was as widows that women had the strongest property rights. The household division documents are replete with evidence attesting to widow control over family property and the process of household division. While widow control was not guaranteed and management of family property could indeed pass to a widow's eldest son, that practice was by no means a universal, if even the general, rule. Many widows could and did manage family property, orchestrate household division, and manage their own *yangshan* property. And widows could and did defend their property in Qing courts.

In sum, the evidence demonstrates that property did devolve to women, and women did have control over individual, conjugal, and family property at various points in the family cycle. But the existence of this women's property complex should not imply that women were equal to men within the property system. The power of men over family and conjugal property was predominant, and women managed it only in exceptional cases and as widows. Individual property, over which women did exert considerable control, was seldom if ever large enough to create a true balance of power between women and men in property relations; nor did women possess such property in ways that allowed them to live independently of the families into which they were born or married.

Qing Law: Code and Practice

A frequently asked question concerning Chinese legal history is, what was the relationship between the Qing Code, the magistrate, and local practices? In terms of legal procedures, as I have stressed, household division was a community, ritualized process that only occasionally went to court. The vast majority of cases were handled by the family, lineage, or community without any relationship to the state.

When the rare case went to court, it was handled not as a penal case for which punishments were meted out, but in a manner of civil law, in which the magistrate decided for one side or the other, or ordered a compromise. Further, the courts protected the rights of individuals, both men and women, and the norms of the community-based procedure. Household division may well have been an exception within codified law, but in this instance, code and practice were in almost complete harmony. The code mandated support for surviving parents and equal division among sons. Custom, with the added guarantees of marriage expenses and dowries, was organized in harmony with the code. This unity of code and practice, I would argue, explains the minimal amount of inheritance law that was written into the codes from the Tang to the Qing. Whether this harmony is better explained by the codes molding custom or perhaps by custom molding code is probably a false dichotomy. In the case of inheritance, this harmony is best explained by the conflation of the political goals of the state, the amount of power in official hands, and the tenacity of custom over time.

The one exception to this harmonious correlation was in the difficult area of adoption, and it may explain why the vast majority of codified inheritance law of the Qing related to adoption. Adoption practices, especially among the poor, were much more chaotic than the code allowed. There was, however, a rough correlation in that *guoji* and *baoyang* adoptions do generally equate to the Qing statutes on adoption, *guoji* meaning adoption from within the lineage and *baoyang*, the adoption of a foundling under the age of three *sui*.

Political Structure and Economic Development

Finally, it might prove interesting to speculate, perhaps wildly, on household division's effects on two other aspects of Chinese history. In the arena of political history, traditional China's greatest achievement was the rise of bureaucratic government staffed by scholars selected through civil service examinations. The possibility for this development stems from household division. When Emperor Wudi ordered the nobles of the Han dynasty to divide their fiefs equally among their sons, he destroyed the economic base of noble power, and, at least in times of political stability, a landed nobility ceased to be an economic and political threat. Then the emperors, and in one case the Empress Wu Zetian, through centuries of trial and error found their way to the scholar-staffed bureaucracy as their preferred and legitimate form of government. Thus equal-male inheritance was central to clearing the way for the rise of China's form of bureaucratic government, one of China's great contributions to world history.

In the arena of economic history, it is increasingly fashionable to ignore the Engels-Habbakuk paradigm that linked family, economic development, and the rise of capitalism. Jack Goody, for example, purposefully severs the connection (1990). Others feel the paradigm is in "crisis" and that we should "break free" of these questions generated from English historical experience (Philip Huang 1991:335).

For me, however, the question explored by Habbakuk remains of direct and primary importance, and this study does suggest that household division produced an economy similar to that he hypothesized. It is now generally accepted that late imperial China's society and economy were characterized by equal-male inheritance, universal marriage, a dense population, property fragmentation, and peasant handicrafts that in many market sectors put up stiff resistance to capitalist imports. Further, economic historians have had a difficult time demonstrating the existence of the type of economic dynamics associated with capitalism—continuing revolution in technology; rising labor productivity, especially in agriculture; and rapid urbanization —from the Ming period up to 1840 and perhaps even through the 1930s. Thus Habakkuk's variables, as described in the Introduction, are all in place.

But the question remains, is his explanatory mechanism—inheritance—the right one? The answer is both yes and no. His description is accurate, and household division may well have been the explanatory mechanism for the simultaneous existence of universal marriage, dense population, fragmented land, and a highly commercialized handicraft economy. But it falls short of explaining why such a constellation of factors fails to generate capitalist growth dynamics. For analytical purposes, let us divide Habakkuk's explanation into two.

His first thesis is that handicrafts tend to resist manufactured goods, thus possibly shutting out an externally generated capitalism. This resistance can indeed be seen in China from 1840 to 1900, but over time this resistance was broken as industrially produced goods became many times cheaper and superior in quality. In time, peasant handicrafts did succumb to industrial goods.

His second thesis is that partible inheritance tends to break down wealth, thus short-circuiting an internal development of capital. While it is true that household division tends to break down wealth, it did not stop some families from accumulating vast quantities of money and land, which could have been used as capital. The key question becomes, at what point does increasing wealth become capitalist-style capital? The question is designed to suggest that no amount of wealth automatically becomes capital. Capital presupposes an array of social structures and relationships in which money can be invested as capital. Thus, while Habakkuk's constellation of social and economic elements may be explained by inheritance, he fails to explain why such an inheritance regime and its related constellation of demographic and economic factors derail the internal development of capitalism.

If Habakkuk is insufficient on this level, what does this study suggest regarding the relationship between inheritance and the pattern of Chinese economic development? The best answer is that there is no direct relationship between household division and the emergence of capitalism, much as Goody suggests. Thus the classic topic of the emergence of capitalism is never directly addressed in this book, but it is hinted at in various sections, and we can speculate on the question by using household division as a window on a possible explanation.

The Old Dilemma: Why No Capitalism?

The relevant evidence only allows for a discussion of the landlord-tenant relationship, which for now must be limited by the distinction between two types of household division documents: those of rich landlords and those of tenants. Rich landlords usually referred to land by a name or a number: the name of the tenant or the amount of rental income. In marked contrast, tenants referred to land by a name and often by the area or the borders that marked it. In other words, landlords divided rental income; tenants divided land. This observation suggests that wealthy landlords had less concern with the exact location of the land and the production process than with rent and who was responsible for its payment. The tenant was concerned with the payment of rent but perhaps more importantly with the land and the agricultural production process.

This conclusion was confirmed by many of my informants: the tenant always controlled the production process. One informant simply laughed and said, "Everybody knows the tenant was responsible for everything." In more abstract terms, in the landlord-tenant relationship, the laborer controlled the labor process, while the landlord collected rent (Liu Wenqing, Li Xingfang, and the Longyan Local Gazetteer Committee interviews).

This situation is the opposite of the requirements of a capitalist-worker relationship. If the owner of capitalist means of production cannot force the laborer to work as the capitalist directs, the capitalist would go bankrupt investing in new, more efficient technology, because he would not be able to force the laborer to use it as required. The conditions for investment in technology that in turn create rising productivity simply do not exist. Thus, in the Chinese landlord-tenant context, investment decisions were left in the hands of the tenant, who had less to invest and, as a renter, little incentive to do so.

In fact, the household division documents of the rich landlords and merchants reveal an interesting pattern of investment. Their portfolios included land, education, commercial activity, and money-lending. There is never a mention of investment in technology.

To make this analysis more convincing would require at least a discussion of owner-cultivator peasants, labor in the handicraft industries such as silk, wage labor in cities and on the Grand Canal, and wage labor in the protoindustrial sector, such as the Zigong salt fields in Sichuan, all topics well beyond the scope of this study. But the hint from the landlord-tenant relationship is instructive. If in most labor situations in late imperial China, the laborer controlled the labor process, this fact goes a long way toward explaining the existence of a commercialized economy that displayed few capitalist growth dynamics. In a society where labor controls the work process, landed and commercial wealth can be accumulated, but existing outside of a well-articulated capitalist–wage laborer social relationship, they can never become true capital.

Appendix 1

China's Laws on Inheritance

Tang Law

All the land, housing, and property to be divided must be divided between the brothers equally. (After the father and grandfather die, and the brothers live separately and do not cook together for three years, or if they have fled and six years or more have passed, or if there is no surviving land, housing, stores, workshops, bondservants, or slaves, there can be no discussion of division.)

The property acquired from the wife's family is not included in the divided property. (If the wife is dead, her natal family cannot take back the property she brought, including all property and slaves.)

If any of the brothers is dead, his son(s) take his share. (The appointed heir is the same.)

If all the brothers are dead, their sons divide equally.[1] (The father and grandfather's permanent and gift lands are also divided equally. The personal share lands should be divided according to the age and status rules [of the equal fields distribution system]. Even if the land is limited in quantity, it should be divided according to this rule.)[2]

If a brother is not married, he gets extra property for marriage expenses; if any [father's] sister or daughter is unmarried and in the house, she gets one–half of a brother's marriage expenses. A widow who is without a son receives her husband's share. If all of her husband's brothers are dead, she receives a share equal to one brother's. (If she has a son, she gets nothing more. She is called the "chaste

widow" who remains in her husband's home and does not remarry. If she does remarry, she cannot dispose of the property—the bond-servants, slaves, land, and houses—in her first husband's house, and all must be divided among the appropriate heirs.)
(Niida [1933] 1964: 245–246)

Song Law

JUNIOR FAMILY MEMBERS STEALING PROPERTY
DIVIDING PROPERTY; SONS AND DAUGHTERS WHO MOVE ELSEWHERE

As for those younger family members who selfishly appropriate family property, if the property they take totals ten bolts they will receive ten strokes, and for each ten bolts more the punishment will be raised one level, up to a total of one hundred. Those who divide but do it unequally will be punished according to the amount taken and according to the law on pecuniary malfeasance, less three levels.

Comment: All those living together must have elders, and when the elders are alive, the younger family members cannot make decisions for themselves. If the younger do not obey the elder and self-ishly take family property, then for ten bolts taken they will receive ten strokes, and for each ten bolts more, ten strokes will be added, up to one hundred. . . . As to the land, housing, and property to be divided, the brothers shall divide equally, and the property from the wives' households is not divided. If any of the brothers is dead, the son(s) inherit his (their) father's share. If this is violated, it is deemed to be unequal. If the brothers are going to divide one hundred bolts of silk, and one brother gets sixty bolts, he is getting ten bolts extra, so he should be punished with eighty strokes, going by the law on pecuniary malfeasance, less three levels.
(*Song xing tong* 1984:197)

Yuan Law—1294

According to the old substatute: as to each person allowed to con-test for real and movable property, a wife's son(s) receive four shares each, a concubine's son(s) receive three shares each, and son(s) born of illicit sex with a worthy person and son(s) of a favored slave girl receive one share each.
(Zhang Xueshu 1986:53)

Regarding dowry lands and other goods that a woman brings into her marriage: from now on if a woman who has once been married wishes to marry again to someone else, whether she is divorced

while her [first] husband is alive, or is living as a widow after her husband has died, her dowry property and other belongings that she brought into her marriage should all be taken over by the family of her former husband. It is absolutely not permitted for her to take them away with herself, as was formerly done.
(quoted in Birge 1992:262–263)

Ming Law
From the *Ming Code*
Younger Family Members Selfishly Taking Family Property

For all younger family members who selfishly appropriate family property without their elders' permission, if the amount taken is twenty strings of cash, they will receive twenty strokes of the light bamboo, and for each additional twenty strings the punishment will be raised one level, up to a total of one hundred strokes of the heavy bamboo. If when living together the elders do not divide the family property equally, the crime is the same.
(*Da Ming lü* 1959, juan 4:10)

From the *Great Ming Commandment*

22. The family's property and land is divided equally among sons of the wife or others according to their numbers without regard to whether they were born of the wife, a concubine, or a slave, with the exception of the beneficiaries of official protection, in which case preference shall be given to the eldest son and grandson of the wife. Bastard sons shall get half the portion of a son. In other cases, if there is no other son, an appropriate successor shall be designated heir, to share equally with the bastard sons. If there is no appropriate successor they may inherit the entire amount.
(Farmer 1995:159)

24. Those who have no sons may designate a nephew from the same lineage *(zong)* and the appropriate generation *(zhaomu)* ... to become their heir. First exhaust the closest relatives with a common father and next the circle of nine-month *(dagong)*, five-month *(xiaogong)* and three-month *(sima)* mourning relatives. . . . If there is none among all of these, then it is permitted to select from among distant relatives anyone with the same surname to name an heir. If, after designating an heir, a natural son is born, the family property shall be evenly divided with the originally designated heir. In no case is it allowed to raise someone from a different surname

as an heir. To do so would disrupt the clan system. When someone of the same surname is designated, the generational hierarchy may not be violated in a way which would disrupt the generational sequence.
(Farmer 1995:159–160)

25. In the event that a wife whose husband dies, leaving her without a son, wants to hold to her vows, and her husband's status ought to be continued, an heir of appropriate ancestry shall be selected by the clan head. When the wife is married a second time, the first husband's property and the original dowry shall both be disposed of by the former husband's family.
(Farmer 1995:160)

27. When a family is cut off, and there is no appropriate heir in the same lineage, the surviving daughters may inherit the property. If there are no daughters, the property shall go to the state.
(Farmer 1995:160)

35. Those sons and paternal grandsons whose grandparents or parents are living may not divide the wealth and reside separately. If father or grandfather permit the division then it is permissible.
(Farmer 1995:161)

Selected Qing Laws

ILLEGALLY APPOINTING AN ELDEST SON

Statutes

Whoever illegally appoints an eldest son will be punished with eighty strokes of the heavy bamboo. For those whose official wife is over fifty and has no son, it is allowable to appoint the eldest son of a concubine. For those who do not appoint the eldest son of the concubine, the crime is the same.

If somebody adopts a son from the same lineage, and they have no natural son (and if the adoptee's parents have a son), and if the adopted son abandons his adoptive family, he shall be punished by one hundred blows of the heavy bamboo and sent back to the control of his adoptive parents. If the adoptive parents have a blood son, and the natural parents have none, and the adopted son wants to return, it is allowed.

Those who adopt a son from a different surname and thus confuse the lineage order shall receive sixty blows of the heavy bamboo. For those who adopt out a son into a different surname group as an heir, the punishment is the same, and the son in returned to his own lineage.

For an abandoned child under the age of three *sui*, even if it has a different surname, adoption is allowed, and he or she can take the adoptive family surname. But such a son is not allowed to be appointed as heir if the family has no son.

For those who adopt an heir from within the lineage, but the order is out of generational sequence, the crime is the same. The son is returned to his line, and an appropriate heir should be found.[3] (*Da Qing lüli*, juan 8:14)

Substatutes

Someone without a son is permitted to appoint an appropriate nephew according to the order of the ancestral tablets to inherit. . . . If, after an heir is named, a natural son is born, the family property will be divided equally with the previously appointed heir.

A woman whose husband dies and who does not remarry will receive her husband's portion. The lineage elders must select, according to the order of the ancestral tablets, an appropriate heir to inherit. She who does remarry must allow her previous husband's property and her original dowry to remain under the management of her previous husband's family. (*Da Qing lüli*, juan 8:15)

LEGAL SEPARATION OF RESIDENCE AND DIVISION OF PROPERTY

Statutes

During the lifetime of the grandparents or parents, any son or grandson who legally establishes a separate residence and divides the family property shall receive one hundred blows of the heavy bamboo, but only if the grandparents or parents make the complaint.

If during the legal mourning period for the mother or father, the sons legally establish separate residences and divide family property, they shall receive eighty blows of the heavy bamboo. In this case the complaint must be made by a close senior relative; but if the division is done in accordance with a parent's will, this statute will not apply. (*Da Qing lüli*, juan 8:28)

Substatute

When the grandparents and parents are alive, the sons and grandsons cannot divide the family property and reside separately. Even

if this division of property and separation of residence does not include legal registration of the residence, it is still illegal and shall be punished as above in full. In those cases where the parents permit the division, it is allowable.
(*Da Qing lüli*, juan 8:28)

YOUNGER FAMILY MEMBERS SELFISHLY TAKING FAMILY PROPERTY

Statute

For all younger family members who selfishly appropriate family property without their elders' permission, if the amount taken is ten taels of silver, they will receive twenty strokes of the light bamboo, and for each additional ten taels the punishment will be raised one level, up to a total of one hundred blows of the heavy bamboo. If when living together the elders do not divide the family property equally, the crime is the same.
(*Da Qing lüli*, juan 8:29)

Substatutes

For sons of wives and concubines, except in cases concerning the *yin* privilege,[4] which must be passed to the wife's first son and grandson, when dividing family property and land, no distinction is made between sons born of wives, concubines, and maidservants, and the property is divided equally by the total number of sons.

A son born of an illicit relationship gets one-half a share. If there is no legal son and an heir is appointed, the heir must divide equally with the illicit son. If no heir is appointed, then the illicit son may inherit the entire share.

When a household has no male heirs, and there is truly no possible heir to appoint from within the lineage, all the daughters shall inherit. For those families without daughters, let the local officials make a clear report and, after deliberation, turn over the property to the state.
(*Da Qing lüli*, juan 8:29)

Selected Republican Inheritance Laws

Chapter 1: Heirs to Property

Article 1138

Heirs to property other than the spouse come in the following order:

1. Lineal descendants by blood;
2. Parents;
3. Brothers and sisters;
4. Grandparents.[5]

Article 1140

Where an heir of the first order provided in Article 1138 has died or lost the right of inheritance before the opening of the succession, his lineal descendants shall inherit his successional portion in his place.

Article 1141

Where there are several heirs of the same order, they inherit in equal shares as *per capita,* unless it is otherwise provided by law.

Article 1142

The order of succession for an adopted child is the same as for a legitimate child.

The successional portion of an adopted child is one-half of that of a legitimate child, but, in case the adoptive parents have no lineal descendant by blood for their heir, his successional portion is the same as that of a legitimate child.

Article 1143

Where a person has no lineal descendants by blood, he may by will designate an heir to the whole or a part of his property, provided that the provisions concerning compulsory portions are not contravened.

Article 1144

Each spouse has the right to inherit the property of the other, and his or her successional portion is determined according to the following provisions:

1. Where the spouse inherits concurrently with heirs of the first order, as provided in Article 1138, his or her successional portion is equal to the other heirs;

2. Where the spouse inherits concurrently with heirs of the second or third order as provided in Article 1138, his or her successional portion is one-half of the inheritance;

3. Where the spouse inherits concurrently with heirs of the fourth order as provided in Article 1138, his or her successional portion is two-thirds of the inheritance;

4. Where there is no heir of any of the four orders provided in Article 1138, his or her successional portion is the whole of the inheritance.

Chapter 2

TITLE III: PARTITION OF INHERITANCE

Article 1164

The heirs may at any time demand the partition of the inheritance unless it is otherwise provided by law or agreed upon by contract.

Article 1165

Where the will of the deceased has determined, or asked a third person to determine the method of partition of the inheritance, the method so determined shall be followed.

Where a will prohibits the partition of the deceased's property, the effect of such a prohibition is limited to twenty years.

Article 1166

Where one of the heirs is a child *en ventre de sa mere,* partition of the deceased's property by the other heirs may not take place unless the successional portion of such child has been reserved.

In regard to such partition of inheritance, the mother acts as agent of the child *en ventre de sa mère.*

TITLE IV: WAIVER OF INHERITANCE

Article 1174

An heir may waive his right of inheritance.

Such waiver must be effected by a written declaration to the court, the family council, or the other heirs, within two months from the time when he had cognizance of the succession.

Chapter 3: Wills

TITLE I: GENERAL PROVISIONS

Article 1187

A testator may freely dispose of his property by a will, so long as he does not contravene the provisions in regard to compulsory portions.

TITLE VI: COMPULSORY PORTIONS

Article 1223

The compulsory portions of an heir is determined as follows:

1. For a lineal descendant by blood, the compulsory portion is one half of his successional portion;

2. For a parent, the compulsory portion is one half of his successional portion;

3. For a spouse, the compulsory portion is one half his successional portion;

4. For a brother or a sister, the compulsory portion is one-third of his or her successional portion;

5. For a grandparent, the compulsory portion is one-third of his successional portion.

(LRPG 1961:338–357)

Appendix 2

Historical Sources and Their Limits

T HE structure of this book is the result of the interplay of purposeful theoretical concerns and, perhaps more important, the serendipitous availability of materials. The core of the book is constructed from household division documents (the rough equivalent of wills in the West),[1] which are extant in various collections. The main collections are the *Taiwan sifa* (referred to as TS in the text), a collection of land, inheritance, and adoption documents collected and published by the Japanese government after their colonial conquest of Taiwan in 1895. A second source is the *Taiwan gongsi cang guwenshu yingben* (referred to as TWGS in the text), a massive collection of Qing family, property, land sale and pawn, and inheritance documents located in the Hoover Institution library on the Stanford University campus. These two collections make Taiwan by far the best documented province in China on the topic of inheritance.

Another large collection is housed at the Economics Institute of the Chinese Academy of Social Sciences in Beijing, which contains just over one hundred documents from Huizhou in Anhui province. A similar collection of Huizhou materials housed at the History Research Institute of the same academy was published too late to have a significant impact on this study.[2] Smaller collections exist from Fujian province in Xiamen University's History Research Institute and in the private papers of Zheng Zhenman, a fellow of the institute. About twenty household division documents are extant at the Zhejiang Provincial Museum. And, finally, there are scattered household division and inheritance-related documents in the lineage genealogies produced in the Ming and Qing periods and available at the Genealogical Society of Utah in Salt Lake City.

From these varied places, I have collected about five hundred household division and inheritance-related documents, and I have closely analyzed 250 and entered them into a computer database. These 250 provide the core of the analysis. The remaining 250 documents are primarily from Taiwan and would merely further document this already well-documented province.

The problems related to these documents are several. First, the largest number of documents and those easiest to find are from Taiwan, and thus it is necessary and time-consuming to search out documents from other provinces to avoid the criticism that Taiwan may have been some sort of exception in inheritance practices. Second, the large extant number of documents might suggest that a serious amount of statistical calculation and comparison would be possible. Unfortunately, this is not the case. The vast majority of the documents are very imprecise in methods of measurement, for example, referring to land by the number of plots rather than by area or market value. And in those cases where measures are more exact, regional variations in measures, such as the use of the *tong* in Fujian,[3] make comparisons impossible. Thus only about twenty-five documents actually allow for serious calculation, and the few statistical comparisons used in this study are meant to be suggestive, not definitive; the book as a whole is a qualitative not a quantitative analysis.

A third weakness is the lack of precise provenance and spatial density for the vast majority of the documents. Because these documents were kept by families and not a more central authority, such as the feudal manors or local parish churches in Europe, the best that can be determined for each document is the province of origin, or perhaps a subregion within the province, and the date of the division. By comparison to Europe, this scattered and thin nature of the documentation makes the study of household division in a particular village or county over time a virtual impossibility. A final weakness of the household division documents is their formulaic style that hides the human drama, emotion, and bitter arguments that must have accompanied the process of household division. These elements must be found elsewhere.

One guaranteed source for insight into the human side of household division is the *Chūgoku nōson kankō chōsa* (Investigations of Customary Practices in Rural China; referred to as *Kankō chōsa* or *KC* in the text). This collection of six massive volumes of interviews with North China peasants from the early 1940s was planned by expert Japanese historians and anthropologists who were particularly concerned with family and household division. Each volume contains page after page of conversations recorded verbatim on the subjects of adoption, family property, family headship, and household division. The detailed nature of the interviews allows for a more nuanced analysis of the personal aspects of household division than what is visible in the household division documents. One problem with the interview materials, however, was the timing. The early 1940s was the period of the Republican revolution and the Japanese occupation. What effects did these two processes have on inheritance practices? I have found the effects of both events to be minimal; the Qing inheritance system remained intact. These two sets of documents, the household division documents and the *Kankō chōsa* interviews, provide the most and best evidence for the arguments in this book.

A third source is legal disputes. One English-language source of pre–Qing dynasty legal disputes is Robert Van Gulik's translation of the *T'ang-yin-pi-shih: Parallel Cases from under the Pear Tree*. A much more extensive source is a series of legal case decisions compiled in the Southern Song dynasty, titled the *Minggong shupan qingmingji*, or the *Famous Judges' Collection of Clear and Lucid Cases* (*Qingmingji* or QMJ in the text). The *Qingmingji* collection provides a detailed, nuanced view of Southern Song inheritance. Most cases are dated between 1200 and 1250, and they were written in the form of a judge's decision on a dispute about family and property. As I. R. Burns has shown in his detailed dissertation (1973), the *Qingmingji* is an exceptionally rich source of information on Southern Song inheritance, family property, and related questions. For the Qing dynasty, I have collected fifty inheritance-related legal disputes from the Baxian archives, now located in Chengdu, Sichuan province.

These legal cases are important in several ways. First, the pre-Qing cases provide some sense of inheritance practices that can be compared to early dynastic law and that provide a baseline to compare to the Qing. The Qing cases are important in that they confirm what the division documents and interviews demonstrate, and they reveal the ways in which the state became involved in household division, an important aspect of civil law. They also provide a sense of the personalities and motivations of the people involved.

One problem with these documents is their sheer numbers. For Baxian alone, there are approximately 113,000 extant items, in varying degrees of completeness. Because there is no truly useful index and reading all of the cases would be impossible, it is difficult to answer questions such as these: Could a woman sue her family because her dowry was too small? Did a magistrate ever invoke the stipulated Qing punishment of twenty strokes of the light bamboo for a father who unequally divided property? Years of work at Baxian alone would be required to decide with relative certainty whether such a case had ever occurred.

A related source also used extensively here comprises the legal codes that guided the governing of the successive dynasties. There are short references to inheritance law for the Qin and Han dynasties, and the Tang, Song, and Yuan codes are extant in varying degrees of completeness. Both the Ming and Qing codes are extant in total. I have used these codes to demonstrate two things: first, the development of a tradition of equal-male division of property, and, second, that inheritance practices, though at times deviating from the law, more often than not were well in tune with the dynastic codes, particularly for the Qing.

A source that I had hoped would prove fruitful regarding inheritance was popular literature. While this genre has proved rich in other areas,[4] the writers of popular literature only rarely turned to the topic of household division. I have used these rare stories to give a sense of personality and motivation. Unlike in England, where an entire genre of literature was based on inheritance struggles, the Chinese family head had little power to determine how family property was to be divided. As I have taken pains to demonstrate, by the Qing the rules of equal division applied, whatever the desires of the parents. Given the relative inflexibility of late imperial Chinese inheritance, storytellers and authors of popular literature in China only occasionally turned to household division for plot lines.

A final group of sources for this book are my own interviews conducted with individuals and groups in Fujian in 1990–1991, while I was there doing dissertation research. I am particularly thankful to Professors Yang Guozhen and Zheng Zhenman for arranging these interviews. I used these interviews first to confirm that the fundamentals of household division, as revealed in the Taiwan documents and the *Kankō chōsa* interviews, were the same in Fujian and second to find any local variations that might have existed. The section in Chapter 3 on postdivision ceremonies was improved immensely from these interviews.

Thus I have tried to use the strengths of one set of sources to offset the weaknesses inherent in others. In weaving together these sources, I hope to have obtained a well-rounded view of household division that analyzes the rules and strategies employed by Chinese families as they passed their property from one generation to the next. It is on the basis of this view that I have attempted to extend the analysis to include household division's effects on important parts of Qing social structure and crucial processes in Chinese historical development.

Appendix 3

Chinese Terms for Weights and Measures

I N the Qing and Republican periods, many terms for weights and measures used in household division documents were, in a superficial sense, standardized. Terms such as *mu*, yuan, tael, and *dan* (often read as *shi*) appear in many different areas and thus may appear to convey a single meaning. In fact, the meaning differed by time and place, often greatly. For example, the term *diao* formally meant one thousand copper coins strung together through a square hole in the middle of each coin. In reality, a *diao* might contain from 160 to 990 copper coins, depending on the locale. The term *jin* (often translated as "catty") formally meant 1⅓ pounds, but in reality it varied from 12 to 42.5 ounces. A *dan* meant one hundred *jin* but varied from 90 to 280 *jin*. *Mu* is usually rendered as one-sixth of an acre (7,260 square feet), but it varied between 3,840 and 9,964 square feet. One standard even featured a *mu* that equaled 18,148 square feet. Therefore, for the terms below, I have given the official meaning of the weight or measure and, where known and appropriate, the range of its regional variations (Bell and Woodhead 1913:83–86).

Term	Official Meaning	Range of Variation
big yuan	one of the many types of silver dollars used in the Qing and Republican periods; *see* yuan	
chi	14.1 inches .358 meters	8.6–27.8 inches

copper	1 copper cash: a round copper coin with a square hole in the middle; same as *wen*	
dan	100 *jin*	90–1,300 *jin*
dan	Song dynasty measure of grain and land: 67 liters	
diao	1,000 copper cash strung together	160–990 copper cash
dou	10 sheng .1 *shi* 629 cubic inches	176–1,800 cubic inches
fen	unit of area: .1 *mu*	
fen	unit of weight: .01 tael	
guan	Song dynasty money: 1 *guan* = 1,000 *wen*	
jia	.97 hectare 11.3 *mu* 2.41 acres	fairly standardized in Taiwan
jin	1⅓ pounds	12–42.5 ounces
liang	*see* tael	
mu	one-sixth acre (7,260 sq. ft.)	3,840–9,964 and 19,148 sq. ft.
ping	in Huizhou, a local measure of grain	larger than a *jin*
qing	100 *mu;* Ming and Qing dynasty measure of land	

qiu	a plot of land, size unstated	
sheng	.1 *dou* .01 *shi*	
shi	100 *jin*	90–1,300 jin
suo	a piece of land, size unstated	
tael	37.8 grams of silver 1.3 avoirdupois ounces	
tong	in Fujian, a grain measuring box	the size varied by village and by landlord
wen	1 copper cash: a round copper coin with a square hole in the middle; same as copper	
xiaoyang yuan	one of the many different types of silver dollars used in the Qing and Republican periods; *see* yuan	
yuan	silver dollar	gross weight: 415–420 grains grains of fine silver: 369–378
zhang	10 *chi* 3.581 meters	
zhong	Song dynasty measure of land	

Appendix 4

Chinese Terms for Guarantors on Household Division Documents, by Province

1. Anhui

jianqin 見親
jianyi 見議
jianzu 見族
ping 憑
pingfang 憑房

pingqin 憑親
pingzu 憑族
qinfang 親房
zaijianqin 在見親
zhongjian 中見

zhongjianpingzu 中見憑族
zhongjianzu 中見族
zu 族
zuzhong 族中

2. Fujian

fangqinren 房親人
gongjian 公見
gongqin 公親
gongzhengren 公証人
jianfen 見分
jianren 見人

jianyiqin 見議親
jianzhengren 見証人
jianzhongren 見中人
jiazhang 家長
pingzheng 憑證
qinqi 親戚

waiqi 外戚
zaijian 在見
zhengguanqin 証關親
zhijianren 知見人
zuqin 族親
zuzhang 族長

3. Hebei

shuoheren 説和人
zhongbaoren 中保人

zhongjianren 中見人
zhongren 中人

zhongshuoren 中説人

4. Shandong

jieyi 街誼

xiangren 鄉人

xiangyi 鄉誼

5. Taiwan

changjian 場見
changjianren 場見人
fangqinren 房親人
gongqinren 公親人
gongren 公人
weigongren 為公人
weizhongren 為中人
zaichang 在場

zaichangfangzuren 在場房族人
zaichanggongqinren 在場公親人
zaichangjianren 在場見人
zaichangren 在場人
zaichangzhijianren 在場知見人

zaijian 在見
zaijianren 在見人
zhijian 知見
zhijianren 知見人
zuqingongren 族親公人
zuzhanggongren 族長公人
zuzhangren 族長人

Appendix 5

Common Terms for Household Division Documents, by Province

1. Anhui
fenbodan 分簿單
fendan 分單
fendanjiushu 分單鬮書
fenguan 分關
fenguanbo 分關簿
fenguanshu 分關書
fenjiushu 分鬮書

fenxijiushu 分晰鬮書
jiushu 鬮書
xichanjiushu 晰產鬮書
yizhubiaofenwenbo 遺囑書分文簿
yizhujiushu 遺囑鬮書
zunyiming fenjia qingdanjiushu 遵遺命
分家清單鬮書

2. Fujian
fencuanjiushu 分爨鬮書
fenguan 分關
fenguanyongyuanzhizhao 分關永遠
執照
fenshu 分書

heyue 合約
heyuejiushuzi 合約鬮書字
jiushu 鬮書
jiushuheyue 鬮書合約
zhijiufenzi 執鬮分字

3. Hebei and Shandong
fence 分冊
fendan 分單
fendanfenbo 分單分撥
fendanwenyue 分單文約
fendanyongyuanzhizhao 分單永遠執照

fendanzhizhao 分單執照
fendanzi 分單字
fenjiadan 分家單
fenjushu 分居書
yongyuanfenqi 永遠分契

4. Taiwan
fenjiuhetongzi 分鬮合同字
fenjiuzi 分鬮字
fenyejiushuheyuezi 分業鬮書合約字
fenyejiushuzi 分業鬮書字
hetongjiushuzi 合同鬮書字
heyuezi 合約字

jiufenyuezi 鬮分約字
jiufenzi 鬮分字
jiushu 鬮書
jiushuheyuezi 鬮書合約字
jiushuyuezi 鬮書約字
jiushuzi 鬮書字

jiuyuezi 鬮約字

zhufenjiuyeheyuezi 囑分鬮業合約字

zhufufenjiuheyuezi 囑咐分鬮合約字

zhushufujuyue 囑書付據約

5. Zhejiang
fenguan 分關

fenguanlu 分關錄

fenguanshu 分關書

fenyue 分約

guanfen 關分

6. All provinces. The *yizhu* 遺囑 was known as
yizhujiuyue 遺囑鬮約

yushi 諭示

zhufu 囑咐

zhushu 囑書

zhushuzi 囑書字

Notes

Chapter 1. Introduction

1. The one exception in the collection is Lutz Berkner's essay "Inheritance, Land Tenure and Peasant Family Structure: A German Regional Comparison," which does tend to confirm some of Habakkuk's insights.

2. Goody is well aware that property devolves more to men, but his point is that in Eurasia women do inherit conjugal property, even if unequally. See Goody 1990.

3. Ch'u defines *li* as "the rules of behavior varying in accordance with one's status defined in the various forms of social relationships, [which] were formulated by the Confucianists for this purpose. They are the means by which differences in status and role are maintained" (1961:230–231).

Chapter 2. Inheritance Law and Practice before the Qing

1. Here primogeniture means that the title passes to the first son of the principal wife, even if the firstborn is the son of a concubine (Ch'u 1972:13).

2. The assumption regarding poor sons is that they had no property and thus married into wealthy families with property but no natural sons.

3. For Japan, see Mass 1989:94–102, Nakamura and Miyamoto 1982:243; for Europe, see Goody 1976:26–27, Berkner 1976:83, and Cooper 1976:199.

4. References to the Song Code as well as the preceding Tang and subsequent Yuan, Ming, and Qing codes can be misleading at times. A code's statutes and substatutes were in effect from the day the particular code was promulgated; but any individual law could be superseded by later legislation, memorials, and rescripts. Thus to be precise on the exact state of inheritance law in a given decade as it mutated over the centuries of the Tang and the Song is well beyond the scope of this study. My purpose here is to point out what I believe to have been the general continuities and a few of the more striking changes. I leave it to

Tang-Song specialists to work out the remaining features, both major and minor, of this crucial transitional period in inheritance and family law.

5. The probable effectiveness of this law is discussed later in this chapter.

6. One of the most probable changes in family law and practice between the Song and the Qing dynasties was the increased use of adoption in the latter period. In the former, adoption seems to have been less frequent, and thus extinct households were more common, forming a tempting target for state taxation.

7. A returned daughter was one who had married out but had returned to her natal home for some reason, possibly because she had been expelled from her husband's home or had been left without a son and property in her deceased husband's household (Bernhardt 1995:305; *Song xing tong* 1984:198).

8. A household division document is similar to a will, and it details the property given to each heir at household division time. See Chapter 3 for a full discussion.

9. See the discussion of sources in Appendix 2 for a detailed presentation of the *Qingmingji*.

10. In the Qing one *mu* equaled one-sixth of an acre, but actual size varied greatly by time period and geographic location. See Appendix 3.

11. The Chinese term for years of age. In the traditional view, a child was born one year old and then added a year at each New Year. Thus seventy-three *sui* would be either seventy-one or seventy-two years old by American standards.

12. A *shi* (bushel) was a measured unit of grain. The exact weight or volume of each *shi* varied over the centuries and by geographic place. See Appendix 3.

13. A *zhong* was an area unit used to measure land. See Appendix 3.

14. Property retained by or given to parents for support in their old age. See chapters 3 and 4 for complete discussions.

15. A piece of land. See Appendix 3.

16. Father Guo had started life without much property, and he had borrowed money from his first son's wife's dowry to get a start in business.

17. For the debate and alternative interpretations surrounding this case, see Bernhardt 1995 and Birge 1992:104–119.

18. The marriages of Xiancheng and Shiguang were not "official," and though Qiuju is referred to as a concubine at one point and Liu is most likely a slave girl, both women are specifically treated as wives by the court. This is just one of several factors that confuse the proceedings.

19. A unit of area used to measure land.

20. An *yizhu* is similar to a will. See Chapter 3 for a complete discussion.

21. My interpretation of the document differs slightly from that of Chen Ping and Wang Qinjin. My feeling is that the first child by the first husband is a son named Jun, not a daughter named Yijun, as Chen and Wang have suggested. Thanks to Zheng Zhenman for his insights in reading this document.

22. As to whether Tang women's property rights did, as the law stated, include the right to a dowry specifically valued at one-half a brother's marriage

expenses, the evidence is silent. Their right to a dowry is clear, but the relative amounts are not discussed.

23. The property rights associated with adoption and postmortem heirs in the Qing was actually more complex and subject to negotiation in each instance. See Chapter 4 for a complete discussion.

24. See Birge 1992:242–244 for a complete translation and discussion of this case.

Chapter 3. Qing Household Division: Why, When, and How?

1. Popular literature is a useful source for household division, but not as rich a one as it is for topics such as adoption (see Waltner 1990). Unlike in England, the Chinese family head of the Ming-Qing period had little power to determine how the property was to be divided. The rules of equal division applied, whatever the desires of the parents. Thus there could be no making and remaking wills, disinheriting one son, or favoring a daughter or a lover, a few examples of plot twists that make up an entire genre of English literature based on inheritance struggles. Given the relative inflexibility of Chinese inheritance, storytellers and authors of popular literature in China only occasionally turned to household division for plot lines.

2. The difficulty of defining class in rural China lies in the nature of the household division documents. Few documents calculate wealth in terms that are comparable. For rural families, size of landholdings, for example, is seldom specified beyond the number of "pieces." Thus it is impossible either to make an accurate estimation of class position, such as between poor, middle, and rich peasants, or to ascertain the link between these classes and the timing of division. In Chapter 8, I will demonstrate that defining class in a more general sense, distinguishing between peasants, gentry, merchants, and pawn-brokers, for example, does reveal differences in inheritance strategies.

3. In theory, a widowed daughter-in-law, as the stand-in for her deceased husband, should have had the power to demand division. But I have found no evidence for this.

4. See Appendix 4 for a more complete listing of guarantor terms on household division documents.

5. See Appendix 5 for a complete listing of household division document names.

6. Sometimes just *pin da, jun fen,* or *pin da jun* was used.

7. Burns states that in the *Qingmingji* there are often references to Song dynasty household division documents being officially sealed (1973:128).

Chapter 4. The Rights of Individuals in Qing Taiwan

1. The surname of Bilan and Bitao is not mentioned in the household division document. Omission of the surname occurs in about 20 percent of the documents from South China, I presume because the surname was so well known to the community that its inclusion was unnecessary.

2. The *jia* was the standard measure of land area in Qing Taiwan and was equal to .97 hectares. See Appendix 3.

3. A *jin* was a unit of weight, roughly equal to one American pound. See Appendix 3.

4. The eldest grandson portion was property granted to the first grandson or, more precisely, the first son of the first son. It is part of the "lineage orientation" of household division common in South China. This practice is described in detail in Chapter 8.

5. See Chapter 8 for a discussion of trusts and common property.

6. This and other exceptions to the equal division rule will be discussed in Chapter 8.

7. As shown in Chapter 2, the Qing Code further specifies that sons born to maidservants were legally entitled to full shares, and sons born in illicit relationships were entitled to half shares. The evidence I have surveyed contains no instance of how these sons were treated in practice.

8. See Wolf and Huang 1980 as an example.

9. A common euphemism for death.

10. Her five sons.

11. A *tongyangxi* was a female baby or little girl brought into a home that had a male baby or a young son. The expectation was that when the two children came of age, they would begin living together as husband and wife. This form of "minor" marriage was often favored because it avoided the considerable expense associated with formal marriage when the children reached their teens or twenties. See Arthur Wolf 1995 for a complete discussion.

Chapter 5. Dividing Different Types of Property in Qing Taiwan

1. If one is standing in the house's courtyard facing the central ancestral hall, the favored location is the rooms next to the hall on the right-hand side. If the parents were living, they continued to reside here, and the eldest son received the second favored location, the rooms on the left side of the ancestral hall.

2. *Qiu* is frequently used in Taiwan household division documents to mean a piece of land.

3. The unequal numbers of *qiu* do not imply that the division was unequal, because *qiu* simply meant "piece," leaving the size and value of the land unstated.

4. The division of the other 40 yuan is not given in the document, though it is likely the elder two brothers received 20 yuan each.

5. *Dazu* most easily translates as "big rent" and *xiaozu* as "little rent," but such translations are misleading since *dazu* was the smaller amount and *xiaozu* the greater. Thus I will retain the Chinese terms.

6. Special gifts will be discussed in Chapter 8.

7. This distinction is maintained in the household documents from most other areas, such as Sichuan, Huizhou, and North China, as well.

8. The pawned commodity could be the land itself or rights to rental income in any of its forms.

9. It is also possible that the brothers knew which plots were likely to be reclaimed and which were not. This knowledge would affect division as well.

10. The danger of shortfall existed because the brothers were promising to contribute grain, but the debt was payable in cash. Since they had to sell the

grain and the market price varied, a low price might leave them short on the repayment.

Chapter 6. Household Division Disputes in Qing Courts

1. A final avenue for peasants to achieve access to yamen courts was through the hiring of a litigation broker. These masters of litigation were usually low-ranking scholars who sold their services as scribes, their knowledge of the law, and their connections in the yamen for a price. See Macauley 1994 for a complete discussion.

2. See Chapter 8 for a discussion of this strategy of phased division.

3. For a complete discussion of what constituted "illicit sex," see Sommer 1994.

Chapter 7. Republican Rural North China

1. The article numbers are from LRPG, pp. 338–360.

2. The use of the term "spouse" is important. It indicates that in life husband and wife are joint owners of family property, and when one dies, the other inherits. It was no longer legally assumed, as had been the case in the Qing, that when a husband and wife were living, the husband was the owner of the property.

3. This waiving of inheritance rights by daughters became a common practice in Taiwan after the Republican government fled there in 1949. The waiver of inheritance in her natal home was usually written up at the time the daughter was married out to another family.

4. The equivalent term in Qing Taiwan was most often *baoyang*.

5. *Yanglao* was one North China equivalent of *yangshan*, meaning the property set aside for the support of aging parents. Another North China term was *yanglaodi,* meaning specifically land set aside for the same purpose.

6. The one significant difference was in the rights of adopted sons.

7. *Yanglaodi* could not be divided after the death of one parent if the other survived (KC 4:71A).

8. Meaning the courtyard.

9. A *chi* was one Chinese foot, and ten *chi* equaled one *zhang*. By national standards, one *chi* equaled .3581 meters, though local usage varied widely. See Appendix 3.

10. *Jingjiao, chadaozui, xiaozuo,* and so forth are names of plots of land. Each plot had a name, sometimes suggesting a shape, a nearby landmark, or a former owner's name. Because most of the names are difficult or impossible to translate, I have opted to leave them in Chinese.

11. *Shangfang* was another term for *zhengfang,* or the main rooms of the house. See Figure 7.

Chapter 8. Region and Class: Exceptions, Strategies, and Orientations

1. See Chapter 2 for a complete discussion.

2. A traditional Chinese holiday when families visit and clean the graves of their ancestors. It usually falls in early April in the solar calendar.

3. A common euphemism meaning after someone dies.

4. The documents from Zhejiang are from the hilly southwest, not the Yangzi Delta or the flatlands.

5. The document does not make clear which county in Fujian the Yangs were from.

6. The three Chinese terms are *xiangsheng, linsheng,* and *gongsheng.* A *xiangsheng* was a graduate of the county school. A *linsheng* was a student at the county school who was given free board by the government. A *gongsheng* was a senior licentiate who had passed the county-level exam and was attempting higher-level exams such as that at the provincial level. All three were grades within the lowest examination rank of *xiucai,* and they carried no hope of entering the Qing civil service.

7. One notable exception is Jerry Dennerline's article on charitable estates and marriage strategies (1986).

Chapter 9. Household Division and Society: Land, Orientations, and Social Mobility

1. The best analyses of the relationship between household division and social mobility are by Lavely and Wong (1984 and 1992). The authors argue that, although division did cause downward mobility for all peasant classes, other variables, such as class differences in the number of male children, market possibilities available in land and for labor, and property accretion over the course of a generation, must also be taken into consideration.

Appendix 1. China's Laws on Inheritance

1. Burns concludes from the Song version of this law that sons or grandsons received on a per capita rather than a *per stirpes* basis, but that this was rare in practice (1973:viii, 131–132).

2. I follow Birge 1992 on this part of the translation. The differing types of land in this section are the creation of the Tang dynasty's equal-field land distribution system. See Twitchett 1970 and Hansen 1995:29–30 for detailed discussions.

3. For a translation of all the Qing statutes and substatutes on inheritance and adoption, see Jamieson 1921:13–17. The translations of the Qing statutes in Appendix 1 are mine.

4. The *yin* (which Farmer translates as "official protection") was a hereditary official privilege that included the right to enter the Qing civil service bureaucracy without passing the normally required civil service examinations. The term can also be defined to include any inheritable title or position in the Qing state or nobility structures (see Jing 1994:53). One example is the family of Cao Xueqin, author of *The Story of the Stone.* Cao came from a noble Manchu family, and his grandfather was Cao Yin, the textile commissioner in Nanjing. When Cao Yin died, his son, Cao Yong, inherited the position (Hawkes 1973:28).

5. For a translation of all the Republican articles on inheritance and succession, see LRPG 1961:339–360.

Appendix 2: Historical Sources and Their Limits

1. See Chapter 3 for a complete discussion of household division documents.

2. See Zhongguo shehui kexueyuan, lishi yanjiusuo, eds., *Huizhou qiannian qiyue wenshu* (1991, 1993).

3. The *tong* is a measure of grain, usually a box, that differed in size from village to village or from landlord to landlord.

4. As an example, see Waltner 1990 on Ming dynasty adoption.

Glossary

banci　半嗣

baoyang　抱養

ceshi　側室

chi　尺

dan (weight)　石

dan (grain and land)　碩

dazong　大宗

dazu　大租

di　地

dian　典

diao　吊

disun　嫡孫

dou　斗

erfang　二房

erfuren　二夫人

fanzu　番租

fanglian　房奩

fen (area)　份

fen (weight)　分

feng mu ling　奉母令

fengshui　風水

fu buguo san dai　富不過三代

ge wu fan hui　各無反悔

gong (common or joint)　公

gong (common or joint)　共

gongsheng　貢生

guan　貫

guoji　過繼

huiguan　會館

hujue　戶絕

jia　甲

jiansheng　監生

jiantiao　兼祧

jieji　捷記

jie yi　街誼

jin　斤

jinshi　進士

juehu　絕戶

junfen　均分

juren　舉人

kaoren　靠人

kong kou wu ping　恐口無憑

laozu　老租

liang　兩

linsheng　廩生

lizhang　里長

minglingzi　螟蛉子

mu　畝

239

muyou　幕友

nao fenjia　鬧分家

pengmin　棚民

pi　匹

pin　品

pin da jun (fen)　品打均分

qi　妻

qie　妾

qing　頃

Qingmingjie　清明節

qiu　坵

sanyifan　散移飯

shangfang　上房

sheng　升

sheng chi ri fan　生齒日繁

shengyuan　生員

shi　石

shu　庶

shu da fen zhi　樹大分支

shuitian　水田

shuoheren　説和人

siti you kui　四體有虧

sui　歳

suo　所

tan ding ru di　攤丁入地

tian　田

ting　廳

tong　桶

tongyangxi　童養媳

weizhongren　為中人

wen　文

xiangfang　廂房

xiangren　鄉人

xiangsheng　庠生

xiangyi　鄉誼

xianzu　現租

xiaoyang yuan　小洋元

xiaozong　小宗

xiaozu　小租

xiaozuhu　小租戶

xiucai　秀才

yang　養

yanglao　養老

yanglaodi　養老地

yanglaofei　養老費

yanglaoshan　養老贍

yangshan　養贍 or 養膳

yangzi　養子

yin　蔭

yuan　元 or 圓

yuandi　園地

yu shi　諭示

zaichang zhijianren　在場知見人

zaijianren　在見人

zhang　丈

zheng chang jing duan　爭長兢短

zhengfang　正房

zhi gong wu si　至公無私

zhong (middle)　中

zhong (measure of land)　種

zhongbaoren　中保人

zhongjianren　中見人

zhongren　中人

zhongshuoren　中説人

zhuangtou　莊頭

zongfa　宗法

zongzi　粽子

Bibliography

Abbreviations

BX	Baxian archive documents
DW	Wakefield, David (documents in Chinese)
JJS	Zhongguo shehui kexueyuan, jingji yanjiusuo, documents
KC	Chūgoku nōson kankō chōsa kankōkai, *Chūgoku nōson kankō chōsa*
LRPG	Law Revision Planning Group, *Laws of the Republic of China*
QMJ	*Minggong shupan qingmingji*
TS	Rinji Taiwan kyūkan chōsakai, *Taiwan shihō (Taiwan sifa)*
TWGS	*Taiwan gongsi cang guwenshu yingben*
ZPM	Zhejiang Provincial Museum documents
ZZM	Professor Zheng Zhenman, private papers
ZZZ	*Zhizuzhai Shifang jiushu*

Sources in Chinese and Japanese

Ban Gu. 1975. *Han shu* (The history of the [former] Han dynasty). Beijing: Zhonghua shuju.

Baxian archive of Qing dynasty documents. Held at the Sichuan Provincial Archives in Chengdu, Sichuan; each legal case is cited by serial number.

BX. *See* Baxian archive

Chang Wei-jen [Zhang Weiren]. 1983. Qingdai fazhi yanjiu (Studies in the Qing legal system). 3 vols. Taipei: Academia Sinica.

———, ed. 1986. Ming Qing dang'an (Ming-Qing Archives). Taipei: Zhongyang yanjiu yu yuan lishi yuyan yanjiusuo.

Chen Ping and Wang Qinjin. 1987. "Yizheng Xupu 101 hao Xihan mu 'xianling quanshu' chukao" (A preliminary study of the Xianling document from Western Han tomb number 101 in Yizheng county, Xupu township). *Wenwu* 1987, no. 1, 20–25, 36.

Chen Zhiping and Zheng Zhenman. 1987. "Pucheng xian Dongtou cun 'wudai tongtang' diaocha" (An investigation into 'five generations under one roof' in Dongtou village, Pucheng county). In *Ming Qing Fujian shehui yu xiangcun jingji*, ed. Fu Yiling and Yang Guozhen, 310–328. Xiamen: Xiamen daxue chubanshe.

Chūgoku nōson kankō chōsa kankōkai. 1952–1958. *Chūgoku nōson kankō chōsa* (Investigations of customary practices in rural China). Ed. Niida Noboru. 6 vols. Tokyo: Iwanami shoten.

Da Ming lü (The Ming Code). 1959. Nanjing Library edition.

Da Ming ling (Great Ming Commandment). 1969 reprint. In *Huang Ming zhishu*. Taipei: Chengwen chubanshe.

Da Qing lüli. See *Da Qing lüli zengxiu tongzuan jicheng*

Da Qing lüli zengxiu tongzuan jicheng (Revised comprehensive edition of the statutes and established precedents of the Great Qing dynasty). 1878. Shanghai.

DW. Documents collected by David Wakefield. Nos. 1–15.

Feng Menglong, ed. 1985. *Xing shi heng yan* (Constant words to awaken the world). Xi'an: Shaanxi renmin chubanshe.

Fu Yiling. 1987. "Fujian nongcun de gengchu zudian qiyue jiqi maimai wenshu" (Rent and pawn contracts and sale documents for agricultural animals in rural Fujian). In *Ming Qing Fujian shehui yu xiangcun jingji*, ed. Fu Yiling and Yang Guozhen, 69–78. Xiamen: Xiamen daxue chubanshe.

———. 1989. *Fu Yiling zhishi wushi nian wenbian* (Fu Yiling: Selections from Fifty Years of Historical Research). Xiamen: Xiamen daxue chubanshe.

Fu Yiling and Yang Guozhen, eds. 1987. *Ming Qing Fujian shehui yu xiangcun jingji* (Society and local economy in Ming-Qing Fujian). Xiamen: Xiamen daxue chubanshe.

Fujian Provincial Library. Documents. Fuzhou.

Guo Jiechang. 1892. *Fuzhou guoshi zhipu* (The Fuzhou Guo family genealogy). 10 juan.

Huadong junzheng weiyuanhui, tudi gaige weiyuanhui, eds. 1952. *Fujiansheng nongcun diaocha* (Rural investigations in Fujian province). N.p.: n.p.

JJS. *See* Zhongguo shehui kexueyuan, jingji yanjiusuo

Kankō chōsa. *See* Chūgoku nōson kankō chōsa kankōkai

KC. *See* Chūgoku nōson kankō chōsa kankōkai

Kunshan Mashi zupu (The genealogy of the Ma lineage of Kunshan). Genealogical Society of Utah Microfilm No. 1129094.

Lü Xisheng. 1988. *Xu Xiake jiazhuan* (Records of Xu Xiake). Changchun: Jilin wenshi chubanshe.

Mao Zedong. 1982. *Mao Zedong nongcun diaocha wenji* (Mao Zedong's collected rural investigations). Beijing: Renmin chubanshe.

Minggong shupan qingmingji (Collection of clear and lucid decisions by famous judges). 1987. Edited by the Song-Liao-Jin-Yuan research group of the History Research Institute of the Chinese Academy of Social Sciences. Beijing: Zhonghua shuju.

Morohashi Tetsuji. 1955–1959. *Daikanwa jiten* (The great Chinese-Japanese dictionary). Tokyo: Taishūkan shoten.

Nanxun Zhoushi jiapu (The genealogy of the Zhou family of Nanxun). 1911. Genealogical Society of Utah Microfilm No. 0770659.

Niida Noboru. 1942. *Shina minbuhō shi* (History of family law in China). Tokyo: Tōyōbunka gakuin.

———. 1959–1964. *Chūgoku hōseishi kenkyū* (A study of Chinese legal history). 4 vols. Tokyo: Tokyo University Press.

———. [1933] 1964. *Tōrei shūi* (Remnants of the Tang statutes). Tokyo: Tōyōbunka gakuin. Reprint, Tokyo: Tokyo University Press.

Pingyuan zongpu (The genealogy [of the Lu family] of Pingyuan). 1906. Genealogical Society of Utah Microfilm No. 1129321.

Qi Sihe. 1981. "Shangyang bianfa kao" (On Shangyang's legal reforms). In *Zhongguoshi tanyan* (Inquiries into Chinese history). Beijing: Zhonghua shuju.

Qingmingji. See *Minggong shupan qingmingji*

QMJ. See *Minggong shupan qingmingji*

Rinji Taiwan kyūkan chōsakai (Temporary committee on research of customs and practices on Taiwan). 1910. *Taiwan shihō* (The common law of Taiwan). 2 vols.

———. 1910–1911. *Taiwan shihō furoku sankōsho* (Reference materials appended to the common law of Taiwan).

Shiga Shūzō. 1950. *Chūgoku kazokuhō ron* (Discussion of Chinese family law). Tokyo: Kombundō.

———. 1967. *Chūgoku kazoku hō no genri* (Principles of Chinese family law). Tokyo: Sōbunsha.

Song xing tong (The Song Code). 1984. Beijing: Zhonghua shuju.

Taiwan gongsi cang guwenshu yingben (Copies of public and private documents from Taiwan). 1983. Series 1–10. Taipei: n.p.

Tang lü shuyi (The Tang code). 1983. Beijing: Zhonghua shuju.

Tōyō bunko mindaishi kenkyūshitsu. 1975. *Chūgoku tochi keiyaku bunsho, Kin-Shin* (Chinese land contract documents, Jin-Qing). Tokyo.

TS. *See* Rinji Taiwan kyūkan chōsakai

TWGS. See *Taiwan gongsi cang guwenshu yingben*

Uchida Tomoo. 1956. *Chūgoku nōson no bunke seido* (The household division system in rural China). Tokyo: Iwanami shoten.

Wakefield, David. Documents collected by Wakefield. Nos. 1–15.

Wu Zuoxi, ed. 1917. *Linghai wushi zupu* (The Linghai Wu family genealogy). Original at Fuzhou Provincial Library.

Wushi zhipu (The genealogy of the Wu family). Genealogical Society of Utah Microfilm No. 1474173.

Yang Guozhen. 1990. *Ming-Qing tudi qiyue wenshu yanjiu* (Studies of Ming-Qing land contract documents). Beijing: Renmin chubanshe.

Zhang Xueshu, ed. 1986. *Tongzhi tiaoge* (The Yuan code). Hangzhou: Zhejiang guji chubanshe.

Zhang Youyi. 1984. *Ming-Qing Huizhou tudi guanxi yanjiu* (Studies in land relations in Ming-Qing Huizhou). Beijing: Zhongguo shehui kexue chubanshe.

———. 1987. "Ming-Qing Huizhou dizhu fenjiashu xuanji" (Selected landlord household division documents from Huizhou in the Ming-Qing period). *Jingji yanjiusuo jikan* 9:79–135.

Zheng Zhenman. 1984. "Qing zhi Minguo minbei liu jian 'fenguan' de fenxi: guanyu dizhu de jiazu yu jingji guanxi" (An analysis of six household division documents from the Qing and Republican periods: On landlord families and economic relationships). *Zhongguo shehui jingjishi yanjiu* 3:32–36.

———. 1988. "Ming-Qing Fujian de jiating jiegou jiqi yanbian qushi" (Development and change in family structure in Ming-Qing Fujian). *Zhongguo shehui jingjishi yanjiu* 4:67–74.

———. 1989. "Mingdai Taiwan jiating jiegou de ruogan tedian" (Several special characteristics of family form in Qing dynasty Taiwan). *Taiwan yanjiu jikan* 2:19–28.

———. 1992. *Ming Qing Fujian jiazu zuzhi yu shehui bianqian* (Family structure and social change in Ming-Qing Fujian). Hunan: Hunan jiaoyu chubanshe.

———. n.d. Private papers.

Zhejiang Provincial Museum. Collection of private family and state documents.

Zhizuzhai Shifang jiushu (The household division document of the Shi branch of Zhizuzhai). 1864. Located in the Fujian Provincial Library, Fuzhou.

Zhongguo kexueyuan lishi yanjiusuo ziliaoshi, eds. 1961. *Dunhuang ziliao, diyi ji* (Dunhuang documents, part 1). Beijing: Zhonghua shuju.

Zhongguo shehui kexueyuan, jingji yanjiusuo (Economics Research Institute, Chinese Academy of Social Sciences, Beijing). Collection of family documents from Huizhou, Anhui.

Zhongguo shehui kexueyuan, lishi yanjiusuo, eds. 1991, 1993. *Huizhou qiannian qiyue wenshu* (One thousand years of contract documents from Huizhou). Shijiazhuang: Huashan wenyi chubanshe.

Zhou Xianghe. 1986. "Qingdai Taiwan jiushu yanjiu" (A study of household division documents from Qing Taiwan). In *Qingdai Taiwan shi yanjiu* (Studies of Qing Taiwan), ed. Chen Zaicheng, Kong Li, and Deng Kongzhao, pp. 300–312. Xiamen: Xiamen daxue chubanshe.

———. 1991. "Qingdai Taiwan nongcun jingjide jiliang yanjiu" (A statistical study of Qing Taiwan's rural economy). M.A. thesis, Xiamen University.

Zhoushi fangpu (The Zhou branch genealogy). 1924. Guizhou. Genealogical Society of Utah Microfilm No. 1085423.

Ziliujing Zhenzhushan Wangshi baoshanci sixiu jiapu (The genealogy of the Wang family from Zhenzhu mountain, Ziliujing, fourth edition). 1911. Genealogical Society of Utah Microfilm No. 1904932.

ZPM. Zhejiang Provincial Museum collection of private family and state documents.

ZZM. The private papers of Professor Zheng Zhenman.

ZZZ. See *Zhizuzhai Shifang jiushu*

Interviews with the Author

Chen Sidong. Fujian Historical Association. Interviewed May 11, 1991.

Li Xingfang, Wu Qingsun, and Xie Jizhong. Group interview with these three residents of the city of Liancheng, Fujian. Interviewed June 25, 1991.

Liu Wenqing and You Zhisheng. Old watchmen at the Quanzhou museum. Interviewed May 10, 1991.

Longyan Local Gazetteer Committee. Group interview with nine members of the editorial committee for the new Longyan Local Gazetteer. Interview conducted June 22, 1991. The members included Chen Renxing, Chen Zheng, Deng Youguang, Guo Chunrong, Guo Danhong, Li Hanzhou, Qiu Zisong, Zhang Yingsheng, and Zhang Youtong.

Qiu Haisen. Resident of Dayang village on the outskirts of Longyan, Fujian. Interviewed June 23, 1991.

Wang Lianmao. Curator of the museum of Quanzhou overseas communication history. Interviewed May 9, 1991.

Xie Tianxi. Member of the Quanzhou Chamber of Commerce. Interviewed May 9, 1991.

Zhang Ruiyao. Resident of Xinquan, Fujian. Interviewed June 26, 1991.

Sources in English

Ahern, Emily, and Hill Gates, eds. 1981. *The Anthropology of Taiwanese Society.* Stanford: Stanford University Press.

Baker, Hugh. 1979. *Chinese Family and Kinship.* New York: Columbia University Press.

Bell, H. T. Montague, and H. G. W. Woodhead. 1913. *The China Year Book.* London: George Routledge and Sons.

Berkner, Lutz K. 1976. "Inheritance, Land Tenure and Peasant Family Structure: A German Regional Comparison." In *Family and Inheritance: Rural Society in Western Europe,* ed. Jack Goody, Joan Thirsk, and E. P. Thompson, 71–95. Cambridge: Cambridge University Press.

Bernhardt, Kathryn. 1995. "The Inheritance Rights of Daughters: The Song Anomaly?" *Modern China* 21, no. 3 (July 1995): 269–309.

Bernhardt, Kathryn, and Philip Huang, eds. 1994. *Civil Law in Qing and Republican China.* Stanford: Stanford University Press.

Birge, Bettine. 1992. "Women and Property in Sung China (960–1279): Neo-Confucianism and Social Change in Chien-chou, Fukien." Ph.D. dissertation. Ann Arbor: University Microfilms International.

Bourdieu, Pierre. [1972] 1977a. "Marriage Strategies as Strategies of Social Reproduction." In *Family and Society: Selections from the Annales,* ed. R. Foster and O. Ranum, 117–144. Baltimore: Johns Hopkins University Press.

———. 1977b. *Outline of a Theory of Practice.* Cambridge: Cambridge University Press.

———. 1986. "From Rules to Strategies." *Cultural Anthropology* 1 (February): 110–120.

———. 1990. *The Logic of Practice.* Stanford: Stanford University Press.

Buck, John Lossing. 1937a. *Land Utilization in China.* Shanghai: University of Nanking.

————. 1937b. *Land Utilization in China: Statistics.* Shanghai: University of Nanking.

Burns, I. R. 1973. "Private Law in Traditional China (Sung Dynasty): Using as a Main Source of Information the Work *Ming-kung shu-p'an Ch'ing-ming-chi.* Ph.D. dissertation, Oxford University.

Buxbaum, David, ed. 1978. *Chinese Family Law and Social Change in Historical and Comparative Perspective.* Seattle: University of Washington Press.

Cao Xueqin. 1973. *The Story of the Stone.* Trans. David Hawkes. New York: Viking Penguin. 5 vols.

Chang, Chung-li. 1955. *The Chinese Gentry: Studies on Their Role in Nineteenth Century Chinese Society.* Seattle: University of Washington Press.

Chang, Tao Hsing. 1935. "Inheritance in China." *Iowa Law Review* 20, no. 2 (Jan. 1935):411–415.

Ch'en, Paul Heng-chao. 1979. *Chinese Legal Tradition under the Mongols: The Code of 1291 As Reconstructed.* Princeton: Princeton University Press.

Ch'u, T'ung-tsu. 1961. *Law and Society in Traditional China.* Paris: Mouton and Co.

————. 1972. *Han Social Structure.* Seattle: University of Washington Press.

Cohen, Myron. 1970. "Developmental Process in the Chinese Domestic Group." In *Family and Kinship in Chinese Society,* ed. Maurice Freedman, 21–36. Stanford: Stanford University Press.

————. 1976. *House United, House Divided: The Chinese Family in Taiwan.* New York: Columbia University Press.

Cooper, J. P. 1976. "Patterns of Inheritance and Settlement by Great Landowners from the Fifteenth to the Eighteenth Centuries." In Goody, Thirsk, and Thompson 1976: 192–327.

Dennerline, Jerry. 1986. "Marriage, Adoption and Charity in the Development of Lineages in Wu-hsi from Sung to Ch'ing." In *Kinship Organization in Late Imperial China, 1000–1949,* ed. Patricia Ebrey and James Watson, 170–209. Berkeley: University of California Press.

Duyvendak, J. J. L. 1928. *"The Book of Lord Shang": A Classic of the Chinese School of Law.* Chicago: University of Chicago Press.

Eberhard, Wolfram. 1987. *A History of China.* Fourth revised edition. Berkeley: University of California Press.

Ebrey, Patricia. 1984. *Family and Property in Sung China: Yuan Ts'ai's Precepts for Social Life.* Princeton: Princeton University Press.

————. 1993. *The Inner Quarters: Marriage and the Lives of Chinese Women in the Sung Period.* Berkeley: University of California Press.

Ebrey, Patricia B., and James L. Watson, eds. 1986. *Kinship Organization in Late Imperial China, 1000–1940.* Berkeley: University of California Press.

Engels, Frederick. 1902. *The Origin of the Family, Private Property, and the State.* Chicago: Charles H. Kerr and Co.

Esherick, Joseph, and Mary Rankin, eds. 1990. *Chinese Local Elites and Patterns of Dominance.* Berkeley: University of California Press.

Farmer, Edward L. 1995. *Zhu Yuanzhang and Early Ming Legislation: The*

Reordering of Chinese Society Following the Era of Mongol Rule. New York: E. J. Brill.

Finegan, Michael. 1985. "Inheritance and Family Structure in Qing China: Evidence from Taiwan and Fujian." Paper given at the Association for Asian Studies annual meeting, March 24, 1985.

Fletcher, Joseph 1986. "The Mongols: Ecological and Social Perspectives." *Harvard Journal of Asiatic Studies* 46, no. 1 (June 1986): 11–50.

Freedman, Maurice. 1958. *Lineage Organization in Southeastern China.* London: University of London Press.

———. 1966. *Chinese Lineage and Society: Fukien and Kwangtung.* London: Athlone Press.

———, ed. 1970. *Family and Kinship in Chinese Society.* Stanford: Stanford University Press.

———. 1979. *The Study of Chinese Society: Essays by Maurice Freedman.* Stanford: Stanford University Press.

Goodrich, L. Carrington. 1959. *A Short History of the Chinese People.* Third edition. New York: Harper and Row.

Goody, Jack. 1973. "Strategies of Heirship." *Comparative Studies in Society and History* 15 (1973): 3–18.

———. 1976. "Inheritance, Property and Women: Some Comparative Considerations." In Goody, Thirsk, and Thompson 1976:10–36.

———. 1990. *The Oriental, the Ancient and the Primitive: Systems of Marriage and the Family in the Pre-Industrial Societies of Eurasia.* Cambridge: Cambridge University Press.

Goody, Jack, Joan Thirsk, and E. P. Thompson. 1976. *Family and Inheritance: Rural Society in Western Europe, 1200–1800.* Cambridge: Cambridge University Press.

Habakkuk, H. J. 1955. "Family Structure and Economic Change in Nineteenth-Century Europe." *The Journal of Economic History* 15, no. 1: 1–12.

Hanley, Susan B., and Arthur P. Wolf, eds. 1985. *Family and Population in East Asian History.* Stanford: Stanford University Press.

Hansen, Valerie. 1995. *Negotiating Daily Life in Traditional China: How Ordinary People Used Contracts, 600–1400.* New Haven: Yale University Press.

Harrell, Stevan. 1985. "The Rich Get Children: Segmentation, Stratification, and Population in Three Chekiang Lineages, 1550–1850." In Hanley and Wolf 1985:81–109.

Hawkes, David. 1973. "Introduction." In Cao Xueqin, *The Story of the Stone* 1:13–46.

Ho, Ping-ti. 1962. *The Ladder of Success in Imperial China: Aspects of Social Mobility, 1368–1911.* New York: John Wiley and Sons.

Holmgren, Jennifer. 1986. "Observations on Marriage and Inheritance Practices in Early Mongol and Yuan Society, with Particular Reference to the Levirate." *Journal of Asian History* 20, no. 2 (1986): 127–192.

Hsu, Cho-yun. 1965. *Ancient China in Transition: An Analysis of Social Mobility, 722–222 B.C.* Stanford: Stanford University Press.

————. 1980. *Han Agriculture*. Seattle: University of Washington Press.

Hsu, Cho-yun, and Katheryn M. Linduff. 1988. *Western Chou Civilization*. New Haven: Yale University Press.

Hsu, Francis L. K. 1967. *Under the Ancestors' Shadow: Kinship, Personality and Social Mobility in China*. Stanford: Stanford University Press.

Huang, Liu-hung. 1984. *A Complete Book Concerning Happiness and Benevolence*. Ed. and trans. Djang Chu. Tucson: University of Arizona Press.

Huang, Philip C. C. 1985. *The Peasant Economy and Social Change in North China*. Stanford: Stanford University Press.

————. 1990. *The Peasant Family and Rural Development in the Yangzi Delta, 1350–1988*. Stanford: Stanford University Press.

————. 1991. "The Paradigmatic Crisis in Chinese Studies: Paradoxes in Social and Economic History." *Modern China* 17, no. 3 (July): 299–341.

————. 1994. "Codified Law and Magisterial Adjudication in the Qing." In *Civil Law in Qing and Republican China,* ed. Kathryn Bernhardt and Philip Huang, 143–186. Stanford: Stanford University Press.

Hucker, Charles O. 1975. *China's Imperial Past: An Introduction to Chinese History and Culture*. Stanford: Stanford University Press.

Jamieson, G. 1921. *Chinese Family and Commercial Law*. Shanghai: Kelly and Walsh.

Jing, Junjian. 1994. "Legislation Related to the Civil Economy in the Qing Dynasty." In Bernhardt and Huang 1994:42–84.

Judd, Ellen. 1989. "Niangjia: Chinese Women and Their Natal Families." *Journal of Asian Studies* 48, no. 3 (August 1989): 524–544.

Knapp, Ronald G. 1980a. "Settlement and Frontier Land Tenure." In *China's Island Frontier: Studies in the Historical Geography of Taiwan,* ed. Ronald G. Knapp, 55–68. Honolulu: University of Hawai'i Press.

————, ed. 1980b. *China's Island Frontier: Studies in the Historical Geography of Taiwan*. Honolulu: University of Hawai'i Press.

Lang, Olga. 1946. *Chinese Family and Society*. New Haven: Yale University Press.

Lavely, William R., and R. Bin Wong. 1984. *Family Division, Reproductivity, and Landholding in North China*. Ann Arbor: University of Michigan Population Studies Center, Research Report Nos. 84–85.

————. 1992. "Family Division and Mobility in North China." *Comparative Studies in Society and History* 34, no. 3 (July): 439–463.

Law Revision Planning Group of the Executive Yuan of the Republic of China. 1961. *Laws of The Republic of China: First Series—Major Laws*. Taipei.

Lin, Yueh-hwa. 1947. *The Golden Wing, A Sociological Study of Chinese Familism*. Reprint ed., Westport, Conn.: Greenwood Press.

LRPG. *See* Law Revision Planning Group of the Executive Yuan of the Republic of China

Macauley, Melissa. 1994. "The Civil Reprobate: Pettifoggers, Property, and Litigation in Late Imperial China, 1723–1850." Ph.D. dissertation, University of California, Berkeley. Ann Arbor: University Microfilms International.

Malthus, T. R. [1914] 1982. *An Essay on the Principle of Population*. London: Dent.

Mao Zedong. 1990. *Report from Xunwu*. Trans. Roger P. Thompson. Stanford: Stanford University Press.

Mass, Jeffrey P. 1983. "Patterns of Provincial Inheritance in Late Heian Japan." *Journal of Japanese Studies* 9, no. 1 (1983): 57–95.

———. 1989. *Lordship and Inheritance in Early Medieval Japan*. Stanford: Stanford University Press, 1989.

Meskill, Johanna. 1979. *A Chinese Pioneer Family: The Lins of Wu-feng, Taiwan, 1729–1895*. Princeton: Princeton University Press.

Myers, Ramon. 1970. *The Chinese Peasant Economy: Agricultural Development in Hopei and Shantung, 1890–1940*. Cambridge: Harvard University Press.

Nakamura, James, and Matao Miyamoto. 1982. "Social Structure and Population Change: A Comparative Study of Tokugawa Japan and Ch'ing China." *Economic Development and Cultural Change* 30:229–269.

Okamatsu, Santaro. 1971. *Provisional Report on Investigations of Laws and Customs in the Island of Formosa*. Taipei: Ch'eng Wen Publishing Company.

Riasanovsky, V. A. [1938] 1976. *Chinese Civil Law*. Arlington: University Publications of America.

Schurmann, H. Franz. 1956. "Traditional Property Concepts in China." *Far Eastern Quarterly* 15:507–516.

Shiga, Shūzō. 1978. "Family Property and the Law of Inheritance in Traditional China." In Buxbaum 1978:109–150.

Sommer, Matthew. 1994. "Sex, Law, and Society in Late Imperial China." Ph.D. dissertation. Ann Arbor: University Microfilms International.

Sung, Lung-sheng. 1974. "Inheritance and Kinship in Northern Taiwan." Ph.D. dissertation. Ann Arbor: University Microfilms International.

———. 1981. "Property and Family Division." In Ahern and Gates 1981:361–380.

Twitchett, Denis. 1959. "The Fan Clan's Charitable Estate, 1050–1760." In *Confucianism in Action*, ed. David S. Nivison and Arthur F. Wright, 97–133. Stanford: Stanford University Press.

———. 1970. *Financial Administration under the T'ang*. Cambridge: Cambridge University Press.

Valk, Marius Hendrikus van der. 1939. *An Outline of Modern Chinese Family Law*. Monumenta Serica Monograph, series 2. Peiping.

van der Sprenkel, Sybille. 1966. *Legal Institutions in Manchu China: A Sociological Analysis*. London: Athlone Press.

van der Valk, Marc. [1939] 1969. *An Outline of Modern Chinese Family Law*. Reprint. Taipei: Ch'eng Wen Publishing Co.

Van Gulik, R. H. 1956. *T'ang-Yin-Pi-Shih: Parallel Cases from under the Pear Tree*. Leiden: E. J. Brill.

Waltner, Ann. 1990. *Getting an Heir: Adoption and the Construction of Kinship in Late Imperial China*. Honolulu: University of Hawai'i Press.

Watson, Rubie S. 1984. "Women's Work and Inheritance in Chinese Society: An Anthropologist's View." In *Women in Asia and Asian Studies*, ed. Barbara D. Miller and Janice Hyde, 7–23. Syracuse: Maxwell School of Citizenship and Public Affairs, Syracuse University.

———. 1985. *Inequality among Brothers: Class and Kinship in South China.*
    New York: Cambridge University Press.
Wolf, Arthur P. 1970. "Chinese Kinship and Mourning Dress." In Freedman
    1970:189–207.
———. 1995. *Sexual Attraction and Childhood Association: A Chinese Brief for
    Edward Westermark.* Stanford: Stanford University Press.
Wolf, Arthur P., and Chieh-shan Huang. 1980. *Marriage and Adoption in China,
    1845–1945.* Stanford: Stanford University Press.
Wolf, Margery. 1968. *The House of Lim: A Study of a Chinese Farm Family.*
    New York: Meredith Corporation.
———. 1972. *Women and the Family in Rural Taiwan.* Stanford: Stanford Uni-
    versity Press.
Wu Ching-tzu. 1973. *The Scholars.* Translated by Yang Hsien-yi and Gladys
    Yang. Beijing: Foreign Languages Press.

Index

About the Author

DAVID WAKEFIELD received his B.A. and M.A. from San Francisco State University, and Ph.D. in Asian history from UCLA. He has lived and traveled extensively in Asia and Latin America. He now lives with his wife Su and son Daniel in Columbia, Missouri, teaching Chinese and Japanese history at the University of Missouri. He is the translator of *The Three-Inch Golden Lotus,* a novel by Feng Jicai.